THE
VIKING ART
OF WAR

This book is dedicated, in sadness, to the memory of Paul Morris

THE
VIKING ART
OF WAR

PADDY GRIFFITH

CASEMATE
Philadelphia & Newbury
A Greenhill Book

Published in the United States of America in 2009 by
CASEMATE
908 Darby Road, Havertown, PA 19083

and in the United Kingdom by
CASEMATE
17 Cheap Street, Newbury, RG14 5DD

 *A Greenhill Book*

ISBN 978-1-932033-60-1

For a complete list of Casemate titles, please contact:

United States of America
Casemate Publishers
Telephone (610) 853-9131, Fax (610) 853-9146
E-mail casemate@casematepublishing.com
Website www.casematepublishing.com

United Kingdom
Casemate-UK
Telephone (01635) 231091, Fax (01635) 41619
E-mail casemate-uk@casematepublishing.co.uk
Website www.casematepublishing.co.uk

PRINTED AND BOUND IN THE UNITED STATES OF AMERICA

Contents

List of Tables and Figures

Tables

Figures

Glossary

Aldeijuborg: Staraja Ladoga

ASC: Anglo Saxon Chronicle

'Battle': Major division of an army (*ie* a 'brigade' or 'division' in modern parlance)

Berserk: 'Frenzied warrior'. Berserks are discussed at length in chapter five.

Biarmeland: see 'Permia'

Blueland: the Sahara and Sahel regions (due to the blue robes of the Berber/ Tuareg nomads)

Bretland: Wales

Boat (in modern usage): Vessel less than 150 feet long – *ie* including all Viking 'ships'

Bonder: Free yeoman farmer (*cf hauldr* or 'holds', or English *thegns*)

C³I: Command, control, communication and intelligence

Centuries: For clarity and ease of recognition these are normally referred to in the text as 'the 800s' for the ninth century, 'the 1000s' for the eleventh century, etc

Corvid: Member of the crow family (ravens, jackdaws etc)

Drapa: Long laudatory poem with refrains

Dreng: Sometimes used to designate a Bonder; at other times just 'a good chap', 'a comrade in arms' or 'a fellow crew member'

Druzhiny: Norse 'friendly battalions' acting as mercenaries to Rus or Slav princes

Earl: *Jarl* or high nobleman under a king (*cf* English *ealdorman*)

Gardariki: Russia (after the *gards* or fortified trading posts established there)

Geld: Money paid by treaty to secure peace or the departure of an enemy army. Often called 'Danegeld'.

Giantland: North Russia to the East of 'Permia'

Hamwih: Southampton

Herfjöttr: 'War Fetter' or 'Foot Terror', equivalent to modern shell shock

Herred: Danish unit of land owing a certain amount of military service (*cf* the Swedish *hund* and the English 'hundred')

Hersir: Norwegian leader of men, ranking at around the 'captain' level

Hird: King's bodyguard and inner circle of advisers, favoured assistants etc

Holmgard: Novgorod

Hringsfjord: Mont St Michel

Jomsburg: Now-deserted Viking site near modern Wollin

Long Hundred: 120 is the number represented by saga references to '100'

Micklegard: Constantinople, or modern Istanbul

Narvesund: The straits of Gibraltar

Nidaros: The original Trondheim, which became the seat of the Norwegian kings

Orcadian: From Orkney

Pafagard: Rome

Permia/Biarmeland: The White Sea and River Dvina area

Reric: Mecklenburg (and not Lubeck as is sometimes claimed)

Rus: The Swedes in Finland and Russia, later identified with the whole Slav population of Russia into which they merged

Scatt: Tax

Scrælings: Eskimoes and/or Red Indians

Serkland: 'Saracen land' or any Arab land (not just North Africa)

Shield wall or *Skjaldborg*: Tactical formation for land combat with more or less overlapping shields but indeterminate depth

Ship (in modern usage): Vessel more than 150 feet long; unknown in Viking times

Skiphired: 'Ship army' or muster of warriors for amphibious military duty

Svinfylkja: 'Swine Wedge', a triangular tactical assault formation with its point facing towards the enemy

Slabland: Possibly Baffin Island, but in any case an island in the Arctic Circle

Sunstone: Cordierite, a substance allegedly used by the Vikings for navigation in cloudy weather (see *Sturlunga Saga*, vol 1 p.470 n)

Swithiod: Sweden, as distinct from 'Great Swithiod' which was Odin's kingdom, identified variously with Russia or the Ukraine

Thing: Local assembly, a democratic meeting of all enfranchised citizens

Valland: The west coast of France

Varangians: Rus merchants or mercenaries operating at Constantinople

Vigfuss: Ready or eager for battle

War arrow: Symbolic token that is passed around all the houses in a region which owe military service, to call the warriors to a muster. Sometimes called a 'war token', but note that it is not the same as a *'thing* token' (to call a court or parliament) or the tokens taken by ambassadors to establish their credentials with foreign dignitaries

Preface

This book is intended to examine what we know of Viking warfare using the methods of modern military analysis. Such an undertaking has been applied to Roman strategy by several authors during the past quarter century; but not to that of the Vikings. The reason for this imbalance is doubtless that we know a great deal more about the Romans, who are also generally considered to have been more important to the development of western civilisation as a whole. They regarded Scandinavia as no more than a barbarian backwater, and were content to leave it well beyond their horizon, whereas the Vikings would later visit such places as Rome and Byzantium with feelings of humility and awe.

It is nevertheless an embarrassing fact that we know very little about the Viking art of war, and much of our perception of it has been formed by the spurious imaginings of post-Viking writers and artists who have had little actual evidence, if any, to guide them. Firm evidence is indeed appallingly scanty, and there is in truth little realistic alternative to 'spurious imaginings' for many aspects of the subject. We may be able to demonstrate that some parts of the popular image are false – for example the Vikings did not wear horned helmets and there was no such thing as a 'blood eagle' – but we do not have much that is solid to put in their place. We know a little about where the Viking armies wandered, but almost nothing about their operational or tactical methods. Almost all of what we are left with is the purest guesswork.

In writing this book I am particularly indebted to Ian Greenwood, who focused my attention sharply onto 'Dark Age' subjects when he set up the innovative *Guthrum's Army* magazine, historiographical experiment and investigative experience, including a very productive conference in 1983. This was all centred on the Anglo-Saxon wars of 865–79, and anything in the present book that is related even remotely to that subject can be attributed directly to Ian and his collaborators. For me, he has indeed been a strong creative influence: not only for his insights into historiographical method, but also for many vital technical aspects of the subject itself. He also sent me many useful texts for the present volume and, above all, he introduced me to the late Paul Morris, to whose memory the present work is respectfully dedicated and who, had he been spared, would surely have made a far better fist of this whole thing than I possibly can.

As an undergraduate I first encountered academic study of this era when I sat in awe at the feet of the late Trevor Aston, whose brand of scholarly dry humour still remains an inspiration. Others who have given me significant help more recently include Peter Bone and Simon Davies, who both offered me free access to their extensive funds of expertise, cogitation and practical experience of Viking-age artefacts. Matthew Bennett, equally, has been a wonderful source of information and ideas. John Davis, Guy Halsall, Heinrich Härke, Jim Roche and Peter Thompson have also each, in their own way, taught me important things about the subject, while Nigel de Lee, in particular, has not only fed me with Viking perspectives over many years, but has also showered me with dozens of translated sagas to help in the writing of this book. I apologise deeply to him for not having recognised the sagas as genuine 'military literature' during my 1980 conference on that subject: but I do not at all apologise to my family for attempting, in the course of 1994, to explain the rambling but subtle 'Viking jokes' that are contained within the sagas. My behaviour in that area, I'm afraid, as they have themselves already concluded, is just something they will have to live with.

I am also very grateful for the professional efforts, on my behalf, of the RMA Sandhurst, Nuneaton Borough and Birmingham Central libraries.

Needless to say, however, none of these persons or institutions is in any way responsible for what I have chosen to put in the present work, since all the mistakes are entirely my own.

Finally, I am extremely grateful to my late parents for taking me round the Norwegian ship- and folk-museums while I was merely ten years old. Without that early experience I do not think I would have been interested at all.

Paddy Griffith
Nuneaton, 1995

CHAPTER 1

A Military Analysis of the Vikings

'You can't run a croft without a second source of income.'
– Jim Webster, in conversation with the author.

The Vikings Defined

Just what do we mean by the expression 'The Vikings'? In terms of strictly linguistic origins they were initially defined as any 'sea pirates', and in some of the Icelandic sagas we find raiding Wends, Esthonians and Slavs described just as easily as 'Vikings' as were the Danes, Norwegians and Swedes. Elsewhere the word is used for any individual thief or racketeer, as in 'an arrant thief and a Viking' (*Saga of Gunnlaug*, p.34) or 'Vikings and outlaws and all the rogues he [*ie* Ulfkel the Wizard, in *Seven Viking Romances*, p.182] could muster'. They are often equated, in turn, with 'Berserks' or 'frenzied warriors' (Berserks are discussed at length in chapter five). Elsewhere again, however, a Viking is taken to be a much more honourable type of operator – either a 'merchant adventurer' or a 'soldier'.

According to these definitions not all Scandinavians should be considered as Vikings, since only a minority of the population indulged in robbery, warfare, extortion or trade; and still fewer did so on a full-time basis. Women, children and senior citizens presumably did not go 'a-viking' – although in the literature we do find some surprisingly young noble boys turning up as participants in, or even directors of, pillaging expeditions. The provocative role of women as the aggravators of male bellicosity is also a recurrent theme of the sagas – and there are even some genuine Amazons – so we should not perhaps dismiss them too easily from participation in the viking process. And as for the old, we find that the mighty pirate-poet Egil Skallagrimsson could still credibly be suspected of committing a double murder even when in his eighties and blind (*Egil*, p.237). Indeed, in *Laxdœla Saga* (p.78) Killer-Hrapp manages to murder quite a large number of people even after he has himself died!

Modern usage, however, mercifully cuts through such semantic perplexities and simply equates the Vikings with all the inhabitants of Scandinavia, and all ethnic Scandinavians wherever in the world they may happen to be settled. Hence an Icelandic farmer's wife living in Newfoundland would qualify as a Viking just as much as a Danish poet in Dublin or a Swedish mercenary soldier in Constantinople – although, of course, by no means all Dublin poets or Varangian Guards were necessarily ethnically Scandinavian.

So far this is simple enough; but we should remember that Scandinavia itself was a far from homogenous unit. For a long time it was divided into very many culturally separate districts ruled by warring minor kings, which merged only gradually and painfully into a series of larger provinces or more major kingdoms. These in turn eventually crystallised – at a very uneven pace – into rough equivalents of the unified nation states that are today called Norway, Sweden and Denmark. Pairs of these states were occasionally consolidated into larger 'empires' for a few fleeting moments during the Middle Ages, and such empires usually also included some far-flung colonies run by a mixture of immigrants from all parts of Scandinavia. In the Icelandic sagas there is certainly a good deal of pride expressed in the sheer geographical extent of Viking influence, and some of the heroes seem to move around almost as freely from the Eastern Mediterranean to the White Sea, from Scandinavia to Greenland, or from Ireland to Western France, as we might do today with the full benefit of air transport. Clearly the idea of a 'Viking world' did enjoy a certain validity at the time, even though the concept of an 'empire' as such may well have been inappropriately premature.

It was probably always the case that the bigger the political unit, the more strained would be the underlying political and cultural divisions between its various constituent regions. Even Canute the Great, who ruled perhaps the largest of the Viking 'empires' between 1018 and 1030, considered himself to be no more than a favoured individual who temporarily happened to be the king simultaneously of several quite different states. He cannot have expected them to stay united after his death, since the administrative and logistical means for holding them together did not yet exist. Indeed, he had already shed Norway from his portfolio five years before he died, by granting it to his son Sven, just as he was known to be exceptionally 'mild' and lenient towards vassals (eg in Scotland; see The Olaf Sagas, p.269) who wished to retain as much as possible of their traditional authority. His kingdoms should thus, perhaps, be seen as equivalent more to a mixed holding of stocks and shares – to be bought or sold individually according to market conditions – rather than to ownership of a single large, centralised, multinational company. In more political terms, we might compare them with the twenty different and diverse states of North America about 1760, rather than with the more modern federal concept of the 'USA' (and even today North America still remains divided, since Canada has not only retained her separate identity but includes a potentially breakaway province in Quebec).

Since 'viking' is an activity closely associated with the idea of sea piracy, one might argue that it is not specific to any particular period of history and hence that 'The Viking Age' is a chronologically meaningless expression. In theory the immediate Scandinavian heirs to the Roman empire – the Baltic and North Sea

Table A

Scandinavian 'Empires' and settlements of the Viking era

A few Scandinavian 'Empires' of the Viking era

'Ivar Vidfarne ruled all Sweden, Denmark, Saxony, the Eastern Baltic and one fifth of England in the mid 800s' (*Sagas of the Norse Kings*, p.37): fictional.

Swedish kings control Hedeby and south Jutland c.890–934; Erik the Victorious unites Sweden and Denmark for a short time in the 980s.

Harald Bluetooth unites Denmark and Norway c.980–86.

The Orkneys officially colonies of Norway from c.880. The Hebrides and other islands pay tribute at different times, but are never so closely subjugated. Iceland becomes Norwegian in 1262–4.

Sven Forkbeard rules Denmark 985–1014 and England 1013–14.

Canute the Great rules Denmark 1018–35 (& his sons until 1047, but Magnus of Norway disputes this, and at times rules Denmark & Norway); England 1016–35 (& his sons to 1042); Norway 1028–30 (& his sons to 1035).

The Viking settlements outside Scandinavia (*ie* NOT the first discovery or first raids)	**First settled from**
Baltic bases from pre-Viking times (Truso, Courland, Staraja Ladoga etc): Some later (Wollin c.950 etc)	Denmark, Sweden
The Shetlands and Orkneys from the 780s (?)	Norway
The Hebrides and Man from c.800 (?)	Orkney (Norwegians)
Dorestadt from c.830s	Denmark
Dublin and other Irish towns from c.840	Orkney (Norwegians)
North Normandy from c.840s	Denmark
Noirmoutier/Cotentin from c.843	Ireland, Norway
Novgorod from 862	Sweden
Kiev from the late 860s	Novogorod (Swedes)
Northumbria from 867	Norway, Denmark
East Anglia from 869	Denmark
Iceland from 870	Norway
Caithness from c.890	Orkney, Ireland (Norwegians)
Greenland from 986	Iceland (Norwegians)
Vinland the Good from c.1000	Greenland (Norwegians)

pirates operating from the Jutland peninsula in the 400s or 500s – ought to qualify as 'Vikings' just as easily as Ragnar Lothbrok in the 800s or Harald Hard-ruler in the 1000s. Indeed, the early marauding tribes showed so much 'Viking spirit' that they colonised England memorably enough for 'the Anglo-Saxon peoples' still to be known by their name today. Nor were these Anglo-

Saxon peoples particularly backward in exploring the Eastern Baltic or establishing trade contacts with the Mediterranean. Although we have found the
remains only of their less impressive boats, for example at Nydam and Sutton
Hoo, it is clear that they knew all about the use of sails and had almost as much
strategic outreach as the Vikings themselves. They raided Spain and even North
Africa, and one of their forces actually stole an entire Roman fleet on the Black
Sea and sailed it all the way home via Gibraltar. This leads us to the conclusion
that the more famous later Viking raiders had by no means invented the arts of
either navigation or piracy. John Haywood's important recent book on *Dark
Age Naval Power* has made this point far more specifically and comprehensively
than earlier authorities, and he states that 'the raids of the Saxon pirates
between the third and fifth centuries are comparable to those of the Vikings in
both range and tactics' (Haywood, p.3 *ff*).

Modern usage does nevertheless insist on limiting 'The Viking Age' to the
later generation of raiders, perhaps because they were able to exploit a distinct
advance in naval architecture which had occurred during the relative tranquility
of the 600s and 700s. This period also saw consolidation and refinement across
the whole spectrum of Scandinavian culture – its languages, arts, crafts and
political structures – which surely did much to help lay a strong foundation for
all the energetic activity that was to follow. Even though there was no iden-
tifiable internal 'revolution' within Scandinavia just before the Viking Age,
there was nevertheless a fruitful 'winding up of a spring' that would finally be
released, with great force, in the spectacular expansion of both trade and piracy
towards the end of the 700s.

The starting point of the Viking Age is normally taken to be the first major
act of pillage in the West for which we have a precise date – the sack of St
Cuthbert's abbey on Lindisfarne in 793. As for the end date, some say it came
when localised minor kingship was replaced by centrally-organised statehood
under 'imperially' minded great kings, around the second half of the 900s or the
early 1000s (for example Eric the Victorious in Sweden, Olaf Tryggvasson in
Norway or Sven Forkbeard in Denmark). This was a time when the native
anarcho-democratic society of old Scandinavia was finally giving way to a more
structured feudal organisation subject to strong foreign influences. In the
Icelandic sagas this royal centralisation is often located a century earlier than
1000, when the rule of Harald Finehair (King of Norway between c.872–85?
and 931 or even 945?) brought a mass banishment – or at least 'an accelerated
voluntary emigration' – of many independently-minded noblemen and warriors
from Norway. Because these migrants often ended up in newly-discovered
Iceland, that island can thus in a sense be said to have begun its life as a Viking
settlement only when the Viking Age was approaching its end in Norway.

Other commentators claim that the true end of the Viking Age should be
taken as the moment when the Scandinavians were converted to Christianity.

This happened around the early 1000s for most of them, although Sweden would see a successful pagan uprising under Sven the Sacrificer as late as around 1100, and Dalarna still remained unconverted in 1177. Yet even in Sweden, St Ansgar had already made some converts at Birka by 830, and elsewhere in the Viking world there were more than a few significant conversions during the late 800s. Guthrum's famous treaty of Wedmore with Alfred in 878, for example, included – among other things – the Danish leader's acceptance of Christianity. Increasing exposure to the Western world certainly worked as a powerful booster in the conversion process – especially by outward Viking migrations to the British Isles and Normandy, but also inwards through evangelistic missions to Scandinavia from the Carolingian empire and the see of Hamburg-Bremen. Equivalent pressures for conversion were also encountered in Russia once it had itself become Orthodox, while even before the Crusades the lure of the Holy Land could often exercise its own particular magic upon those who had voyaged as far as Gibraltar ('Narvesund') or Constantinople ('Micklegard').

However it came about, the moment of religious conversion represented a traumatic turning point at which the whole time-honoured pantheon of pagan gods – from stalwart Thor of the thunder to wily Odin of the ravens – suddenly found itself consigned to that particular Valhalla which is 'the dustbin of history'. The extinction of a long-standing religion must surely be a very rare and significant event especially when, as in this case, it also seemed to mark the transition from an excitingly heroic age into a drabber, more disciplined – although sometimes perhaps slightly more charitable – way of life. There can be little wonder, then, that conversion to Christianity is often seen as a very major landmark in Scandinavian evolution.

Another school of historians, however, claims that the key change came rather later than that, at the moment when the Vikings finally became indis-

Table B

The conversion of the Viking lands to Christianity

England – Treaty of Wedmore 878 (Guthrum).
Normandy – Treaty of St Clair sur Epte 911 (Rolf the Ganger).
Kiev – 989 (St Vladimir).
Iceland – 1000 (following the mission of Thangbrand).
Sweden – c.1000–1100 (cf St Ansgar had failed 829 etc).
Ireland – c.1020 (Sigtryg Silkbeard).
Norway – c.995–1028 (Olaf Tryggvason and St Olaf).
Denmark – c.1060s (Sven Estrithson, Harald and then St Canute; cf St Ansgar had failed 826).

---

tinguishable from the foreign native populations into which they had settled: when they 'turned bamboo' and allowed the balance of their culture and institutions to be swayed by the alien influences around them. Thus we can talk of Harald Hard-ruler's failed 'Viking' invasion of England directly from Norway in 1066, but of William's successful 'Norman' one from Rouen in the same year. By that time the Normans had apparently ceased to be Vikings, even though the whole outreaching thrust of their culture had first been activated by the insertion of hyperactive Scandinavian settlements and sailing skills into the otherwise very French (or 'Frankish') Seine valley. By 1066 the Normans had absorbed all external influences and had settled down into a distinctive 'post-Viking' way of life, war and politics. Indeed, something quite similar could also be said of the defeated English king Harold himself. Not only did he, like all Anglo Saxons, speak a language that was more or less comprehensible to the Vikings, but he had personally assimilated many Viking influences from his Danish mother and from the whole court of King Canute. He followed a hybrid style of Anglo-Scandinavian kingship that was fairly widespread in those times, and in his final campaigns he seemed to draw upon such Viking military traditions as mobility and boldness. This was itself reminiscent of his 'thoroughbred English' father, Earl Godwine, who had employed mariners who were 'sailors by profession and pirates at heart' (Stenton, p.559). Harold was therefore almost as much of a Viking as William, even though neither of them was known by that description at the time, and their culminating 'English vs Norman' battle at Hastings was very much a clash of post-Viking rather than of truly 'Viking' armies. Because the name 'Viking' has been removed from the nomenclature at Hastings – although less so from the substance – we must accept that we have by that time effectively entered a new age.

The Vikings became assimilated to a varying degree in each different host country, depending on the relative numerical, military–political and cultural balance between the invaders and the invaded in each particular case. In Novgorod and Kiev it apparently did not take long for a small number of Swedish merchant adventurers to adapt to Slav habits and transform themselves into 'Rus', who could no longer be considered as Vikings in any meaningful sense. This process seems to have been complete by about 1030, if not earlier. In Ireland, too, the Vikings provided a great boost to the coastal towns and trade, but failed to overwhelm the inland clans and so 'went native' almost as quickly as the Rus. The speed of assimilation would doubtless have been accelerated by the Vikings' short life expectancy, since it is second generation immigrants who will adopt the habits of their host country most easily, and will be left free to do so more quickly if their parents live for only thirty years rather than seventy.

In Iceland, by contrast, there was no indigenous population for the Vikings to merge into, apart from a few Irish anchorites who were disposed of as quickly as the first Scrælings to be encountered in Vinland (although in the latter case they would eventually take revenge). The Vikings in Iceland were thus left free to follow their own anarchically decentralised way of life for much longer than had been possible in other settlements, or even in Scandinavia itself. In Iceland they experienced only rather distant and intermittent cultural intrusions from Orkney, Scotland, Ireland or Norway. Of these it was the ambitions of the Norwegian kings which proved to be by far the most influential, achieving conversion to Christianity in 1000 and full political annexation in 1262-4. Yet even after that final upheaval there was still a thriving production of nostalgic saga literature, marking out Iceland as a distinctively Viking country long after most of its fellows had succumbed to the European mainstream. The Viking influence also remained strong in the Orkneys, Hebrides and Man up to around the same era, although in those cases there was no literary output in any way comparable to that of Iceland.

Nevertheless, apart from a few special cases like Iceland and the Western Isles, the Viking Age in both Scandinavia and the colonies was definitely coming to its end around 1050. This is often conveniently rounded up to the more 'memorable' date of 1066, although that is not exclusively because of the battle of Hastings. 1066 also happens to have been the date of Harald Hard-ruler's doomed expedition from Norway to York. This was one of the last North Sea ventures of its kind, although by no means the end of Scandinavian military manoeuvres in the area. King Sven Estrithson of Denmark would make two more attempts against eastern England in 1069-70 at the head of a very large fleet – although admittedly he contrived to snatch an even more crushing defeat from the gaping jaws of victory. His successor St Canute also made an abortive expedition to England with some 200 boats in 1075, and was on the point of trying again in 1086, in alliance with King Olaf of Norway and Count Robert of Flanders, when he was murdered. In a more westerly sea, Scandi-navian mercenaries from Ireland could still make appearances in North Wales as late as 1144.

In the Viking world as a whole, 1066 looks far less like a 'magic number' than it does to the modern English reader. Danish, Norwegian, Scots and Orcadian rulers continued to fight it out around the North Sea and the Irish Sea for over two centuries longer. Conversely, the English reader might reflect that the foreign seizure of the throne in 1066 was, in many ways, little more important than Canute's earlier accession in 1016. In both cases a powerfully-armed invader came across the sea and took over the government of the whole country, leaving a strong (but not necessarily overwhelming) cultural imprint.

Nevertheless, the peculiar resonance of 1066 to the English reader will always remain, and we will be using it as our end-date – at least as a rough guide – throughout the present book. Thus we can say that our 'Viking' subject matter covers almost three centuries, between 793 and 1066, and represents the period when 'post-Anglo-Saxon' waves of Scandinavian trader-pirates spread out from their homelands, established important overseas settlements and left their distinctive mark, but then gradually faded back into the general mainstream of European development.

Table C: A few definitions of 'Ages'

Ancient Period – From the Garden of Eden to the Birth of Christ, or to the end of the Roman Empire (or even possibly up to the Battle of Bosworth, 1485, or the 'Discovery' of America, 1492).

Classical Period – The rise and fall of the Ancient Greek and Roman states.

Roman Iron Age – (*ie* 'The Decline and Fall of the Roman Empire' in North Europe) – c.0–400 AD.

'The Dark Ages' – Normally taken to be c.400–1066.

Early Germanic Iron Age = essentially the same as:
   Migration Period (*ie* the era following Roman Departure) – c.400–575.

Later Germanic Iron Age = essentially the same as:
   Vendel Age – Era of Swedish wealth before the Viking Age – c.575–800.

Early Middle Ages – c.751 (King Pippin starts to rule the Franks) or 987 (Hugo Capet rules) – 1066 (or 1100).

Viking Age – Defined in this book as 793–1066 (but there are many alternative definitions!).

Age of the Settlements (in Iceland) = essentially the same as:
   The Saga Age – c.874–1030 (*ie* the period described in most Icelandic sagas).

The Age of the Sturlungs (in Iceland) – c.1180–1264 (*ie* the period in which most Icelandic sagas were written, and in which national independence was lost).

High Middle Ages – c.1066 (or 1100)–1350 (the Black Death started in 1348).

Late Middle Ages – c.1350–1485 or 1492.

The Renaissance – c.1450–1600.

The Meeting Between Civilian and Military

Most recent books about the Vikings have attempted to describe their entire culture and way of life, at peace as well as at war, without concentrating exclusively upon their specifically military attributes. For the general historian this is the normal approach to any past society, and even among military historians there is a strong modern movement towards an all-embracing 'war and society' style of analysis. This is indeed a particularly appropriate method of study in the case of the Vikings, since they did not themselves always make a very clear distinction between commerce and piracy; between fishing trips and raiding trips, or between settlement and invasion.

Admittedly we get a warning from *Orkneyinga Saga* (p.215, although discussing events around 1150 rather than before 1066) that notorious Vikings like Sven Asleifarson might actually regard farming as a more central activity than 'viking'. In this perspective the latter is seen as an overseas piratical adventure that is to be pursued specifically at the times of year when relatively little effort needs to be put into agriculture. Each year the seasons pass in the same sequence – sowing, spring viking, harvesting, autumn viking, Yule feast and over-wintering of the crews. In *Egil's Saga* Bjorn Brynjolfsson seems to have made a somewhat similar distinction when he 'divided his time between viking raids and trading voyages' (*Egil*, p.81). Nevertheless, even within the general category of 'viking' there was still likely to be just as much pure economic activity as there was military activity or piracy. Later in *Egil's Saga* Egil himself goes raiding in the Eastern Baltic and collects much loot; but instead of bringing it home he uses it as trade goods while he is still in Courland. This was, in effect, a 900s equivalent of the 1700s British slavers' triangle between West Africa where the slaves were procured, the New World where they were exchanged for more negotiable commodities such as sugar or cotton, and the home port of Bristol or Liverpool where that produce was finally converted into cash, land and social prestige.

Also very instructive is the case of the Halogalander Carl, who in 1026 sailed his trading vessel to Biarmeland (*ie* 'Permia', on the River Dvina, or modern Karelia) in company with the boat of Thore Hund. They first attended the local market and bought furs – in return for money or trade goods – as honest merchants. Once they had left the market, however, they realised they were thereby excused from the 'truce' under which they had been trading – so they decided to return to shore as plunderers. They robbed some rich graves and a temple, escaping to Finmark only to fall out among themselves. Carl was killed and his boat destroyed, leaving Thore to take home all the loot, as the sole beneficiary of the escapade (*The Olaf Sagas*, pp.271–6).

All three of the instances cited come to us through the sagas, and are therefore of highly questionable authenticity. However, it is worth noting that Sven Asleifarson, Bjorn Brynjolfsson and Thore Hund are not portrayed as having conducted their activities on a particularly grandiose scale. A very different type of warfare was surely simultaneously being undertaken – with far more centralised purpose and single-minded continuity – by bigger men who had bigger armies and fleets at their disposal. For example, we find plenty of cases in the literature of even quite small viking expeditions which lasted for most of a year, coming home only for an extended Yule feast, even before we start to read about the very common practice of over-wintering in foreign parts. A single sea voyage could itself sometimes take many weeks before landfall – depending on the distance and the weather – so a raider could scarcely guarantee to get back at just the right time for the harvest unless he was operating relatively close to home. In modern criminological parlance the 'twice a year' Viking was therefore presumably acting rather like a local burglar against his fairly close neighbours, whereas an 'all year' or 'over-wintering' Viking was acting more like an international fraudster or drug baron.

Even so, the primary purpose of the marauding armies emanating from Scandinavia during the Viking era was probably seen to be less a matter of fighting battles than of pure economic activity – *ie* of raising money by the easiest means. If that meant looting and pillaging in the manner of Egil and his friends it might well be profitable, but it might just as easily lead to violent, messy and unfortunate consequences, with very grave dangers to life and limb. If, on the other hand, it meant merely using the processes of civilised diplomacy to negotiate a lump sum of Danegeld, or the reluctant concession by one lord of what another lord believed to be legally his due, then it could be expressed as merely a legitimate act of taxation or politics. If it meant finding apparently under-utilised land for settlement and cultivation, it could be portrayed as 'making the desert bloom' – regardless of the wishes of the pre-existing population. After all, one man's invader is another man's administrator or farmer, just as one man's aggressive imperial general staff is another man's boring government bureaucracy.

Modern authorities seem to be divided on the question of whether or not the Vikings ever possessed anything resembling a true regular army; but it is clear that if one ever existed at all it was relatively small, and very localised in both time and place. The overwhelming majority of Viking campaigns were planned and manned by much less 'military' groups. They might be temporary musters of local or clan militias; expeditions of merchant adventurers or of yeoman fishermen; gangs of landless bandits; the retinues or household circles of particular lords, or almost any other category of essentially part time, amateur or unofficial soldiers that one could possibly imagine. In some cases these men might live the life of a warrior for many years on end – although more often it would be less – but the key point remains that they were not true 'professional soldiers' in the way that term is normally understood today. They may admittedly have conducted recognisable military operations following some rough equivalent of an operational doctrine, while their tactical doctrine was surely a well established and well-practised reality; but this should not be taken to imply that they saw their loyalties as lying primarily with the army or with the profession of arms. They did not really recognise a higher abstract 'art of war' in any modern sense of the term, although they doubtless followed certain general principles in a practical and instinctive way. Instead of constructing high-faluting theories about an art of war, they would almost always have tended to play things according to their pragmatic self-interest mixed with a basic code of honour, loyalty to one's lord, and probably even to law, custom, religion and tradition. This code was doubtless rooted far more in civilian attitudes than in specifically military ones, in a way that would appear strange to a modern soldier, or even to a Roman legionary. Hence we can say that few

Viking warriors should be counted as regular soldiers.

Most Vikings surely did little more than bring a high awareness of what we might today call 'security issues' into the conduct of their normal civilian transactions. To a Viking, the best definition of a soldier would surely have amounted to little more than 'an ordinary citizen who understands that he's living in a dangerous human environment'. He has to carry personal protection and to be a master of lethal force when necessary, although this may not mean he is any less of a handyman, a navigator, a husband or an athlete. In a society with very warlike codes of social, religious, literary and legal practice this definition would mean that almost all adult males might be counted as 'soldiers'. We should remember that Odin the wily war-god was worshipped even by poets, and cruel human sacrifices were sometimes associated even with the cult of Frey, the supposedly benign god of fertility and life. Who, after all, could possibly doubt that sword and shield were needed to defend croft and boat, just as plough and fishing-line were needed to bring forth the wealth of land and sea respectively? War and peace were indeed inseparable in Viking society, as has been very well understood by most modern scholars.

As a reaction against the bad old 'predatory' stereotype of the Vikings, there has certainly been a scholarly modern attempt to emphasise the non-military aspects of their lives. This has partly been the result of a splendid extension of archaeology in recent years, which has greatly expanded our appreciation of the Vikings' farming, fishing and family activities; but it has also represented a reaction against the many classic images portraying the Vikings as no more than blood-stained pirates or seaborne gangsters. The problem has perhaps been that too much of the original literature about the Vikings – whether from nostalgic but very bloodthirsty Icelandic sagas or from scandalised European clerics – portrayed them mainly as predatory warriors who were 'heroically self-defining' enforcers of their own laws. They too often lived by the sword, and so they came to be seen as essentially 'military'.

During the nineteenth century this image was taken up by romantics or Scandinavian nationalists who, frustrated by the complexities of modern technological life, looked back to a golden age of free enterprise and untramelled empire-building. During the twentieth century the same movement sometimes degenerated into outright fascism and an admiration of barbarism as a good in itself. The Nazi SS, in particular, drew a special inspiration from the legends and runes of its mythical Aryan past. In more recent times the 1994 Viking-pagan revival in Norway, associated with 'black metal' music, has continued the same theme. It is all this which much of modern scholarship has, quite rightly, been concerned with reversing and putting into a true perspective. From today's point of view, for example, the brutal 'eugenics' of *King Gautrek's Saga* (*Seven Viking Romances*, pp.142–4), in which spare or useless mouths are expected to jump over a cliff in order to conserve food stocks for the survivors, can be shown to have been intended as amusing satire rather than the directly literal call to action that half-educated Nazis may well have assumed.

About the only thing that can be said in favour of the 'heroic barbarian' image of the Vikings is that it did at least serve to enhance their international profile and make them familiar figures in Western culture. This has had an oddly positive effect upon their reputation, to the point where they seem to have escaped the linguistic fate of other 'barbarians' such as the Huns, Vandals, Tartars or Mongols – all of whose names have in recent times been used as terms of abuse. People are not insulted today by being called 'Vikings', since the Vikings are somehow seen as having grown out of, or atoned for, their early barbarism (even eventually converting to Christianity) in a way that is not true of all those other barbarian tribes. Nevertheless, there is still a strong Western liberal revulsion against what is perceived to be the underlying malice and violence of the Vikings. Right up to very recent times their odious image has been perpetuated in mass culture by the general thirst for garishly violent characters and 'bad guys'. For example, it is not very difficult to find modern animated cartoon films and video games which portray the evil villains as wearing 'Viking style' horned helmets, even though it is now very well established that such items of headgear were completely unknown among real Vikings.

A large proportion of what has been said about the Vikings amounts to historical and archaeological rubbish. Experts in the field have always been painfully aware of this, and so during much of the twentieth century an ever-growing scholarly counter-attack has been mounted against the bad old caricatures. This new wave of scholarship has been at pains to demonstrate the full and true glory of the Vikings' achievement as brilliant artists or poets, boat-builders or traders, explorers or board-gamers, stoical fisher-folk or crofters ... or simply as ordinary human beings possessing no fewer but no more heroic warrior qualities than anyone else. If their lives often tended to be nasty, mean, brutish and short, it had more to do with their relatively low technology in a harsh climate than with some general moral failure of their religion or law. Nor do we even have to see the Vikings as symbolising a 'dark' age or the near extinction of Western culture, since there is plentiful evidence that some of their most helpless victims – notably the English under King Aethelred the Unready – were actually flourishing both economically and artistically at precisely the same time as they were being subjected to some of the worst Scandinavian assaults. Indeed, it was precisely because they were so rich that they could afford to pay out such glittering piles of Danegeld, time after time, without apparently suffering very much financial pain.

Today, the much-needed academic 'war and society' counter-attack has successfully come to dominate our view of the subject, and it has in effect become a new orthodoxy. There is a difficulty, however, insofar as it sometimes fails to confront the idea that, for all their highly cultured and creative skills as civilians, it was mainly by naked force of arms that the Vikings were able to create their globally significant near-empires. Hence the inner secret of their success and historical prominence surely lay in their qualities as warriors (or 'pirates') first of all, and in other things only afterwards.

To the present author it therefore now seems a good time to stop and take stock – if only to gain a contrasting perspective – before we allow ourselves to be frog-marched too uncomplainingly or too rapidly into the 'war and society' lobby. At the risk of appearing retrogressive or anachronistic to the modern historical purist, I am therefore hoping in this book to re-insert a wee small wedge between the military and civilian aspects of Viking activity. The present work is intended to concentrate specifically on the Viking achievement in the art of war, rather than in such fields as architecture, agriculture, local government or the manufacture of soapstone bowls. It is intended to be a contribution to that honourable strand in modern military literature which is concerned not with glorifying barbarism, but with analysing the development and history of 'the art of war' as a distinct subject in its own right.

Apart from anything else, one excellent reason for limiting the present study to the art of war is that an extensive and entirely military analysis of the Vikings has not, apparently, been attempted recently by any practising military historian or student of strategy and tactics. Although the 'war and society' scholars have completely revolutionised our view of the Vikings during the past two generations, the one thing they have steered away from is a strictly military view. Yet military history itself has also moved with the times, and we can now review the military structure of past imperialism with new eyes. In the process we may even be able to give a new and stimulating, albeit perhaps slightly unconventional, polish to the findings of modern civilian scholarship.

It seems doubly timely to write such a book today because the 'war and society' school has, in effect, now won its campaign to counter-balance the wild bogey-man image that the Vikings used to generate in their rôle as warriors. We surely no longer need to be quite so 'politically correct' and onside with the civilian scholars as we might have been some forty or fifty years ago since, unlike then, they have now made their point stick pretty universally in the academic world, if not always with the wider public. Today we can surely afford to look around a little more widely without fearing that it will, in some sense, betray scholarship or archaeological science.

Finally, it is perhaps worth adding that the expansion of the British Empire between around 1600 and 1919 may be seen as a relevant parallel to the spread of Viking influence between the 800s and the 1000s. The British, like the Vikings before them, were in some ways exquisitely civilised at home but still capable of massive barbarities in their far flung colonies abroad. It has also been said that the British Empire was created in 'a fit of absence of mind', being based more upon blundering in the dark than upon some carefully-prepared blueprint. It was never really planned, but depended largely on local individual commercial, missionary or piratical initiatives, supported by a ferocious military culture. In all this the similarities with the Vikings are striking. Yet the haphazard nature of the British Empire does not prevent scholars from treating its military aspects as a distinct subject worthy of study, and there is in fact an important body of analytical military literature which dissects it – starting with the works of Julian Corbett and Colonel C.E. Calwell and progressing into the 'low intensity conflict' era of Frank Kitson and Robert Thompson. But if this is true for the British, why should it not apply almost equally to the Vikings? It is the contention of the present book that we should not be debarred from analysing the Viking art of empire-building as a distinct subject – and even as a distinctly military subject – any more than we have been for the British equivalent.

Perhaps the main difference between the two cases is that in the era of their empire-building the British did not often engage in internecine combats between themselves, but presented a more or less unified front to foreigners. Admittedly the foundation of the East India Company in 1600 preceded almost 150 years of fitful civil war and Jacobite rebellion inside Britain and, like the Norwegian migrants to Iceland around 900, many of the early British settlers in the New World were motivated as much by a fear of persecution at home as by the agricultural or piscatorial attractions of their intended destination. Nor did such tensions entirely disappear after Culloden, since there was a British civil war in America between 1775 and 1783 which was followed by many spasmodic agrarian, industrial and constitutional disputes within England itself, not to mention the greater endemic conflicts in Ireland.

By and large, however, these internecine troubles of the expanding British Empire can scarcely be compared in significance with those experienced by the Vikings. Whereas the British fought by far the majority of their wars against foreigners, the Vikings surely fought most of theirs against other Vikings. A Viking king could count himself lucky – or even in some cases deeply dishonoured – if he died peacefully in his bed. This is dramatically illustrated by the fates of the Norwegian kings during the Viking era (see Table D). Thus out of sixteen kings, two abdicated voluntarily and later died in bed (12.5%); three died in office from accidental or natural causes (18.7%); two were murdered (12.5%), and six fell in battle (37.6%, including two who had already been forced out of Norway). The remaining three were forced out of Norway before they died of natural causes (18.7%), making a grand total of eleven who were forced out or killed by enemies (68.8%) and only five who were not (31.2%). There would indeed appear to be a solid factual foundation for the old Viking saying that 'a king is for glory, not for long life' (Foote & Wilson, *The Viking Achievement*, p.144). By contrast the British Empire also had a total of sixteen rulers between 1600 and 1919; but only Charles I was killed and only James II and Richard Cromwell were forced definitively out of office by their enemies (*ie* 18.8% of the total). If the start of British imperial expansion is taken to be 1700 rather than 1600, furthermore, then not one out of ten rulers was removed from office by enemy action.

This turns out to be a not very much better record than that of the 20 kings of Wessex and England between 802 and 1066, who had only two murdered (Edward the Martyr and Edmund, son of Edward the Elder) and only one killed in battle (Harold Godwinson at Hastings). The remaining 85% fought many battles, not always against Vikings, and had varying experiences of success and failure. Not all of them held on to all of their territory all of the time. Alfred the Great and Aethelred the Unready each suffered particularly notable reverses, although admittedly the former – in common with his grandfather Egbert who had temporarily been banished to Frankia by Offa of Mercia – did go on to become *Bretwalda* (or chief king of all England). Nevertheless, they all died of natural causes as far as one can tell, and so their level of personal risk at the hands of internal enemies would seem to have been dramatically lower than that of their Norwegian contemporaries. Maybe one could massage the statistics by taking out the three Viking kings of England (Canute, Harold and Hardacanute, all of whom happened to die in bed) and adding the (significantly

Table D

The fate of the Norwegian kings

Gudrod the Magnificent: murdered by the wife he had abducted.
Halfdan the Black: accidentally fell into a hole in the ice.
Harald Finehair: voluntarily abdicated and died naturally.
Eric Bloodaxe: exiled to York; killed in the battle of Stainmore.
Hakon the Good: killed in the battle of Fitjar.
Harald Greycloak: killed in the battle of Lymfjord.
Earl Hakon: murdered by a spy.
Olaf Tryggvason: drowned in the battle of Svold.
Earl Eric: transferred from Norway to Northumberland then died of disease.
Earl Sven: chased out by St Olaf, died of disease in the Eastern Baltic.
St Olaf: chased out of Norway: killed in battle of Stickelstad.
Earl Hakon: lost at sea off Orkney.
Canute the Great: voluntarily abdicated and died naturally.
Sven: chased out of Norway but died naturally.
Magnus the Good: died naturally.
Harald Hard-ruler: killed in the battle of Stamford Bridge.

---

more accident-prone) kings of Mercia, Northumbria and East Anglia to the list. But even so, the impression still remains etched upon our minds that the Vikings followed a far more quarrelsome, reckless, primitive and dangerous style of kingship than anyone else.

Of the Norwegian Viking kings, all sixteen had to face at least one major rebellion on home territory sooner or later (*ie* 100%), whereas only eight out of sixteen rulers of the British Empire had to do so between 1600 and 1919 (*ie* 50%, which also happens to be the same percentage as for 1700–1919; and probably the Wessex/English kings of 802–1066 did not have to face a markedly higher level of specifically English rebellion). Hence we can say that the British Empire at its height may to some extent be characterised as an exploitation of relatively peaceful times at home, a release mechanism for national energies that might otherwise have led to domestic trouble. For the Vikings, however, the exact opposite seems to have been the case. For them the overseas colonies were very much an afterthought, and a secondary consequence of the main business of defeating domestic enemies or defending the homeland against assaults from other parts of Scandinavia.

Although Norway was attacked very often between 793 and 1066, it was almost never attacked by non-Viking races. Denmark admittedly suffered endemic border (or 'marcher') warfare with the stalwart Wends and Caro-lingians, while Sweden was frequently raided from the East. In neither of these last two cases, however, did these wars add up to anything like as much fighting as there was between the Viking states themselves. By the same token the Viking attacks on Frisia, Britain, Ireland, France, Spain and Russia were rarely conducted by a major Scandinavian king until the colonisation process was already well under way, and even then many of the campaigns turned out to be directed against rival Viking armies. Offensive operations against genuinely foreign foes were more normally run by freebooters, landless 'sea-kings' or princes who were either working their 'apprenticeship' for high royal office, or trying to win some compensation for banishment from the home country.

If we are looking for the 'Viking art of war', therefore, we should look at Viking warfare against other Vikings every bit as much as we look at their attacks on other cultures.

Myth and Reality

There is certainly nothing mythological about the Vikings' readiness to take up the sword. They did often fight each other; they did often go raiding; and they did conduct many major campaigns by both land and sea. Unfortunately for us, however, the record for most of this has been handed down through sources that are notoriously very difficult to interpret, whether they be contemporary accounts by non-Vikings, or the Icelandic sagas of a considerably later era. In both cases we can often detect that something very important did occur at roughly some particular time and place: but we will probably not have any reliable details about just what the 'occurrence' actually comprised.

The death of St Edmund is a classic case in point. In their entry for late 869 the various versions of the *Anglo Saxon Chronicle* tell us only the following:

> In this year the host went [or 'rode'] across Mercia into East Anglia, and took winter-quarters at Thetford: and the same winter St Edmund the king fought against them, and the Danes won the victory, and they slew the king and overran the entire kingdom, and destroyed all the monasteries to which they came (the names of the leaders who slew the king were Ingware and Ubba). (*ASC*, pp.70–1.)

We also know from a strong early tradition that the king was killed on 20th November and finally interred at Bury St Edmunds, while the chronicler Asser adds that he had fought fiercely but was killed 'with a large number of his men, and the Vikings rejoiced triumphantly.' (Keynes & Lapidge, *Alfred the Great*, p.78.) A cult formed around the martyred saint, and it was flourishing after around 900 ... and that's more or less all we do know about the incident.

Later chroniclers asserted, variously, that it all happened in either Hoxne or Hellesdon and not Thetford, and that the king was killed during the battle, or

Figure 1   **The distance of sources from the Vikings**

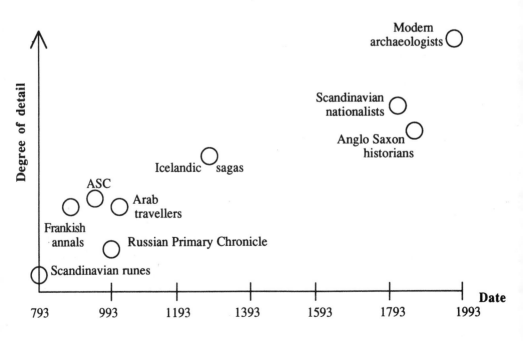

possibly in a second battle after he had actually won the first one. We also have a long speech that he is supposed to have given before he voluntarily surrendered himself to a certain fate (either by accepting battle against the odds, or by literally surrendering to the enemy). Most writers, however, seem to have had the martyrdom of St Stephen high in their minds, since they deny that Edmund actually went down fighting, or even that he voluntarily surrendered, but tend more towards the view that he was discovered hiding under a bridge after the battle (whichever one it was) had finished. He was then tied to a tree, scourged, shot dead with arrows (or possibly only wounded by the arrows) and finally beheaded. Alternatively, some say that this was not in fact the case, but that he was treated to the notorious 'blood eagle' instead. Bishop Hunbeorht may or may not have been killed with him. Anyway, in 1848 someone claimed to have found one of the original arrowheads embedded in an ancient oak tree at Hoxne, even though the burial mound for the fallen is supposed to be at Thetford. Just to ensure an equilibrium of uncertainty, the most recent historians of the event seem to prefer the Hellesdon site to either of these two places.

Oh dear – the whole thing quickly becomes very confusing, and all we can really say for sure is that we really do not know very much at all about the death of St Edmund, except that it happened somewhere in East Anglia and probably on 20th November 869. All the rest is highly unreliable later gossip, probably embellished into a longer story by writers who knew no more than is in the *ASC*, but who didn't want to disappoint the martyr's devoted followers by such a short account. We certainly have nothing like military detail for the battle, or battles – some even say it was a *siege* and not a battle at all. We do not know how many men were on either side (recent guesses have varied between 1000 and 20,000), and there is absolutely no record of how the battle developed or what tactics were used. We do not know the scale of casualties suffered by either side. Most accounts follow the *ASC* in saying the Danes came by land but Abbo of Fleury, writing a century after the event, thought they came by sea. The reader is left entirely free to pay his money and take his choice.

Cases like this cannot tell us much about 'the Viking art of war', particularly not about the precise sequence of events on a given day. It is only by piecing together dozens of similar cases that we can begin to get even a general idea of what sort of actions may have been normal or standard operating procedures. Sometimes we are lucky enough to get a pretty strong piece of evidence from a given incident about one particular aspect, even if there is nothing at all for others. This can then be compared with complementary cases where we have better evidence for the other aspects but not for the first, and so on. Sometimes the archaeological record can supply vital clues, and gradually a picture of sorts can be pieced together. Nevertheless, it must be stressed that we simply do not know much about the Viking art of war. More or less informed guesswork is really all we have.

When we come to the Icelandic sagas of the 1200s, the same problem becomes still more acute, since they usually tempt us with longer and more attractive stories which are often centred specifically around warfare. They amount to a far more interesting and extensive body of literature than we have, for example, from either Germany or England before – and maybe even during – the time of Chaucer. The sagas are also written by Vikings for Vikings, and therefore have a certain credibility and sympathy for their subject which is frequently lacking in the works of moralising Western churchmen. Even though Iceland had generally abandoned overt paganism long before the sagas were written, it still adhered to many other Viking customs and was relatively sheltered from some of the more uncompromisingly progressive aspects of continental European thought. It is also highly relevant to remember that the general conditions of travel and combat around 1200 cannot have been all that different from those of 900, even if the specific events and personalities of the earlier era were often too far in the past to be reported with any accuracy. Hence the sagas often seem to be on somewhat firmer ground regarding general conditions than they are in respect of specific events and people.

A relevant comparison is that although today we do not know as much as we would like about the private lives and precise thought processes of Wellington or Napoleon, and not even the grandchildren of their contemporaries remain alive today, we can still recognise some important features of their world, from which many commonplace stories, quotations and jokes about them have come down to us. 'Up Guards and at 'em', for example, or 'Not tonight Josephine', were both ringing phrases in twentieth-century music hall, even if neither quotation can actually be authenticated. It is in this sort of way that we should perhaps see the saga writers' perception of their ancestors, and so, albeit only by somewhat indirect means, we ought to be able to draw a certain amount of information, or at least attitudes, from them.

What we should be careful to avoid, however, is the recurring temptation to read the sagas as if they are all composed of literal and well-attested fact. As with a good Dracula movie, a saga story can often start with a reasonable enough everyday life scenario which lulls the reader into accepting its plausibility – but it may then gradually descend into extremes of magic, mystery and horror which, though it may have had some basis in legend, clearly has none at all in fact.

The case of Ragnar Lothbrok – the most famous and widely-reported Viking hero of them all – is instructive. In Saxo Grammaticus' supposedly serious *History of the Danes* (written by a Dane, but drawing upon some Icelandic sources), Ragnar is portrayed in several different and contradictory roles. At one moment he might be a local king of Sjaelland fighting against Jutes and/or Scanians in a moderately credible way (Saxo p.281 – although his '300 boats' still seem rather a lot for such a local magnate); then at another he might appear as a highly improbable emperor ruling all of Ireland, Orkney and

England as well as the whole of Scandinavia, bequeathing a fleet of 1700 boats to his sons (p.292). He invents a useful set of snake-repellant leggings combined with non-metallic body armour (p.281 and especially footnotes), as well as some workable bronze tanks that rout the Permians (p.286). He goes on to win spectacular victories in 'Hellespont', not to mention defeating the great Emperor Charlemagne and quite a few fire-breathing dragons besides. It is commonly recognised that in all this Saxo has stuffed together all sorts of disparate references (mostly dating from later than 1100) which describe many different historical and legendary figures – tapping perhaps as many as two dozen quite separate traditions. Maybe someone in Sjaelland really did defeat the Jutes and/or Scanians in the early 800s, and maybe some Danish king really did once win a temporarily important victory against Charlemagne's allies. (This is probably a reference to King Godfred's burning of the Abodrite town of 'Reric' in 808 and kidnapping of its merchants to Hedeby, after which he went on to take £100 in geld from the Frisians in 810 'with 200 ships'. Both these victories, however, were soon negated when Charlemagne imposed a peace upon Godfred's successor, Hemming.) The idea of a North Sea Empire that included all of Ireland and Britain as well as Scandinavia must surely come from the time of Canute the Great in the early 1000s, and not from Ragnar Lothbrok's early 800s at all.

For an even more extreme example, let us look at the saga of Arrow-Odd. It too begins with an air of normality, describing the youth and upbringing of a noble Norwegian warrior who soon starts to go a-viking in search of loot and reputation. So far so good, and the story remains credible enough. It is only gradually that we come to realise that this is really a tale of Arrow-Odd's combat against some pretty powerful sorcery, and that his main weapon consists of enchanted golden arrows which incorporate an automatic boomerang-return feature. Before very long he is being flown around the European air lanes suspended beneath a giant vulture, after which he begets a son from a troll giantess at least four times his height. His first wife has by this time already given him a magic shirt which includes some unusual properties that would be the absolute envy of any 'survivalist' today (*Seven Viking Romances*, p.52). It is proof against cold, fire and iron weapons. It also prevents fatigue and hunger and, being silk-based, is remarkably light to wear. The only thing it cannot cure is cowardice – but since Arrow-Odd does not suffer from that particular complaint, it does not bother him very much. From a modern perspective one may perhaps wonder how it might have fared against nerve gas or depleted uranium bullets; but however that may be, one should surely not imagine that it can give us any hint at all about how real Viking armour may have been constructed.

With the 'lying sagas' or 'romances', such as Arrow-Odd's, it is not too difficult to detect that the authentic historical content is small. Indeed, they have many resonances – and occasionally even whole anecdotes – in common with Arthurian or Robin Hood legends. Thus the main question today may be more a matter of 'did Arrow-Odd exist at all?' rather than 'did he really do all the things that are claimed for him?'. Did Ragnar Lothbrok actually exist? Maybe such romantic heroes are indeed based upon great warriors or bandit chieftains who really did live (and one of whose names might, indeed, even have been Ragnar). Grettir the Strong, the biggest and hunkiest Icelander of all (although his virile member was paradoxically reputed to be somewhat inadequate – see *Grettir*, p.195) seems to have been a real person, and his name and family are historically attested in Icelandic genealogy, although nothing more than that is known for sure (*ibid*, p.v). Certainly many of the places specifically mentioned in all three of these sagas exist, even if the dragons, giants, witches and magical phenomena never did.

Perhaps the main difference of such sagas from the basic ground-rules that apply to the Arthurian or Robin Hood cycles is that Ragnar extirpates Christianity, Grettir has apparently nothing to do with it, while Arrow-Odd accepts it only rather reluctantly, imperfectly and late. The code of chivalry which he takes up is certainly somewhat under-developed in its small print. This code is admittedly very sound on rape and the need to rescue maidens in distress, although perhaps a little too pernickety in its taboo against eating uncooked meat. King Arthur or Robin Hood would also surely have felt at least a little mean and unchivalric if they had ever adopted Arrow-Odd's formula for pillage, which amounts to what J.K. Galbraith might have called 'the ideal of a zero growth economy'. This was summed up in Arrow-Odd's ominously flexible claim that 'I never rob merchants or peasants beyond the occasional raid to cover my immediate needs.' (*Seven Viking Romances*, p.49.)

The sagas certainly contain many hints of what we today think of as late medieval Western European romances – or even as Grimm's nineteenth-century fairy tales. The great warrior tends to go out on a quest and is promised the hand of the princess, and at least half her father's kingdom, if only he can kill the dragon or – more usually, and in fact far more credibly – collect some outstanding taxes or land rights from one of her father's recalcitrant subjects. Treasures of great price are very meaningfully exchanged; loyal bands of hand-picked, high-value knights are nurtured and/or squandered in battle; and evil sorceress-queens are cleverly outmanoeuvred before being finally crushed to death by boulders or wooden clubs at the very altars of their unclean pagan temples (eg *Seven Viking Romances*, pp.116, 120, 164–9, etc). Although we can be certain that very little of this actually happened in anything like the way portrayed, it seems rather important to point out that the 'basic ground-rules' for it all are very probably located in some sort of genuine historical understanding – and even 'truth'. Newly-converted Christian kings in the Scandinavia of the 900s or 1000s surely did see it as an important boost to their personal status (or political outreach, if you will) if they could kill Odin-worshipping rival kings and queens, preferably with extremes of torture and in the smoking ruins of their outmoded temples. Why, we have seen politically active priests killed at their altars even in our own day, and places of worship are still being attacked very much as an integral part of the political process.

Arranged dynastic marriages were also surely the norm for royal princesses in Viking times, and in fact they have been the very essence of international diplomacy for much of the world's history, right up to modern times. Once one starts to link the idea of dynastic marriage to the idea of geo-political diplomacy, one is really not very far away from the sort of raw, power-political deal implied by a saga (or fairy tale) offer such as: 'Defeat my enemy, my boy, and I will let you marry my daughter as well as shower you with silver coins'. One does not have to look very much further than the present-day British royal family to see that a widely-accepted myth of royal magic can actually have some very earthy and simple explanations in everyday reality; and yet, even today, it can still be accepted almost unquestioningly by a surprisingly large number of supposedly cynical courtier-politicians, sophisticated experts, and self-proclaimed 'constitutional specialists'.

One interestingly chivalric military detail which pervades the Icelandic sagas is the idea that most battles should be seen as formal duels or 'trials by battle'. In post-Viking terminology we can call them a type of tournament, which, of course, was already a commonplace idea in the European romances of the 1200s. At one point Arrow-Odd himself is even supposed to have gone jousting (as the champion of his whole army), using very un-Viking 'great long lances', four of which are broken before he and his half-phantom opponent finally agree they are equally matched, and therefore that their two armies should not fight – even though they eventually do, albeit for somewhat different reasons (*ibid*, p.117).

It is certainly common in the sagas that a particular time and place is agreed in advance for two opposing armies to meet (with or without equal numbers of men or boats – the accounts vary from one occasion to another). If the battle is on land, the field should be fenced or marked out with hazel branches, exactly like the defined areas used for individual duelling and very similar to a modern boxing ring. There may be rules laid down concerning weaponry or tactics just as, in individual combats, the rules allow each protagonist to have three shields and maybe also a named second to carry them. We will discuss some of the implications of all this in later chapters; but for the moment it is simply worth noting that modern historical opinion is very sceptical that such formality ever really attended any of the battles so described in the sagas, except possibly in the case of some sea battles, which needed specially calm and sheltered conditions to be fought at all. There was probably often plenty of diplomacy and legal wrangling between the two sides, and their battle lines on land were doubtless clearly defined and understood as occupying one piece of ground rather than another – but the complexity and chivalry of the arrangements that are sometimes implied by the sagas should be taken with a pinch of salt.

Chivalric ideals of honour made something for the scribes to exercise their imaginations about but – as in the case of most Scandinavian civil law codes surviving from this period – it probably had only the very vaguest basis in reality. (See extensive discussions of the laws in Foote & Wilson, *The Viking Achievement*, and p.379 for the rules of individual duelling.) Such local codes as the Trondelag 'Frostathing Law' or the Sognefjord 'Gulathing Law' were written down in an apparently meaningful form during the 900s, including provisions that may cast light on social stratification (based on the fines to be raised for various classes of injury on various classes of people), and on the provisions for mobilising the population for war. These law codes may, perhaps, represent some sort of ideal that the Vikings believed they should aim for; but it still seems likely that few of their provisions were ever actually translated into literal reality.

If the 'romances' require some careful disentanglement of fact from fiction, then the same is true to a far greater extent for the 'kings' sagas' (especially *Heimskringla*), which attempt to give a truthful and comprehensive historical record and look alluringly credible on the surface. On closer examination, however, they suffer from many of the same distortions as we find in Arrow-Odd, especially the crippling obstacles to accuracy resulting from their great distance in time and place from the events they describe. The more intimate and moralising, but also still supposedly truthful, 'family sagas' are based on some detailed Icelandic family records but nevertheless present very similar problems. There are many potential pitfalls, and we must approach all of the sagas with extreme scepticism, remembering that even the apparently least 'lying' of them were still often tales designed primarily for amusement, to while away the long Icelandic winter nights. Even though they are sold as 'true stories', they probably bear about as much relation to the events they describe as do modern cinema renditions of Custer's last stand or the gunfight at the OK Corral.

The case of the so-called 'blood eagle' makes a telling cautionary tale about the dangers of accepting specific military details as retailed in the sagas. Not only do the sagas today suffer from all the normal risks of translation (in this case from medieval Icelandic into modern English), but the medieval saga writers themselves can also be shown to have made some wildly inaccurate assumptions when they first translated the Icelandic scaldic verses which dated from perhaps two centuries earlier. As Roberta Frank has recently demonstrated very convincingly in the *English Historical Review*, the key text for all the allegations of blood-eagling is the original scaldic verse for the killing of the

(possibly only legendary) King Aella at York in 867. When it was first conceived, this was intended to say only that the victim was killed and left as
metaphorical food for eagles (and it could just as easily have been crows, ravens
or vultures, which were equally favoured by poets). Such literary images were
utterly commonplace at the time, and there is no real reason to believe that
anything unusual had happened apart from the simple fact that Aella had been
killed, in circumstances that we cannot today even begin to know. Indeed, one
of the main normal devices of the scaldic verses was precisely the use of clever
metaphors and images (called 'kennings') that were designed to make elaborate
metaphors and riddles which deliberately complicated and concealed very
simple events or things. The subsequent saga writers knew all about this
process, but it did not stop them misunderstanding the poetic image of King
Aella as carrion, and leaping to the false assumption that it was incontrovertible
evidence that he had had the shape of an eagle either carved on his skin or
sculpted out of his intestines, and that then, maybe, salt had been rubbed in
before the victim finally died. It is this story which – like 'send three and
fourpence, we're going to a dance' – has grown and grown ever since, so that all
the saga writers soon began to believe that execution by the blood eagle was
indeed a very common practice among the Vikings. A whole mythology –
exactly as in the case of St Edmund's martyrdom – soon began to accrete
around it.

When viewed in the cold light of day, there actually seems to be no contemporary evidence whatsoever for the blood eagle, regardless of whether it
implied the carving of an eagle on the victim's back, or his artistic evisceration.
It turns out to have been entirely a much later literary conceit, based on a
mistranslation, in just the same way that the alleged Viking habit of drinking
out of human skulls turns out to have been simply a mistranslation for their
actual habit of drinking out of animal horns. These false legends should
therefore be treated in exactly the same way as Arrow-Odd's (alleged) 'survivalist' silk shirt, or St Edmund's (alleged) long parting solliloquy as imagined
by Abbo of Fleury. The whole blood eagle phenomenon was entirely invented
in the Iceland of the 1100s, and its only link with poets vaguely contemporary
with the actual event is every bit as unsubstantiated as the technical details of
just how the execution itself may have been carried out.

None of this is in any way to question the revolting ferocity that must surely
habitually have attended Viking executions by torture, since there is absolutely
no evidence to suggest that they were anything less than revoltingly ferocious.
We must remember that the ritual of hanging, drawing and quartering was still
considered to be a suitable spectacle for the general public as recently as the
seventeenth century – and that more countries in the modern world still
routinely practise torture than do not. Even in our own supposedly humane
society there are many people who would very much like to return to public

executions and floggings, so it is surely a certainty that the Vikings did not shrink from such things. But the point that should be made in the present case is simply that the blood eagle as such did not exist, even though a very great deal of ink has delineated its ominous outline during the past 800 years.

The Icelandic sagas and the non-Viking chronicles can each tell us certain things about how the Vikings operated, about the people who led them, and about what they actually did: but we must beware that a very great deal of what these sagas say is false – often quite deliberately and artfully – and that they still tell us absolutely nothing about many of the military details that we would most like to know today. For example, the question 'did the Vikings have compasses?' is a matter of absolutely crucial importance to any appreciation of their skill as mariners – but the answer seems to be that 'we really haven't a clue', or at least that 'we have no conclusive proof'. Exactly the same is true of key questions like 'did they have any sort of maps?', 'did many of them wear helmets?', 'did they have many mail shirts?' or 'did they have any concept of battle drill?'.

It is perhaps worth making one general reflection at this point, which is that the Vikings – in common with all other peoples in all periods of history – were a complex mixture of the primitive and the advanced. If we remember that for much of the Viking period they measured the value of silver coins by their raw weight rather than by their face value or the denominations stamped upon them, then we have to believe that in many respects they must have been a pretty backward bunch – and so the answer to all the above questions is very probably 'no'. But if, on the contrary, we remember that the Vikings discovered America, founded both Dublin and Normandy, and attacked Constantinople at least three times, then we may begin to revise our perceptions somewhat. After all, it was none other than the supposedly 'backward' Soviet Union that defeated Hitler and then led the way into space.

In the present book we can offer some more or less informed guesses about all of these questions, but ultimately we lack the sort of certainty enjoyed in better-documented periods of history. Hence whenever the present author finds himself carried away into making dogmatic statements and definite assertions that some particular fact about the Vikings is 'true', then it is the reader's personal duty to make the mental addition of 'perhaps', 'maybe' or 'it's really all only guesswork anyway'.

CHAPTER 2

The Causes of Viking Expansion

If you are going to study the Vikings, you will have to study the whole of European history, covering a third of a millennium.
– Matthew Bennett, in conversation with the author.

It is indeed notable ... how raids slackened as they grew more dangerous and less profitable.
– H.R. Loyn, *The Vikings in Britain*, p.31.

The Legacy of the Romans

The immediately pre-Viking northern world had in many essentials been set up for future development in a very direct way by the Roman Empire. It was the Romans who had first brought Angles and Saxons (as soldiers) into England, and the Romans who had inserted both Christianity and the Latin language into the whole of Gaul west of the Rhine, some centuries earlier than either of them would definitively percolate beyond that particular *limes*. It was the Romans who determined that the Germanic peoples inhabiting most of England, northern France, Benelux and southern Germany would be brought heavily under the influence of Romance culture during the first half-millenium AD. They also built roads and developed an extensive waterborne trade around the coasts and up the rivers which linked the North Sea and the Baltic with the Mediterranean and the Levant. They established a generally successful way of doing things within all these areas, and quite a lot of it managed to survive the departure of the legions in the early 400s.

Admittedly many of the Roman towns quickly evaporated or at least shrank, and some of the old certainties, such as a secure coinage, were discarded. There were plenty of wars and invasions among the successors to the Romanised areas, not least the invasion of England by Angles, Saxons, Frisians and Jutes. For all that, however, there remained a strong Romance cultural legacy among the Germanic peoples of Britain and 'former North Gaul', and it even possessed the power to reproduce itself and spread. St Augustine's successful mission to convert England to Roman Christianity came in 597, and the last pagan king of Mercia was killed as early as 655 ('strong in the faith of his ancestors', as his belated obituary in *The Times* would report in 1965). Both the artistic achievement of the Anglo Saxons and the political consolidation of the

Figure 2

The Roman northern world

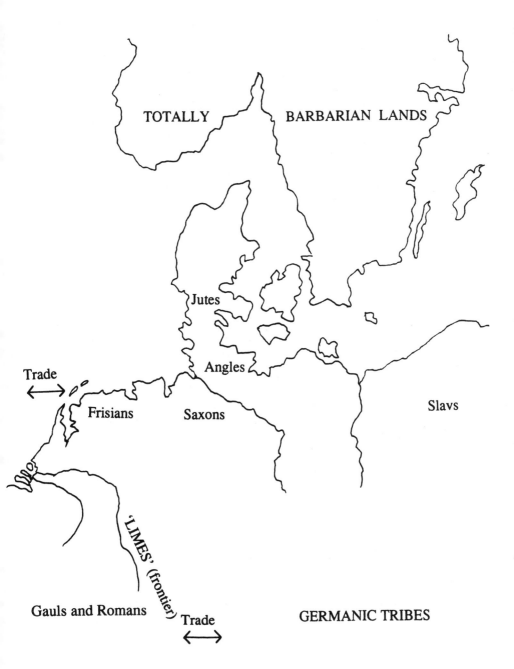

Merovingians were blossoming and being exported by the 700s. By the early 800s Charlemagne's empire became as strongly defended against external barbarians as the Roman empire itself had been in those areas. Important new trading centres, such are Dorestadt, Hamwih (Southampton) and London were being established, just as were the arts of seamanship. This period cannot simply be dismissed as inactive or moribund.

However, the Romans had largely failed to understand or penetrate the civilisations of the Irish, the Picts, the Saxons, the Slavs and, especially, the Scandinavians. The Romans possessed relatively little knowledge of these tribes that seemed so peripheral to the world of their Mediterranean empire. Scandinavia and the Celtic fringe were particularly shunned as strange and inhospitable terrain with treacherous seaways and unpredictable weather. They represented something like an ultimate barbarism, lying beyond even the dark forests of Germany in which Varus had lost his legions in 9 AD. They were, nevertheless, areas that were widely settled and cultivated at that time. Scandinavia certainly contained a race of hardy farmers, fishermen and sailors who knew all the wiles of the sea and all the arts of the crofter. Their more adventurous spirits were already voyaging abroad to participate in the network of trade which joined northern Europe to the Mediterranean, the Middle East and even to distant Cathay. There were Scandinavian settlements on the Eastern Baltic coast long before the Viking Age began. If the Romans failed to discover this area in full, therefore, that did not stop the Scandinavians either from interacting with their own immediate neighbours or from discovering the civilisation and wealth of the Roman Empire itself, and of its successors in the Greek Byzantine empire and in the Arab empire of Islam.

Besides, the former Roman Empire was populated in part by many active Germanic peoples who shared much common stock, including language and religion, with the Scandinavians. The Frisians, Saxons and Franks were close neighbours who between them had been the leading North Sea mariners and traders before the Viking Age. They must have had much in common with the Scandinavians, and must have known them well. We might even go so far as to see the eventual Viking campaigns as almost civil wars between all these Germanic peoples. There had certainly been many Viking-style operations conducted by many of the non-Viking Germanic races before the Vikings themselves erupted onto the scene, so we should beware of falling into the trap of regarding the Vikings as an entirely unique or special phenomenon. Their culture could boast its own distinctive artistic styles and laws, but it often held to the same language, religion and art of war as its neighbours south of the Baltic.

During the Vendel Age the Scandinavians were certainly flourishing, and we have many archaeological finds to testify to their building methods, their naval architecture, their boat burials and their extensive trading contacts with the

Table E

Principal entrepots

Norway

Halogaland starts to be opened c. late 700s (merchant? barracks in Stavanger).
Kaupang (= Skiringsal near Oslo: less rich than Hedeby) = 800–950.
Oslo, Tønsberg, Trondheim start in 1000s (but Trondheim already politically important).
Bergen = 1070.

Sweden

Helgö Island (400–late 700s) replaced by Birka in late 700s (ends c.975), which is replaced by Sigtuna c.975.
Västergarn (Gotland) = c.800s.

Denmark

Hedeby (plus Hollingsted to West) = 700s. Swedish c.875–925. Hit by Slavs c.1000; moves to Schleswig c.1050.
Lund, Roskilde, Odense, Ålborg, Schleswig start c.1000.
Århus starts c.900 (and later Viborg).
Ribe (West Denmark opposite Hedeby) starts and growth of imports in 700s.
Hamburg sacked 845 (by Danish king Horik).

North Sea

York already a trade centre, but boosted by arrival of Vikings.
Dorestad, founded c.625, became the biggest trade centre in North Europe (for Rhine trade). Vikings raid it 834 etc, capture it c.850–60 and raid it again 863, by which time it is in final decline – partly due to changes in the river lines. Tiel and Deventer take over the trade.
London significant throughout the period, but trade moved from the Strand to the (ex Roman, walled) 'City' by the Vikings in 870s. Big German influence in 900s.

Irish Sea

Dublin = 830s – and later many other coastal centres: 841 Base at Kilmainham: 849 Dublin recaptured by Irish; 851 Danes challenge Norwegians in Ireland: 902 Dublin Vikings all expelled. Dublin left by Vikings 1067 (= third time).
Viking bases on North coast re-captured by Irish 866.

Channel

Hamwih (near Southampton): as at London, the trade centre was moved by the Vikings to a walled site, c.870s.
Quentovic (near Étaples): an important trade centre raided by Vikings 842, and abandoned in the late 800s.

Table E continued

Baltic

Reric (near Mecklenburg) big by 800: destroyed by King Godfred 808, to man
   Hedeby.
Grobin, Latvia = pre-Viking Swedes (as Truso etc).
Rügen (North of Berlin) = Slav trade station by 800: near Ralswiek island for Viking
   and Slav traders from 700s.
Kurland (Courland): 852 Slavs make a successful defence – but Swede king Olaf
   finally triumphs at about this time.
Wolin: a key centre, from the 900s.

Russia

Staraja Ladoga = late 700s (from c.760): destroyed by fire 860, but rebuilt and
   fortified.
Novgorod, Kiev, etc = c.860.
Bulghar (confluence of Volga and Kama): northern limit of Arabs (arrive c.775).
   Already big in 921, as end of caravan route from Oxus.
By 944 there is an annual fleet down Dnieper (Kiev, Novgorod, Smolensk) to
   Constantinople each June.
   – Trade to Byzantium cut c.550–750/770 (*ie* apart from via Germany) due
     especially c.650 by rise of Islam, but re-opened by Rus until c.960s (or before),
     when Germany started to take over and raiding on Volga stopped (better local
     defences). Note c.910 arrival of Afghan silver minted coins via Bulghar (*ie* by-
     passes Khazars). 1041 Ingvar's expedition is last desperate gamble.

---

wider world. The hoarding of treasure against raiders seems to have been more
common in the 400s and 500s than in later times, so we can assume that peace
and prosperity was more the norm during the 600s and 700s. It was in this
period that the more northerly parts of Scandinavia began to be opened for
trade and even settlement, although the main centre of wealth would continue
to be located in the Western Baltic, especially at Helgö and then Birka (both
near modern Stockholm) and Hedeby (in south-east Jutland).

Nevertheless, there still remains the important question of just why did the
relatively rich and well-established societies of Norway, Sweden and Denmark
– which were in any case more concerned with internal squabbles than with
external aggression – suddenly spill out onto the world stage towards the end of
the 700s, and make such a nuisance of themselves for the next few centuries? A
number of theories have been put forward, although ultimately nobody can be
very certain just how much weight should be attributed to each. There is some
evidence that the Scandinavian population was growing beyond its normal level
of around two million, spilling out onto marginal land but finding it so poor for

cultivation that it soon had to be abandoned. This may have created a pressure to expand into the outside world, although it was felt only in some places (especially within Norway), and not in others. New farmland within Scandinavia was always being brought under cultivation throughout the Viking period, as well as abandoned, so it did not necessarily have to be found in foreign parts. Nor does the Viking migration to a trouble-free place like Iceland ever seem to have exceeded 80,000 (at the highest estimate: cf Foote & Wilson, p.53, who put the figure at 20,000 during the Age of Settlements), which does not constitute a particularly large total. The extreme difficulty of sailing there must surely have acted as a powerful deterrent against mass immigration, but at the same time was an important part of the country's appeal. Not only did it restrict immigration but, until the Second World War, the long and precarious line of communication to Iceland effectively prevented the arrival of any European armies on Icelandic soil. The Icelanders therefore enjoyed free security from external threats, and their only military exposure came in the internecine 'saga warfare' between their own people – although, by the Sturlung Age, this was often being fomented for external purposes by agents of the Roman church and the Norwegian king.

One should view with deep suspicion the widespread claim that very large numbers of civilians were habitually shuttled around the early medieval world by sea. John Haywood has convincingly demonstrated that such movements were almost impossible under oars alone; but his corollary that the addition of sail made them very easy (Haywood, p.73) should not be allowed to pass unchallenged. Sail did of course make things easier all round for the sailor: but that in itself surely never really made things very much better than 'still very difficult'. Even with the full benefit of sail, the preparation and successful execution of a voyage was still being seen as a very major undertaking as late as the sagas written in the 1200s. Nor should we immediately assume that because an area like Frisia suddenly became depopulated in the 500s due to changes in the water table, its population must therefore necessarily have moved away to somewhere else. They may simply have died where they stood, as we see only too shockingly often in our modern television reports from places like Ethiopia or Rwanda.

With a fair wind it was perhaps possible to sustain high speeds throughout a long crossing under sail, and in 1024 Thorarin Nefiolfsson is alleged to have reached Iceland just four days after leaving Møre in Norway, making a distance of something like 600 miles at between six and seven knots (*The Olaf Sagas*, p.261). This remarkable tale is actually consistent with the performance of a replica of the Gokstad boat which was sailed across the Atlantic in 1893, including one day in which it succeeded in averaging eleven knots (cited in Arbman, p.16). However, it was far more normal for the sagas to reckon 'one day's sailing' as rather less than 100 miles, making an average speed of four knots or less – but still seven to eight knots if one sleeps on land every night. The account of their voyages given to King Alfred by Wulfstan and Othere suggest that 400 miles in five days was a normal standard of reckoning, although it was only in some voyages, and not others, that they landed every night (cited in Gwyn Jones, *A History of the Vikings*, pp.111, 159; *The Norse Atlantic Saga*, p.11).

Nevertheless, the biggest problem still remains – namely, that fair winds could never be predicted or relied upon with any degree of confidence whatsoever. There is plenty of saga testimony to back up the belief that in difficult weather the crossing from Norway to Iceland could easily take all summer – or it might even have to be aborted entirely. It would certainly tend to run against the trade winds unless one made a detour well to the north. Equally, no one crossed and re-crossed even the North Sea more than once or at most twice a year if they could help it. They did not operate anything remotely resembling a weekly or monthly ferry service between York and Oslo or between Harwich and the Hook of Holland. For a Viking, each and every long voyage was surely seen as something like a desperate game of Russian roulette – a deadly gamble in which one risked instant death and the violent loss of all one's worldly possessions; but in which one also hoped to win a massive multiplication of one's wealth and status through spectacularly successful robbery, extortion or trade. No one should ignore the distinct gambling element in the whole Viking approach to seafaring.

In his book *The Age of the Vikings*, P.H. Sawyer has made some eloquent and justly famous arguments to the effect that the Vikings probably did not migrate in very large numbers, even to places where their cultural influence unquestionably became crucial, such as the English Danelaw. Without needing to follow his reasoning too slavishly – and it has been hotly contested, notably by N.P. Brooks – we can at least surely agree that there is relatively little evidence that the Vikings really did move very great numbers of people out of Scandinavia into such colonies as Iceland, England, Russia or France. The major concentration of soldiers during the second half of the 800s was the 'Great Army' operating in England, France and Belgium; but there was only one such army, and other groupings of Viking forces were surely considerably smaller. However, the effect of merely a few invaders was usually quite enough to create a local perception that the area had been well and truly 'Vikinged'. A small Viking raid could easily become the subject of a major entry in the annals, just as a small settlement could come to dominate the culture of an entire local area.

Nevertheless, even if the scale of population transfer was probably relatively minor, we are still left with some important questions about just why the Vikings moved out of Scandinavia in the first place. Changes in the climate have sometimes been cited, but modern research seems to show that the weather became notably adverse only after the Viking era had finished, and remained

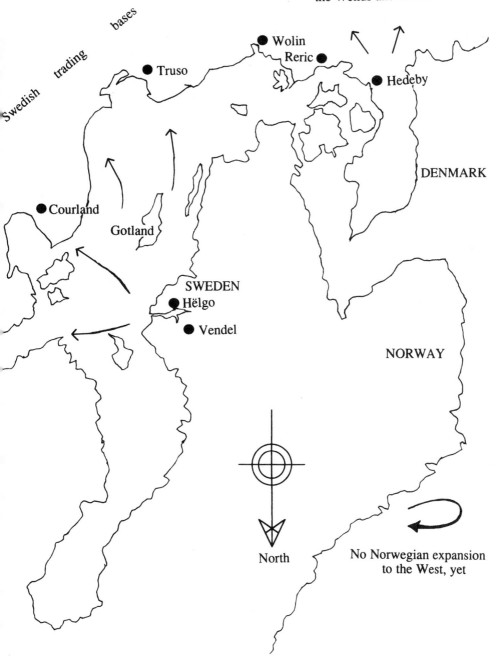

'Marcher' wars against
the Wends and Saxons

Swedish trading bases

Truso

Wolin

Reric

Hedeby

DENMARK

Courland

Gotland

SWEDEN

Hëlgo

Vendel

NORWAY

North

No Norwegian expansion
to the West, yet

Figure 3

Viking expansion in Vendel times

generally favourable while it was in progress. In theory this should therefore have made the Vikings want to stay at home to enjoy the sunshine rather than go off to damp places like Ireland and Brittany, or cold, uninviting places like the deliberately-deterringly named Iceland and 'Giantland' (or 'Permia', *ie* North Russia). Indeed, there is some evidence suggesting that exceptional psychological persuasion was later needed to enhance the attractions of such regions to travellers. Despite the special pleading of some modern commentators, the very name of Greenland is clearly deeply misleading, especially since the earliest accounts specifically mention the snow-clad mountains by which the place could be recognised (though Adam of Bremen apparently believed that the name derived from the colour of the inhabitants themselves, whom he supposed got their pigmentation 'from the salt water': quoted in *The Norse Atlantic Saga*, p.77). Newfoundland was given the more alluring but apparently highly deceitful description 'Vinland the Good' (*ie* 'the good land of wine'), to which the still more outrageous claim was also originally added that 'there is no frost in the winter'. One knows from long experience that the North Americans love to use superlatives whenever they can get away with it, but this very first example of the genre is positively numbing in the scale of its effrontery.

Another explanation sometimes offered for Viking expansion has been the flow of Islamic silver into northern Europe. As Sawyer has explained in both his books, this grew to important proportions during the later 700s, peaking in 800 and still more so around 900 and on to 955. It demonstrates robust Swedish traffic through Russia, and it clearly both motivated and financed their outward thrust in that particular direction. It certainly seems to coincide with the start of the Viking Age very nicely, and must be considered a major spur to Swedish activity. However this silver does not start to circulate in Norway and Denmark until around 900, which is rather late for the Viking Age and so does not explain the Westward drive from those places during the 800s. Then the flow was interrupted altogether in around 970, which doubtless provided an incentive at that time to find wealth from other sources; but since this was already two centuries after the Viking Age had started, it is scarcely a phenomenon that can be said to cast very much light on whatever it may have been that had originally started that era in the West.

Instead of population pressure, bad weather or Islamic silver, it is improvements in the Vikings' boats that have most often been cited as probably the most important of all the reasons for their international expansion towards the end of the 700s. It is alleged not only that the boats then became lighter and more flexible, for the same lifting capacity, but that they also converted from oars alone to the winning combination of sail and oars together. This has sometimes been portrayed as giving the Vikings a decisive technological superiority over all their rivals, equivalent to that of steam over sail in the nineteenth century, or even of nuclear propulsion over oil in the twentieth.

Table F

___

Pressures for international movement

A) *Pressures to get out of Scandinavia*

Pushes	Pulls
Deteriorating climate?	There is more sunshine further South
Deteriorating hunting and fishing?	Fish, whales, walruses and furs are better abroad
Growing internal wars and deportations	Foreigners' crimes must be avenged (*eg* 865 by Ragnar Lothbrok's sons against King Aella?)
The enforcement of Christianity	There are still some pagan lands abroad
Centralising kings interfere with trade	Trading and slaving is best if international
Boredom and low income at home	Join the army for excitement and loot
Second sons need a career	Other family members already prosper abroad
Population pressure on farmland	Travellers say land is plentiful abroad

B) *Pressures to stay in Scandinavia*

Pulls	Deterrents to leaving
One's own king makes the best patron	Service in foreign courts can be suicidal
One's immediate neighbours are weakly armed and highly plunderable	Most foreign Empires are horribly well armed
The best life is at home	Travel is dangerous: 'Bad winds, fog and pirates'
Farming wins wealth and social respect	Trade is financially and socially dubious
Big Christian missionary opportunities at home	There are strange religious practices abroad
Scandinavians are the best people	Foreigners are not nice people

___

With this in mind, the student may certainly notice that there is a striking coincidence of dates between the alleged development of naval technology and the extension of Scandinavian activities overseas. It was apparently during the 700s that the Vikings went beyond their earlier rowing boats and inshore sailing dinghies to the far more adaptable and sea-worthy ocean-going sailing boats, with big sails, which would soon become their distinctive hall-mark.

Figure 4   **The flow of Islamic silver**

(Based on P.H.Sawyer, *The Age of the Vikings*)

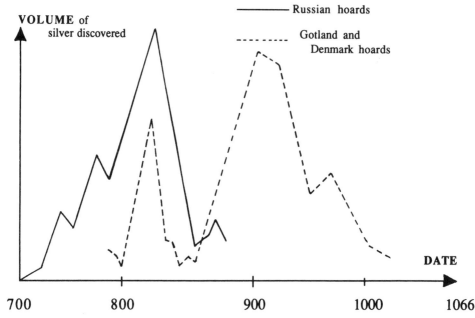

When Arrow-Odd demonstrated the advantages of sail over oars to his doubting troll-giant foster father (later his father in law), it metaphorically summed up a highly important historical change in technology (*Seven Viking Romances*, pp.77–87, and *cf* p.28 for Arrow-Odd's ability to 'get a wind even in calm weather', simply by using sail).

This theory, alas, is badly damaged by John Haywood's recent book *Dark Age Naval Power*, which convincingly shows that most Western European ships had probably already used a combination of oars and sail since at least around 100 AD, inspired by Roman models. He bases his analysis upon what the fleets actually did (as derived from literary sources) rather than exclusively upon the particular boats that happen to have survived from this era; and he demonstrates that in order to do what they did, the fleets must necessarily have deployed technically superior boats to most of those that remain. There was a circumnavigation of the British Isles in 83 AD, for example, which would have been quite impossible without sails. Pirates from the Zuyder Zee area were already reaching the Bay of Biscay around 170, and the Mediterranean itself by about 200. We are reminded that the Romans had been importing silk, by sea, all the way from China, and that they had certainly known all about 'galleys' which spent most of their time under sail. Haywood further disputes the orthodox idea that the bigger boat-finds, such as those at Sutton Hoo and

Nydam, were incapable of carrying sail. Naval historians are therefore surely wrong to assume that sails were introduced only in the 700s, or that the Vikings were particularly leading the way towards them.

It may well be that the Vikings improved their own naval architecture during the 700s, to catch up with the standards already obtaining elsewhere. This improvement in their capabilities may indeed have been a *sine qua non* of their later world-wide expansion; but that is not at all the same thing as the suggestion that they were technologically far ahead of their neighbours. We will return to some of the technicalities in the next chapter; but for the moment it is worth noting that the naval architecture explanation of the sudden Viking outburst in the late 700s now needs to be approached with some caution.

More Defeats than Victories: Expansion Attempts, 793–911

Perhaps the most credible explanation for the start of the Viking expansion is simply that new ideas about kingship were starting to create bigger and more ambitious power struggles within Scandinavia than they had done earlier – including more incentives for the defeated to venture abroad, either as fugitives or seekers of allies, and for the victors to chase after them. These civil wars also, perhaps, led to the building of bigger and more coherent armed forces, linked with a widening of horizons from just the local fjord to more distant provinces beyond the immediate horizon. Thus what had previously been a small scale neighbourhood tradition of piracy and voyaging, confined within the Baltic and along the Norwegian coastline, became just that little bit more ambitious and more internationally noteworthy towards the end of the 700s. Perhaps it did not take very much to tip the scales from local piracy to international campaigning in this way. Nor, as we shall see, did the shift always necessarily lead to more success. Until the collapse of Carolingian coastal defences around the time of Louis the Pious' death in 840, the Vikings actually enjoyed relatively scant success except in the Celtic fringes of Britain. They established themselves in the Orkneys and Hebrides, but whenever they came into contact with a united, properly organised and well-defended state, they were very liable to be defeated. Most of their operations were also on a pretty small scale during this period, although they were to grow into wonderously great enterprises thereafter, once the central determination and political willpower of the Frankish empire had degenerated into internal dissension and localism.

The Viking expansion therefore seems to have been very much a matter of trial and error, running the risk of heavy losses at every turn, rather than a story of unmitigated military victory. Such victories as there were usually turned out to be very mitigated indeed, and we should beware of seeing the Vikings as some sort of fighting supermen. Nevertheless, they did go out and try to make their own impact upon the wider world, which is more than they had tended to do in the years before about 780. They therefore earned their place in the story for their high level of activity after that date, if for nothing else.

Besides, we should remember that the Vikings ventured overseas for very many different reasons – sometimes as traders, slave-drivers, explorers or refugees, and only at other times as soldiers or aggressors. We should not think of their operations as always automatically falling into the same category or always being organised in the same way. Probably the early moves by the Swedes into Russia and by the Norwegians to the Orkneys were conducted as private speculations by a few relatively junior adventurers, and extended in scope only gradually as the settlements grew and the stories of success percolated back home. The notorious raid on Lindisfarne in 793, for example, may not have involved many men or boats at all. That on Portland in 789 is reported in the *ASC* as having comprised just three boats, which looked so inoffensive to the local king's reeve that he made the literally (and instantly) fatal mistake of trying to arrest them. There were in fact only three other raids on England recorded in the *ASC* between then and 835, which scarcely adds up to a major threat during a time of endemic internal war between the various English kings, and between them and their neighbours the Welsh. We should remember that this was supposedly the time when, or at least not long after, King Offa of Mercia created the greatest military earthwork ever built by the inhabitants of the British Isles – over twice as long as Hadrian's Wall, and twice as long as Haig's portion of the Western Front in 1916. Beside the staggeringly grandiose conception of Offa's Dyke, the occasional Viking pinpricks before 835 must surely have seemed to be strategically very minor indeed.

It was not until after about 830 that we start to hear of large armies of Danes joining in the attacks on England and France; and even then they did not begin

Table G

Time chart phase one: *RECONNAISSANCE*, approximately 793–835

Before 793: Norwegian footholds established in Shetland, Orkney and Hebrides.

793–835: Scandinavia: Little-documented petty kings continue to have power.

British Isles: Tentative small-scale raiding South from Orkney: Sometimes successful, especially in Ireland.

Carolingian Empire: Many but normally unsuccessful Danish raids against good defences in Netherlands and France: Denmark itself counter-invaded 815. Increasingly successful Danish attacks on Dorestad, Frisia, Walcheren, Antwerp etc around 830.

Russia: Unrecorded tentative Swedish probing inland from the Baltic coast.

Everywhere: Unrecorded free-enterprise piracy at sea.

---

to over-winter in Ireland until 840, France (Noirmoutier) until 843, and England until 851. Something similar can be said of the Viking (mainly Swedish) 'Rus' activities in Russia. By the early 800s the local Slavonic populations had already established some towns and trading networks on the great inland waterways which flowed from the Staraja Ladoga–Novgorod area through Smolensk and Kiev on the Dnieper to the Black Sea frontier of the Byzantine Empire; or through Bulghar on the Volga to the Caspian Sea gateway to the Islamic and even Chinese empires. However, new Rus arrivals from Scandinavia between about 800 and 860 seem to have had a flair for taking over these Slav towns, strengthening their arrangements for both defence and taxation, and especially for foreign travel and trade.

The key developments are often identified as the arrival of Rurik and his two brothers in Novgorod in 862, to establish a North Russian principality (including Beloozero, opening another route to the Volga), followed soon afterwards by the takeover of Kiev itself by Earls Hoskuld and Dir, and then the unification of both these zones by Oleg of Novgorod in 882 to make an impressively wide pagan Russian kingdom. Nevertheless, it is likely that significant Viking forces had already been operating in all those regions throughout the preceding generation, since the first major (and surprising!) attack on Constantinople occurred in 860, before Rurik is supposed to have arrived even at Novgorod. This suggests that the whole area was already accessible and very well known to the attackers, right down to the precise dispositions of the Byzantine forces at the moment of the attack (when they were almost all absent from Micklegard). We must remember that many of the Russian rivers are half a mile wide, so one could manoeuvre great fleets upon them without necessarily having to capture the towns on their banks until a later stage of colonisation (see especially the books by Blöndal and Obolensky).

The complete assimilation of the Swedish Rus into the Slav population probably did not come very long after the year 1000, and some Soviet scholars have even tended to deny their separate cultural existence altogether. We can probably agree that in these areas the Viking Age may have lasted only a few generations at most, although there was doubtless a continuing influx of new Swedish travellers throughout the 1000s, who were still keen to exploit the fast through-route to Constantinople that these rivers could offer.

On the more easterly Volga route to Baghdad, by contrast, penetration by the Rus probably both started and finished earlier. The flow of Islamic silver to Sweden and Gotland is eloquent of their energetic activities through the 800s and most of the 900s; but their political hold of the area was never very great, and their big military campaigns were generally less successful even than those directed to the Black Sea. For example in 944 they over-wintered in Azerbaijan, but were soon repulsed; while in 1041 their final fling on the Caspian produced Ingvar's notoriously massive débâcle. On the Volga the Rus could never be

Table H

Attacks on the Byzantine Empire by the Rus

Before 860: One raid to the Crimea, another to the south coast of the Black Sea.

860: 200 boats (Earls Hoskuld and Dir) scare Constantinople but finally are defeated and dispersed.

907: Oleg holds the defence to a 'draw' (quite favourable treaty, 911).

941: Igor surprises and outflanks the city, but badly defeated at sea while retiring.

944: New expedition bought off by diplomacy before it reaches the city (Ingvar's treaty less favourable than Oleg's).

967–9: Sviatoslav invited to help against Bulgaria, but takes more of it than expected.

971: Devastating counter-attack by Byzantine army and fleet regains Bulgaria and makes a treaty unfavourable to the Rus.

988–9: 6000 Rus (Vladimir) help Basil II defeat a revolt; some form the Emperor's guard, but others attack Crimea to enforce the delivery of promised rewards.

1024: 800 Rus warriors (under 'Chrysocheir', or Edmund?) ravage Propontis until killed.

1043: 400 boats mount major invasion but badly defeated on sea and land (treaty in 1046).

---

much more than traders and supplicants at court (and would only rarely venture south of Bulghar itself), since the Bulgars held effective military command of the middle reaches of the river; the Khazars held its lower reaches; and south of that one was well into the zone of the Islamic Abbasid Caliphate – one of the most powerful empires of the day. For a plucky little Viking to conduct profitable trade with Baghdad through such an unlikely mesh of well-armed middlemen, it probably took a maximum slice of the initial enthusiasm and *chutzpah* that was available in the early years of Norse expansionism, and these were apparently assets that had wasted away almost entirely by 970.

Nevertheless, it remains true that both in the East and the West, Viking armies – which grew to quite considerable sizes by the middle 800s – were probably still not officially sponsored as 'royal' armies, and even then their leaders may have had little recognised authority at home, or even anywhere else beyond the reach of their strong right arms and their mighty battleaxes. If we want to find the truly 'high royal' Viking figures, such as Harald Finehair in Norway and later Gorm the Old in Denmark, we have to look back to their home countries themselves, and even for these important figures we really have astonishingly little hard evidence to work from. We do at least believe that in those places the big kings were starting to be especially potent in asserting their authority over minor kings around the late 800s; and this often had the effect of sending new waves of the losers overseas. Eric Bloodaxe was an important case in point, when he was banished to York in 945; but the Icelanders also believed that many of their own earlier colonists had come from similar backgrounds and histories. What we do not see at this period, however, is active participation in overseas campaigning by unquestionably 'royal' Scandinavians who were in the direct line of succession within Scandinavia itself. We have plenty of earls, minor kings and entirely landless 'sea kings': but not the truly genuine article. For this we have to wait until the later 900s, when the operations can at last start to be called official and proper wars run by more official armies, rather than just unofficial banditry or the equivalent of unsolicited highway robbery.

Despite its undoubted and immediate psychic shock to churchmen, therefore, the Viking Age really started rather slowly and tentatively, taking around fifty years to build up into a serious assault on the West. Apart from the Swedish efforts in Russia, the main thrust seems to have come both north-about from Norway around Orkney and the Hebrides into Ireland and North-west England and, somewhat later, south-about from Denmark to the Netherlands

Table I

Time chart phase two: *BREAKOUT*, approximately 835–911

Scandinavia: Increasing centralisation of kingship (notably Harald Finehair from c.870 – battle of Hafrsfjord, 800). Iceland discovered and settled.

British Isles: Norwegian enclaves around the Irish coast (especially Dublin). Isle of Man and much of the West coast of Scotland settled. The Danelaw in North and Eastern England settled as result of Great Army operations.

Frankia: The Carolingian Empire fragments. Danes settle on lower Rhine to raid up-river; at mouth of Seine form Great Army to raid inland; at Noirmoutier to raid up Loire (very actively, although with a much smaller force than Great Army), south to Bordeaux and to Spain (and beyond) 844, 859–62. Norwegians (from Ireland) settle the Cotentin.

'The Great Army': Assembles originally on the Seine. To England 865–79 (establish Danelaw, reinforced from Ireland, but defeated by Wessex); then to Northern France/Belgium (equally mixed success); then defeated in England 892–6; then win limited success in Northern France and disperse – apart from official Frankish recognition of the Duchy of Normandy, 911.

Russia: Rus establish their power at Staraja Ladoga, Novgorod, Smolensk and especially Kiev, then attack Byzantium three times: make treaties. Meetings with Arabs on Volga.

Everywhere: Unrecorded free-enterprise piracy at sea.

---

and thence into northern France and South-east England. The two arms of the pincers seem to have met in Dublin about 851, in Northumbria towards 868, and in the Cotentin a little later – sometimes even on moderately friendly terms. Both Northumbria and Cornwall seem to have been raided alternately by the Orcadian or Irish Norse and the Norman Danes; but King Alfred in Wessex was probably troubled almost exclusively by the Great Army from the Seine, as well as by some of its minor freelance offshoots. However, it would seem that most Viking armies in the West, regardless of their origins and leadership, probably contained an indiscriminate mixture of Norwegians, Danes and even some Swedes, not to mention Icelanders and doubtless also non-Vikings, such as uprooted natives of Dublin, Rouen or York. These armies must have been pretty polyglot, so it may not be particularly important to remember where they originally came from except in terms of the strategic geography of their route into the theatre of war.

The relatively small colony of Vestfold Norwegians who first wintered on Noirmoutier island in 843 seem to have kept themselves somewhat apart from both the Dublin and the Rouen Vikings, concentrating mainly on the Loire valley (into which they eventually transferred their permanent base), and Brittany (where they made little headway against the local Dukes, and sometimes formed alliances with them against the Franks). During the middle years of the 800s they mounted some famous but wildly speculative operations – first to the Gironde, then the rest of the Bay of Biscay and onwards to Spain, Algeciras, Provence and Italy. Nevertheless, these never really amounted to very much more than an experiment that was not, as it happened, particularly successful. Thus the 844 expedition to Seville received a distinctly bloody repulse, whereas Hasting and Bjorn's epic tour in 859–62, with sixty-two boats, managed to reach Pisa, though it returned with only twenty boats. In both cases the well-organised defences of established empires proved to be far superior to the pinprick attacks of small Viking fleets – exactly as had been demonstrated by the Carolingian Empire in the Netherlands before about 835.

One should not assess the Western Vikings' achievement mainly on the basis of their wilder flings towards such exotically distant places as Italy, Iceland–Greenland–Vinland, or Permia. Instead, their real business in the later 800s was taking place mainly in Orkney, in the Scottish islands, in the Irish entrepôts, in the English Danelaw and on the lower Seine. In every case the successes can be attributed less to Viking strength than to either the agreement or weakness of the local leaders. In clannishly-divided Ireland, for example, the Vikings' coastal entrepôts were tolerated only on sufferance; but they survived because they were normally as useful to the Irish as they were to the traders themselves. Whenever there was a Viking attempt to push back the inland clans – and there were many – the Irish reacted strongly and effectively, and they were even able to flex their muscles by ethnically cleansing Dublin itself in both 849 and 902.

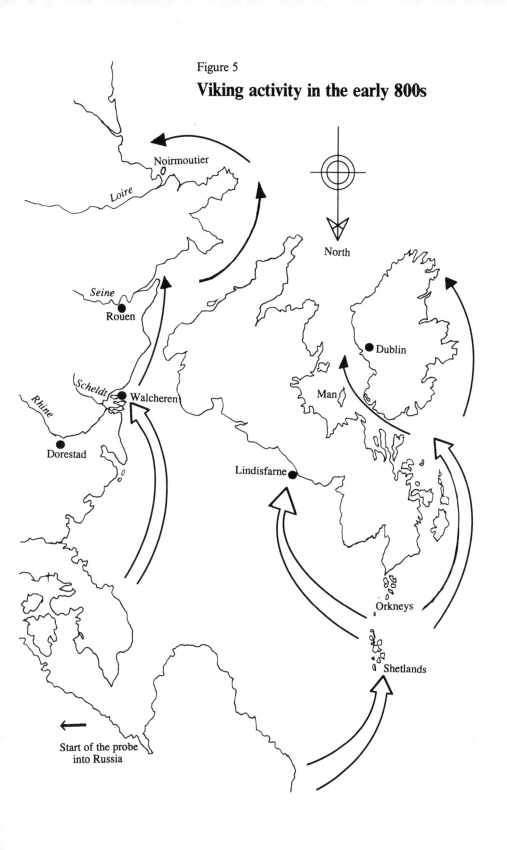

Figure 5

Viking activity in the early 800s

In Northumbria, Mercia and East Anglia, equally, the Great Army of 865–79 seems to have made headway mainly because it could exploit political divisions among the (normally militarily effective) political classes of those areas.

Much of Eastern England was successfully settled by the Vikings, but their efforts up to 879 failed to overcome Alfred in Wessex. By about 890 he was so much better organised that their renewed attacks stood no chance at all. The disputed Carolingian succession also turned out to have left as many weak spots in the political fibre of North-west France as the warring English kings had left in their own areas. Nevertheless, the local regimes still proved to have considerable resilience. Admittedly Charles the Bald, Charles the Fat and Charles the Simple did not often seem to have much luck in their campaigning, and the Treaty of St Clair Sur Epte (signed in 911) was unquestionably an historic milestone insofar as it finally recognised the establishment of a Viking state in Normandy. But we should not forget that the Vikings had been significantly defeated at Saucourt in 881, at Paris in 885–6 and on the Dyle in 891. They may well have won Normandy by the Treaty of St Clair, but that treaty is silently loud in its refusal to give them any of the rest of France. Something similar may be said of the Netherlands, where the Vikings sometimes won concessions on the coast in Dorestad, Walcheren or Frisia, in the hope that they

Table J

More defeats than victories

As a notional (and entirely unscientific) statement of the statistical scoreline or 'odds', the Viking achievement might perhaps look something like this:

| Type of target | Overall success: | | Recommended |
	Vikings	Enemy	Viking policy
Sophisticated empires (Arab, Byzantine, Franks to 830):	0	10	Keep well clear/Fish offshore
Normal kingdoms (England, Ireland, Russia) once Vikings are familiar:	2	8	Trade and Diplomacy
Remote tribes (Skrælings, Permians):	3	7	Slaving, exploitation, defence
Divided empires (Later Franks):	5	5	Threaten, and demand geld
Normal kingdoms before Vikings familiar:	7	3	Try to conquer and occupy
Totally uninhabited areas:	10	0	Settlement and total takeover
Other Vikings:	10	0	Act as seems best

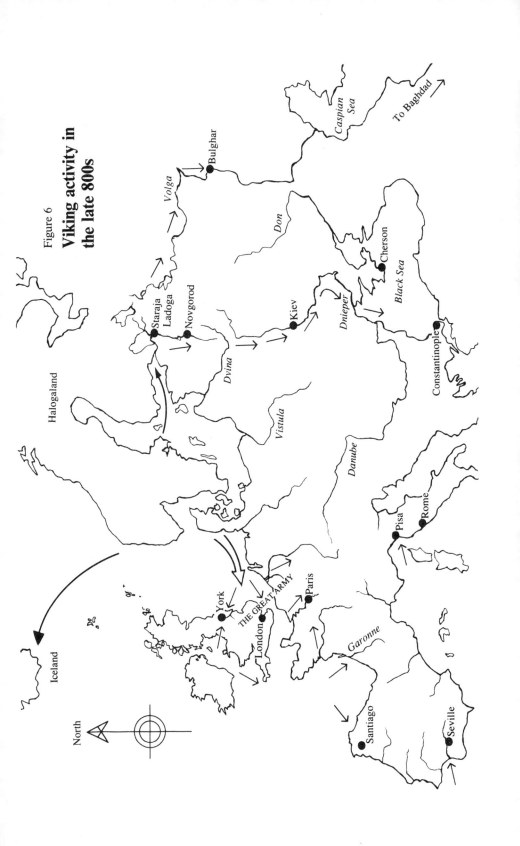

Figure 6

Viking activity in the late 800s

would become allies of the Frankish king, but they were beaten off whenever they tried to venture further inland.

In Ireland, Britain, France and the Netherlands, therefore, the first century of the Vikings' expansion saw them making inroads and establishing cultural influence, but still being held to relatively limited territorial gains. The same was also true in some parts of Scotland, while in the Mediterranean they seemed to bounce off the local defences just as resoundingly as they kept on doing in North Germany itself. It was only around the northern and western rim of Scotland, in the Orkneys, Hebrides and Man, and in Iceland, that they established really lasting Viking states. If they 'played ten', therefore, the Vikings can also be said to have 'lost at least five' and probably nearer seven.

The Second Viking Onslaught, 911–1066

Throughout the early and middle years of the 900s the Vikings can generally be said to have taken on a more quiescent attitude than they had done during the second half of the 800s – except in Russia, where the Kievan kings were still very active; in Ireland, where there was still plentiful trouble; and in the Bay of Biscay, from which both the French coast and Spain were again attacked, especially between 964 and 970. Meanwhile the Vikings were normally in retreat in England until around 980: but they then once again took to the warpath in a very big way.

We have considerably better sources for this second offensive than we have for the first, since a number of factors were combining to increase the quality of the manuscript record by a significant margin. The big Viking kings were becoming more powerful and, as part of this process, they were turning to the more pliable, centralised and especially literate Christian religion. Their non-Viking opponents were also writing more – or at least leaving more writings that have survived – while the eventual golden era of the Icelandic sagas was itself two centuries nearer in time than it had been when Lindisfarne was originally sacked. The sagas are frustratingly very vague and imprecise about kings and dates around 800: but their quality improves markedly for events around 1000.

By about 995 Aethelred's 'unreadiness' (or 'ill-advisedness') was starting to be obvious to all, and some really large 'gelds' began to be paid, first to Sven Forkbeard and Olaf Tryggvason, then to Thorkell the Tall and finally to Canute. Just as it had done a century earlier, Viking Normandy lent a friendly helping hand in some of these campaigns, and offered a refuge and base that was close enough to the English coast to obviate the need for long voyages, but far enough away to be secure from counter-attack. In 1012 Thorkell did not take a geld so much as hire out his services as 'protection' to the English, and after Canute's accession to the throne in 1016 this system became regularised on almost an annual basis. Altogether something like a quarter of a million

Table K

Time chart phase three: *NORMALISATION:* Approximately 911–980

Scandinavia: Norway disputed between the line of Eric Bloodaxe (banished 945, killed in battle of Stainmore 954) and all comers (including Danish allies). Gorm the Old and Harald Bluetooth powerfully consolidate Denmark and introduce Christianity.

British Isles: Vikings defeated in their Danelaw kingdoms (battles of Tettenhall, 910; Brunanburh, 937). All England eventually ruled, once again, by English kings; but Ireland retained as an area of high Viking activity.

Frankia: Normandy expands from the Seine to the Breton border and defeats attackers (including Vikings opposed to 'Frenchification'). Spain raided soon after 960. Meanwhile the Magyars make a short but incisive Westward thrust by land into central Europe, mopping up whatever enclaves have escaped the Viking assault from the sea, while the Arabs temporarily carve out parts of SE France as their own 'Danelaw'.

Russia: Trade with Byzantium flourishes, although Viking attacks on it fail in 941, 944, 971.

Everywhere: Unrecorded piracy is in general decline.

---

pounds of silver are thought to have been paid within a thirty year period, with a big payment on average once every four years. These gelds were certainly celebrated on runestones all over Scandinavia, and they may have helped the general consolidation of kingship – and also of centralised religion in the shape of Christianity – under such figures as the two Olafs in Norway and Harald Bluetooth, Sven Forkbeard and Canute himself in Denmark. But it also turned out to be an excellent time for internecine fighting between these Scandinavian monarchs, who laid into each other with not inconsiderable regularity.

The gelds taken from England must have gone a long way towards replacing the Islamic coins that were no longer reaching Sweden up the Volga from the Caspian – which must be considered to have been an area where the Vikings ultimately failed quite completely. The Vikings were nevertheless far more successful on the Dnieper, albeit only at the expense of assimilation with the local people, just as in Normandy or Northumbria. Whenever they made a direct military attack on the Byzantine Empire, furthermore, they won at best a draw and on at least three occasions an extremely bloody nose. Yet they did actually score two distinct successes in 'loveliest Micklegard', by indirect means, which cemented a mutually beneficial relationship between the two powers. The first was that the Rus were always valued very highly for their trade, since it was as much in the Byzantines' interest as it was in the Vikings' to maintain a continuous flow of goods and money between the frozen North and the sun-soaked South. This trade, unlike that of the Volga, never dried up during the time that the distinctively 'Viking' nature of Scandinavia thrived.

Secondly, the very well-named 'Byzantine' nature of imperial diplomacy meant that in strategic terms it was always essential for the imperial governors of the Crimea (based at Cherson) to enlist the help of barbarian allies all around the northerly fringes of the Black Sea. While the threat was coming from the Rus, Magyars or Bulgarians, it meant the Khazars would have to be bought up and enrolled for service, as they were very successfully until around 900 (notably with the building of a brick fort for them at Sarkel on the Don in 833). Then when the Pechenegs pushed the Khazars out of this area, it was they who immediately became the chosen ally of Byzantium, just as the Alans were enrolled into the Khazars' former role in the North Caucasus. This all amounted to a virtuoso performance in imperial diplomacy, since the Kiev Rus were actually very impressed by Pecheneg power, especially their ability to interdict the lower Dnieper. The system started to fall apart only with the Byzantine attempt to buy up the Rus themselves in 967, which led to a very threatening Viking occupation of the Dobrudja at the mouth of the Danube,

Table L

Time chart phase four: *THE SECOND AGE:* Approximately 980–1066

Scandinavia: Olaf Tryggvason (killed in battle of Svold, 1000) and St Olaf (killed in battle of Stickelstad 1030) impose Christianity and centralisation on Norway; Eric the Victorious in Sweden not as successful (Christianity firmly established only in late 1000s) – but Sven Forkbeard's son Canute creates a huge 'empire' for Denmark. Greenland (c.980–90) and Vinland (c.990–1000) discovered. Iceland converted to Christianity 1000.

British Isles: Major Viking offensives and gelds from 991 (battle of Maldon) until Canute becomes king in 1016; no more Englishmen as king until Edward the Confessor 1042–66. Irish counter-attacks on Vikings become effective (battle of Clontarf 1014), *cf* the Orkney 'empire' reaches its widest extent c.1050.

Frankia: Normandy now assimilated into the 'French' way of life, although there are still occasional (externally based) Viking raids on Spain, Brittany and the Netherlands. The two (equally important) main Norman thrusts around 1066 are to England and to Sicily. Major German silver mines open during the 1000s, while Magyar and Arab attacks fade away (and in Spain the Christian counter-attack begins as the Arabs fall out with the Berbers and with each other).

Russia: Routes blocked; Arab silver supply dries up. Ingvar's defeat on Caspian Sea 1041.

---

effectively at the invitation of Constantinople, from which it would take three years of hard warfare to eject them. Thereafter the Kievan Russians were forced to make a treaty which eventually almost amounted to a recognition of Byzantine overlordship, especially in the spiritual domain. The decisive act of this alliance was Vladimir's expedition to rescue the Emperor from a revolt in 988, which led to the epochal conversion of Russia to Greek Christianity in 989 (although it was only in 1036 that the Pechenegs would finally be pushed off the Dnieper).

Linked to all this was the growing dominance of the Viking–Rus 'Varangians' as the major imperial bodyguard at Constantinople, especially under the Emperor Basil II (976–1025), as well as their active participation in most imperial campaigns by land and sea. The Varangians were never expected to be assimilated into Byzantine culture at all, since that might have made them politically suspect, but were intended to be held apart as a mercenary centre of excellence for all the Vikings' military skills. It was only when Harald Hard-ruler helped topple the Emperor Michael V in 1042 (and then put his eyes out) that the Varangians took an independent role in palace politics. Nevertheless, they continued to be an important feature of the Byzantine military structure for over a century thereafter, albeit increasingly taken over by Englishmen following the Norman invasion of England in 1066. Ironically the ex-Viking Normans themselves were also being used as mercenaries by the Byzantines in the Adriatic before this time, until in 1040 the contingent of 300 serving with Harald in southern Italy and Sicily rebelled and killed a large number of Varangians. A significant Italian–Norman state would then be founded in Apulia by Robert Guiscard 'the Fox' in 1042. It may not have been seen as such at the time, but an historian on the lookout for key moments might be tempted see this event as the final completion of a Viking circle all around Western Europe.

The early 1000s was certainly a period of crisis for the whole Viking edifice, and perhaps its most poignant moment came when the doomed and widely-mourned expedition by Ingvar to the Caspian Sea was destroyed in 1041. Too few participants lived to tell the tale, with the result that we still remain in ignorance of what actually happened, although we do have some 25 surviving runestones to commemorate the fallen. Once due notice has been taken of the time-lapse between the two events, therefore, this is surely almost an equivalent to the plethora of war memorials that we see in our own towns and villages commemorating the battles of Passchendaele and the Somme. We must also remember that in 1041 Viking power was known to be receding quite quickly, in a way that was perhaps not very exactly matched by British power in 1916–17. The battle of Clontarf in 1014 had finally destroyed Viking hopes of conquering Ireland, just as the arrival of Edward the Confessor as king in 1042 was actually a sign of terminal Viking decline in England. The Normans and the Rus themselves had 'gone native' to such an extent that they could no longer reasonably be considered to be true Vikings at all. Both Greenland and Vinland the Good had admittedly been discovered during the final quarter of the 900s, but neither of those could exactly be considered as assets to be measured in the scales alongside the lost kingdoms of Northern France or England itself. Perceptive people might even think them to be doomed assets where the marginal climate, unpromising flora, hostile 'Scrælings' and, especially, the tenuous line of communication to Europe, would tend to reduce their days of productive viability down into years rather than centuries. Like many of the European colonies seized during the age of Queen Victoria, they represented expenditure rather than income. In summary, therefore, the international picture seemed to look very bleak indeed for the Vikings in around 1050, except insofar as they could console themselves with the rather 'offside' view that the future seemed to belong mainly to the Normans and the Rus and also – of course, and as always – to the native royal houses of Norway, Sweden and Denmark themselves.

The Vikings and their Neighbours

THE FRANKS

Of all the Vikings' neighbours, it was the Slavs and the Franks who gave them the most trouble, simply because they were the nearest. Immediately south of Jutland the Danes had traditionally faced the Saxons, with the Frisians further to the west; but at the very start of the Viking Age both these doomed nations found themselves at the top of Charlemagne's list of strategic priorities, and they were both duly overwhelmed. The Saxons were finally defeated in 803 and the Frisians in 810, bringing the borders of the Frankish empire right up to the Danish frontier wall, the 'Danewirke', covering Hedeby. Nor was Charlemagne inclined to stop there, since he fomented trouble among the petty Danish kings and prepared an invasion of the mainland which was carried out posthumously (albeit inconclusively) in 815. The Danish-Frankish border continued to be a flashpoint for conflict for many years thereafter (eg Otto II's invasion of 974), serving to delay and then limit the eventual Viking expansion towards the coast of the Low Countries and France.

As a military leader Charlemagne enjoys one of the highest reputations in world history especially since, like Napoleon's after him, the growth of his empire seemed to depend upon constant expansion at the expense of a succession of rich victim states on the frontier. This empire was not based on solid internal administration, but it managed to hold together as long as it continued to bring in regular, fresh supplies of plunder. In about 800, however, Charlemagne's offensive impetus failed because his supply of rich and vulnerable local victims dried up. The sprawling Frankish empire itself suddenly became the most eminently plunderable entity in Western Europe, so throughout the 800s it had to change its posture from offensive to defensive, and place a major new emphasis on the rapid mobilisation of mass levies for local defence. This meant a switch from relatively small bodies of noble warriors who could finance themselves in offensive operations, to a wider base of more reluctant conscripts, who might be called upon at shorter notice than had previously been the case. In addition, when river-mouth and coastal defences failed against the Vikings around 840, there was a switch to heavily fortified bridges further up-river, especially on the Seine, which proved to be at least half an answer, although the multiple pressures on each of the Frankish kings meant that they could never concentrate their attentions exclusively on the Viking threat.

The main problem with the turn to defensive strategy during Charlemagne's last fifteen years, and increasingly in the reign of his son Louis the Pious, had really been less military than political. In the absence of rich external neighbours to plunder, the leading Frankish soldiers had set about plundering each other and establishing their own independent fiefdoms. There followed a bewildering succession of civil wars and political re-alignments which destroyed the whole cohesion of the empire. Yet there were still numerous campaigns to be fought against external enemies, who kept coming in from every point of the compass. The Slavs, the Bretons, the Basques, the Serbs, the Bulgars and then the Magyars all posed major threats at different times, as did the Byzantines in Italy, while the Mediterranean frontier with the Arabs, including part of Northern Spain, was long and vulnerable. Among all these potential opponents the Vikings were seen as only one among many, although they did apparently enjoy a certain reputation as being especially tricky to deal with. This was because they liked to exploit difficult terrain and attack at unexpected times of day or night, or when they were thought to be in retreat. It would take over a century for the Franks to tame them because their attacks were so persistent and the Frankish kings were so often distracted by other wars elsewhere. (See the articles by Karl Leyser and Timothy Reuter.)

By the 900s the Frankish military system was reverting from a mass levy back towards smaller forces of heavily-armed, mounted knights anchored to a chain of earth and timber fortresses. The latter would evolve into stone constructions during the 1000s, thus providing the foundation for the classic feudal or 'high medieval' military establishment so familiar to the modern mind, upon which the Normans, for example, based their own practice. In terms of equipment Carolingian armies had always deployed the most modern weapons and armour, and the quality of Frankish arms enjoyed high international prestige throughout the Viking Age. The designs were notably improved during the 800s, and these were widely procured or copied by the Vikings as well as by the Arabs (see the article by Simon Coupland). They included everything necessary for fighting either mounted or on foot, but their bows were perhaps less impressive than other items, while both the throwing spear and the two-foot fighting knife or *Sax* seem to have fallen out of use during the 800s.

To the south-east of Denmark lay the Wends or Slav tribes, who were in many ways just as effective raiders and traders as the Vikings themselves, but who succeeded in remaining solidly pagan for much longer. The Northern Slavs had already settled in the area of modern Brandenburg and Poland by about 600, alongside Baltic tribes further to the East such as the Prussians, Lithuanians and Letts. The Slavs operated a warrior democracy of fragmented petty chieftain-ships each with its own stronghold, leading the Vikings to call the Berlin area a 'land of forts' by the 1100s – although by that time many of the clans were coalescing around larger fortresses and a more structured political organisation. They were noted as exporters of fish, pottery and horses, and one Arab traveller in 965 noted that they were particularly well armed with helmets, mail and swords – presumably because they were accustomed to fighting in 'the big league' against the Franks (see *The Northern World*, p.184 *ff*).

The Slavs were always under threat of attack from the Vikings as well as the Franks, but they nevertheless succeeded in maintaining active trade from Baghdad and Constantinople through Russia to their entrepôts at Schleswig, Oldenburg, Mecklenburg, Reric (sacked by the Danes in 808), Arkona and Ralwiek on Rügen island, Menzlin on the River Peene and later Wolin and Stettin at the mouth of the Oder, with Kolobrzeg and the Prussian port of Truso at the mouth of the Vistula. They also gave as good as they got, in military terms, sacking Hedeby in 1000 and harrying Denmark, Gotland, Oland and southern Sweden to such an extent that the Western Baltic was sometimes called the *Mare Rugianorum* after the pirates of Rügen. The pre-valence of treasure-hoarding in southern Sweden during the 1000s has led modern archaeologists to believe that the threat was indeed a very serious one, and the Icelandic sagas themselves often seem to assume that 'Vikings' in the purely piratical sense were almost as likely to be Wends as Scandinavians.

By the 700s these Northern Slavs were being joined by Eastern (or 'Ilmen') Slavs in the Gulf of Finland, who must also have come into frequent conflict with the Vikings, especially once the Swedes began their great inland push to establish the Rus principalities. However they do not appear to have been as militarily efficient as their more westerly cousins, and must have provided the Rus with most of their slaves for both domestic use and export to the markets of the Black Sea and the Caspian. The Rus also mounted many small scale raids even further to the North, as did Norwegians coming around the North Cape to the mouth of the Dvina. Both groups would often have visited the Finns of 'Permia' and the Lapps of 'Halogaland' and the White Sea in search of furs and slaves. These peoples tended to acquire a semi-magical aura as a result of their primitive hunter-gatherer way of life and their strange religion, not to mention their simple powers of survival in such remote and desolate regions. However *Orkneyinga Saga* (p.24) reports some instances when the Lapps in turn were overawed by the Vikings' great swords and war cry.

THE ANGLO-SAXONS

England lay further afield than either the Slav or Frankish lands, but as a strategic objective it was every bit as rich and tempting as they were – especially once a ring of Viking outposts had been properly established around North-west Scotland and then in Ireland and on the lower Seine. It was a country of notoriously warlike and well-armed kingdoms; but the Vikings seem to have known that many of them were in fact politically divided and relatively short of fortifications. Operationally, too, the English were unready to receive the Great Army when it came visiting between 865 and 879. Although winning quite a few of the battles when they could assemble their levy forces ('Fyrd') at the right time and place, they lost many of the wars when this was not possible.

Having lost so much ground in the middle of the century, Alfred naturally found it difficult to claw it all back again from 892 onwards – but that is indeed what he and his successors actually achieved within a third of a century. Alfred set the tone by instituting a comprehensive programme to build warships to his own design that, with sixty or more oars each, were larger than either the Viking or Frisian ones (*ASC* for 896). He also built fortified boroughs (*burhs*) that were permanently manned by their own dedicated garrisons and supported by a revived system of local levy service for more mobile operations. In 893 his levies around London were even split into two divisions, so that one of the two could always be in the field at any time, even though there were some pre-dictable problems associated with the switch between the two. All of these initiatives were followed and expanded by his immediate successors, who built many more *burhs* and harried the Danelaw very effectively.

The result was that England was strong and well protected until the middle of the 900s, although her navy was never strong enough nor her sailors con-fident enough to contemplate a counter-invasion of Scandinavia. Besides, the new defensive arrangements seem to have fallen into decay thereafter (Abels in Scragg, ed, *The Battle of Maldon*, p.143), to be revived only with the new threat from 991. However, this coincided with the weak leadership of Aethelred (978–1016) – as well as a Viking revival of their long-defunct Great Army – and produced the series of accidents which eventually put Canute on the throne. Thereafter all the institutions of English government and warfare, whether they happened to be manned by Danes, Englishmen or Normans, seem to have been indelibly marked by Viking influences, in a way that was true for neither the Franks nor the Western Slavs.

As far as military opposition is concerned, the Vikings appear to have enjoyed quite an easy (and early) ride through the Shetlands, Orkneys and Hebrides to the coasts of Ireland. Isolated monasteries could often be found which had no defences, but fat pickings – in Britain, Lindisfarne in 793, Jarrow in 794, Iona in 795 and 802; and in Ireland Innismurray and Inisbofin in 795, Skellig Michael in 824 and many more before about 830. By then the Vikings had established their own over-wintering bases throughout the northerly islands, and in 840 they wintered in Ireland for the first time, on Lough Neagh, leading to the establishment of Viking Dublin the next year and an intensification of the military effort. This, however, led to a strong reaction on the part of the Irish kings. Although not united among themselves, they were now at last able to identify some fortified Viking bases, which became fixed targets that could be hit. In a series of sieges and battles in the late 840s the Irish kings scored a number of significant successes and stemmed the Viking tide, retaking Dublin and Cork. However, they were still forced to accept a Scandinavian presence in coastal enclaves, since it turned out that no one could manage to unite all the clans against the invaders. For example when Mael Sechnaill, king of Tara, tried to do so in 860–2, he assembled the forces of Leinster, Munster, Connaught and South Ulster; but the kings of North Ulster, Brega and Osraige made alliances with the Vikings.

The events following 860 did, nevertheless, help to divert at least some of the Vikings' energies elsewhere – both to Iceland and to the Great Army with its new Danelaw in England. Dublin Vikings always showed a great interest in Northumbria, and several of them became kings of York until the English reconquest was complete in 945. They were also drawn to Wales – where their raids were frequent if impermanent – and to mainland Scotland, where the resistance of Kenneth MacAlpin (who united Picts and Scots in 844) had hitherto held them at bay. Here they succeeded in dominating the old Irish kingdom of Dal Riada (Argyll), and in 870 the great Dublin Vikings Olaf and Ivar captured Dumbarton Rock, capital of the kings of Strathclyde. Scottish influence was thus gradually rolled back eastwards. Nevertheless the kings of Scotland did manage to maintain themselves and continued to play a significant part in Viking history, allying with one faction against another, or against the English on occasion (*eg* at the battle of Brunanburh 937, probably located in Cheshire, and in 1014 or 1016 at the battle of Carham to capture Lothian). The Picts of the highlands and islands, by contrast, seem to have succumbed completely. In particular Caithness was overrun from Orkney soon after 890, leaving the Vikings free to pursue their own internal squabbles throughout the area.

External and internal warfare continued sporadically throughout Ireland,

Figure 7
Ireland in the Viking Age

DIRECTION OF INITIAL VIKING APPROACH
(Norwegians)

To Dal Riada and Hebrides

North

To Isle of Man

L Larne

L Neagh

Inismurray

ULSTER

L Strangford

CONNAUGHT

Inisbofin

Clontarf
Dublin

To Anglesey

LEINSTER

Limerick

MUNSTER

Waterford

Cork

LATER VIKING APPROACHES (Danes)

sometimes with Vikings fighting Vikings and Irish fighting Irish, during the following century. The Irish Vikings assimilated with the natives to a considerable degree and took the lead in commerce from their bases in Dublin, Ulster and, later, Waterford and Limerick. Nevertheless, they were often joined by new raiding fleets from outside (eg Kells sacked in 920, Clonmacnoise in 822 and 836), so that lasting peace was always elusive. Finally the rise of Brian Boru from about 970 marked a decisive move towards the sort of centralisation of Irish kingship that had been so notably absent in earlier times. His victory at Clontarf in 1014 did not bring the Viking presence to an end, but it laid to rest Viking ambitions to conquer the whole of Ireland.

THE BYZANTINES

Micklegard was in some ways the ideal exotic destination for a Viking, in that it was both an easier gateway to the sunny Mediterranean than either Baghdad or Gibraltar, just as it was the acclaimed successor to the Christian Roman Empire. It was more active and significant in this period than less accessible Rome, although that also made it a particularly tough military nut to crack. The city of Constantinople had been heavily fortified in stone by the Romans, and there was a chain boom across the Bosporus to stop shipping when necessary (*Sagas of the Norse Kings*, p.171). The Byzantine Empire's diplomatic corps was possibly the most advanced in the world, while its armed forces were surely not far behind, with the levy troops and other soldiers and sailors in each of twenty-three territorial 'themes' totalling some 80,000 men, quite apart from a standing imperial army and navy that totalled something like 60,000. In terms of numbers alone this made them vastly superior even to the Viking 'Great Army' which operated in England and France (which was never replicated on the Eastern Front), although in fairness nothing like these numbers could ever be mobilised at any one time and place. The Emperor Nicephorus II (963–9) stated that a corps of 5000–6000 expert cavalry was essentially all one needed for any campaign, and doubtless field armies did not usually swell to much larger sizes. We should, however, recognise that, in addition to raw numbers, the Byzantines could also boast a particularly high level of military discipline, strategic science and weapon technology (see Blöndal's *The Varangians of Byzantium*).

Their cavalry was heavily armoured; their archers had advanced composite bows; their engineers and artillerists had a variety of ingenious machines and engines; and their fleet possessed the very potent secret of Greek fire. This particular weapon is thought to have instantly disposed of Viking fleets in the Black Sea in 860, 941 and again in 1043, which must surely have put it into a highly 'magical' category in the Viking imagination. Something like the same effect must also have been produced by the fact that Byzantine capital ships were big enough to hold crews of 220 on an habitual basis, or over twice as many as the Vikings could squeeze into even their biggest boats. It is noticeable that the Varangians in Byzantine service tended to be relegated to the fast flotilla for chasing Arab pirates, where 110 would be the maximum crew per boat – although even that size of crew must surely have seemed impressive to them.

As an empire Byzantium was constantly skirmishing with the Arabs over Syria, Asia Minor, Bari, Sicily, Cyprus or Crete; with the Khazars and Pechenegs in the Crimean area; and with the Bulgarians and Magyars in the Balkans; and sometimes against the Russian Vikings themselves. Imperial fortunes often went down as well as up; but in the late 900s there was quite a marked Byzantine military revival linked to a particularly expansive diplomatic posture. Even so, the empire still always seemed to be fighting against some-body somewhere, with the result that it was always in need of good new troops. Varangian mercenaries had therefore been welcomed as a useful addition to the order of battle, especially by Basil II, and it was they who brought the battleaxe back into Mediterranean warfare. But it should be noted that service in Basil's Varangian Guard was seen by Vikings as almost equivalent to the grand tour of later days, since it could show a Scandinavian nobleman (or just plain 'tourist') most of the classical sites of the Eastern Mediterranean and the ancient world in general. It was doubtless one such Varangian who left runic graffiti at Piraeus, near Athens (perhaps in 1018?).

THE ARABS

The Arabs were met by the Vikings in two distinct theatres. Most produc-tively and profitably they were encountered as traders at Bulghar on the middle Volga, and all the way down through Khazar lands to the Caspian Sea. The Vikings sometimes tried to bully their way down to the Caspian by force of arms; but in every case they were beaten off and violently reduced to a less aggressive posture. When they were posing as peaceful traders, how-ever, we do have a number of reports of their activity from Arab travellers. The most memorable and garish comes from Ibn Fadlan, who accompanied a caravan from Baghdad to Bulghar in 921–2 (averaging 130 miles per month, or just four and a half miles per day), although it is not entirely clear if he could distinguish a genuine Viking or Rus from a Finn, a Slav or a Khazar. Whatever the truth of his reports, it is certain that Baghdad, capital of the Abbasid Caliphate, was indeed the key entrepôt and cultural centre of the whole Western trade with Arab lands, and their link in turn with the great Silk Road from China which reached its highest development at around this time. 'The art and civilisation of the Silk Road, in common with that of the rest of China, achieved its greatest glory during the T'ang Dynasty' (ie 618–907: Hopkirk, p.28). The road's terminus at Ch'ang-an (or Sian) had a population of two million – equal to that of the whole of Scandi-navia – and in many ways must be considered as much of a cultural refer-

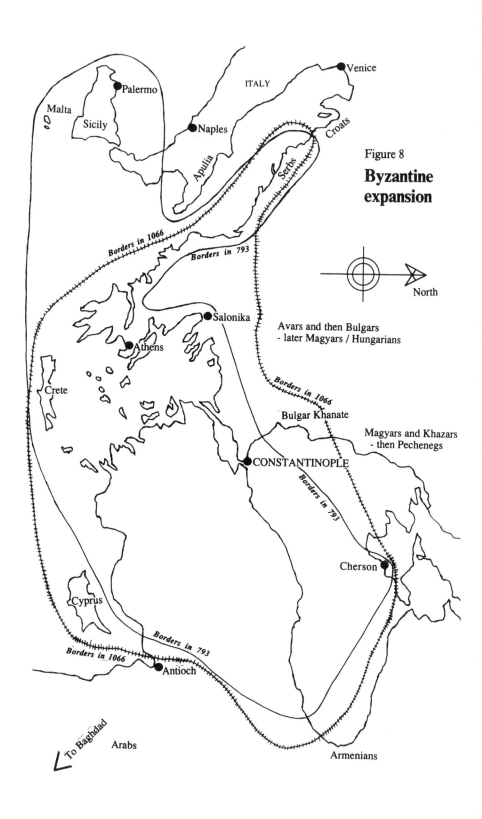

Malta

Palermo

Sicily

ITALY

Venice

Naples

Apulia

Croats

Serbs

Borders in 1066

Borders in 793

Figure 8

Byzantine expansion

North

Salonika

Avars and then Bulgars
- later Magyars / Hungarians

Athens

Borders in 1066

Crete

Bulgar Khanate

Magyars and Khazars
- then Pechenegs

CONSTANTINOPLE

Borders in 793

Cherson

Cyprus

Borders in 793

Borders in 1066

Antioch

To Baghdad   Arabs

Armenians

Figure 9

The military solidity of the Vikings' neighbours

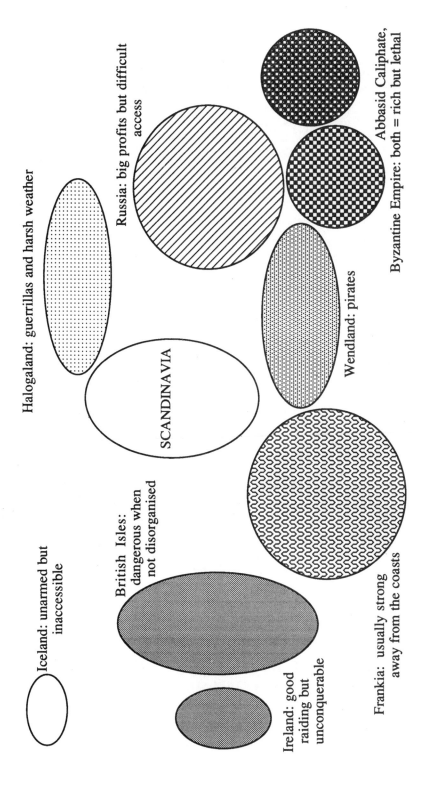

Iceland: unarmed but inaccessible

Halogaland: guerrillas and harsh weather

Russia: big profits but difficult access

SCANDINAVIA

British Isles: dangerous when not disorganised

Wendland: pirates

Abbasid Caliphate,
Byzantine Empire: both = rich but lethal

Ireland: good raiding but unconquerable

Frankia: usually strong away from the coasts

ence point to Viking-age Europe as Los Angeles has been to Europe during the past fifty years.

Less peaceful or profitable were the Western (Umayyad) Arabs of Morocco and Spain, who were occasionally raided by Vikings when Southern France seemed too dangerous or too poor. Unfortunately for the Vikings, however, these Arabs (in common with the non-Arab corridor all along the northern edge of Spain) were themselves highly dangerous both to pirates and *as* pirates, and were very well organised to beat off attacks with fortifications, fleets and readily-mobilised armies. Cities like Seville or Algeciras proved to be not only very rich, but also very well populated, armed and fortified. Any Vikings who managed to get that far found it paid them better in the short run to go elsewhere and hit the soft under-belly of the Frankish lands in the Camargue or up the Rhône to Valence – although in the long run they still had to sail home through the Straits of Gibraltar, where they were very likely to be intercepted by Arab fleets once again. All in all, therefore, the Mediterranean option cannot have enjoyed a very good reputation in the mead-halls of Noirmoutier, Rouen or Dublin.

Scrælings

When the Vikings first arrived in Iceland they found no one but a few Irish anchorite monks who 'went away' (whether free, in chains or in coffins is not specified). As they moved further west to Greenland they found traces of earlier habitation by Eskimoes, and then in Labrador and Newfoundland they increasingly encountered indigenous peoples whom they called 'Scrælings'. These consisted of a few Dorset-culture Eskimoes (thought not to have had kayaks) and some rather larger groups of Point Revenge Indians with birch bark canoes, of which three different tribes have been identified as having lived in the area at that time. These were all stone age peoples and hence techno-logically inferior to the Vikings, but they could still make up for that by outnumbering the invaders. The Indians, at least, were heavily armed with bows, javelins and the dreaded 'balista', made of a rock attached to a throwing stick. They were militarily effective enough to chase off Karlsefni's expedition of 160 (or sixty) men in c.1020. Then in the 1200s Thule-culture Eskimoes (with kayaks) had arrived in Greenland and helped build up pressure on the Viking settlements, possibly by concerted assaults but more likely by sporadic small-scale skirmishing. They certainly helped in the extermination of the entire Western settlement by 1342, and made a significant contribution to the eventual demise of the Eastern settlement soon after 1500 (Gwyn Jones, *The Norse Atlantic Saga*, pp.96, 130 *ff*).

CHAPTER 3

Strategic Mobility

'I don't like the idea of cramming myself into any of those little overloaded boats ... they might sink and drown the lot of us'
— Hrolf Sturlaugsson, in *Göngu-Hrolf's Saga*, p.37.

The Alleged Reliability of Viking Navigation

No one today can possibly think of the Vikings without also thinking of their boats, especially since so many remarkable examples have been preserved. These boats may perhaps have been technically slightly superior to those of the Franks, Saxons and Frisians although, as Haywood has argued, all three of these peoples probably had efficient sailing boats for some centuries before the Viking Age (and a similar point is made in Foote & Wilson, p.240). The Franks were especially quick – at sea as well as on land – to understand and react to the Viking threat when it eventually materialised. They undoubtedly possessed considerable naval experience of their own, even though the Vikings may have been able to draw upon deeper reserves of men who were familiar with the sea.

Whatever the truth of Frankish, Saxon and Frisian equivalence with the Vikings as mariners, it is likely that the boats of the Viking Age did represent a distinct improvement upon the Scandinavians' own earlier practice. It may well be that they progressed during the 700s from a mixed fleet of small sailing boats and large galleys towards bigger types that combined both sails and oars. This development would have greatly enhanced their strategic range, although there is little directly useful evidence to amplify the speed or scale of such a change. The two deep-keeled boats of the 700s found at Kvalsund in Norway have been seen as belonging to a transitional period between oar and sail; but since they do not have mast-steppings they are somewhat debatable as indicators (see *eg* Muckelroy's *Archaeology Under Water*, p.72). We can have more confidence, from boat finds, that the Vikings had efficient sailing galleys in the 800s and later, than that they did not have them earlier.

But just how expert really were the Vikings as sailors and navigators? They certainly have an awesome reputation, and they did indeed reach places as far apart as Gibraltar, the Holy Land and Vinland the Good. Modern reproductions of some of their boats (both warships and merchantmen) have been sailed across the Atlantic to the complete satisfaction of their crews and, although it is very unlikely that the Vikings had either chronometers or any sort of compass to guide them, they do seem to have been expert in some basic forms of direction-keeping. For example, it seems certain that they could hold to a particular latitude, although not to a longitude, using rudimentary instruments combined with observations of the noonday azimuth of the sun, and of the direction of the Pole Star. Add to this that it is received wisdom among experienced offshore sailors that a number of other essential pieces of information, such as the weather forecast or the estimation of a ship's speed, can usually be guessed perfectly well by a trained and experienced mariner without recourse to instruments at all. Admittedly such guesses will lack the mathematical precision that instruments might provide, but the point is that a long and intimate personal experience of the sea can make up for many deficiencies of precision.

The Vikings were certainly reputed to have possessed a keen sensitivity for distant evidence of approaching land, such as changing cloud formations or patterns of bird life. They had no charts or maps, but they surely memorised verbally-transmitted lists of landfalls for any given journey, expressed in days of fair weather sailing expected from one headland or island to the next. They may not always have known exactly where they were, but they surely usually had a pretty good idea. (See the interesting discussions in Gwyn Jones, *A History of The Vikings*, pp.162, 192–4; *The Norse Atlantic Saga*, passim, and Foote & Wilson, *The Viking Achievement*, p.255.) In summary, therefore, we can feel fairly confident in accepting the general view that the Vikings had more or less mastered such navigational sciences as were generally available in their day.

What is less well known, however, is that the sagas report very numerous cases of erroneous navigation and even shipwreck, especially as the result of fog (when they could not take sightings) or storm (when they could not control their direction). Admittedly the sagas are a very dubious form of evidence; but it is still striking that one of their most recurrent themes is the very high level of uncertainty that was still apparently associated with seafaring in the Icelandic 1200s. Matters surely cannot have been all that very different in the Viking 800s or 900s.

Let us first consider some examples of unsuccessful navigation:
– One of the very first Norse landings on Iceland happened by mistake, c.860, while Naddod the Viking was trying to find the Faroes (*The Norse Atlantic Saga*, pp.40,156–7).
– Greenland was first discovered by mistake, c.920 (?), by Gunnbjorn Ulf-Kraukuson while he was trying to find Iceland (*ibid*, pp.73, 186).
– Newfoundland was discovered by mistake by Bjarni Herjolfsson, c.986 or 1001 (?), while he was trying to find Greenland (*ibid*, pp.115, 190).
– Thorstein Eiriksson set off from Greenland for Vinland but failed to find land all summer. He returned to the wrong part of Greenland and there died of illness (*ibid*, p.197).

- Harold Godwinson was blown off course to Normandy, c.1064, where he was forced to make rash promises to William that he would regret at Hastings (*Sagas of the Norse Kings*, p.220).
- Gudleif got lost in a storm, didn't know which country he landed in (actually it was Ireland), and was soon taken prisoner (*Eyrbyggja Saga*, p.193).
- The sons of Njal got lost at sea and didn't know which land they had reached until they were in a naval battle against the Scots (*Njal*, p.145).
- Helgi's ship on the way to Iceland was blown off course towards Greenland. The crew almost died before land was eventually found (*Tale of Scald Helgi*, p.65 *ff*. Note that there is another 'magical' storm on p.69).
- Onund Treefoot had a rough passage from Norway to Iceland and hit only its north-east tip, forcing him to sail north-about the island rather than south-about. Even then he lost a yard and was blown out to sea for several further days (*Grettir*, p.15). By contrast Odd of Mell seems to have been reputed for the accuracy of his navigation, and was 'unusually lucky on his voyages ... for he never made landfall north of Eyja Fjord or west of Hruta Fjord' (*The Confederates*, p.45).

In all this there is a deep irony that many of the most famous Viking explorations and discoveries – upon which so much of their fame as sailors has been based – seem to have happened by accident, in rather the same way that Columbus accidentally discovered the West Indies by setting out to look for the East Indies. There is also a strongly fatalistic tendency in the literature to denigrate the navigator's role by seeing him as almost entirely subordinate to the whims of the weather. In the next section we shall see that the Vikings may have preferred to sail close to the wind only for special emergencies, if they could do it at all, and that for most of their operations they probably would not need or want to use this capability very often. Therefore they were very dependent upon a following wind for most of their movements by sea, and we constantly hear of them 'waiting for a fair wind'. Yet even in the special emergencies when they did need to sail close to the wind and tried to do so, there seem to be good indications that the Vikings were often totally defeated by extreme weather – just as today we can still find oil tankers equipped with the latest navigational technology being sunk on the Orkney rocks, or Ro-Ro ferries turning turtle within the shelter of peaceful Belgian harbours, or indeed in the Baltic itself. For the Vikings, such embarrassing facts could at least be glossed over in the literature by attributing the weather to the actions of sorcerers or witches.

Sometimes it is the hero of a saga who is supposed to be able to navigate more effectively than his opponents because he can overcome or determine the weather with his own spells – for example with a magical gold ring (*Göngu-Hrolf's Saga*, pp.57, 60), or a 'weather hat' (Saxo Grammaticus, p.288 and footnote). We may, however, perhaps speculate that in many cases a particular

Viking might become a hero precisely *because* he had won a reputation as a good navigator and knew how to outsmart his enemies in this department, without actually needing any recourse to magic at all.

More telling, perhaps, is the malignly magical aspect often attributed to bad weather conditions – both fog and storm – which habitually upset the careful calculations of even expert navigators. This is especially common in the 'lying sagas'; but it also appears in many supposedly more factual works such as *Heimskringla*. For example, in *The Olaf Sagas* (p.59) the pagan warlocks who are creating mist to cover their attack on the evangelising Christian King Olaf Tryggvason themselves get lost in it and are captured, while later (pp.68–9) Raud the Strong uses witchcraft to get a good wind to escape, then a storm to stop pursuit, until Olaf's bishop uses counter-magic to get some decidedly more Christian weather. However, it is perhaps significant that these last two examples of 'weather witchcraft' are both located in Salten fjord, which even in more recent times is still noted for its quirky and dangerous currents. We are reminded that the original 'Maelstrom' was also a Western Norwegian hazard to shipping. Equally the North Atlantic around Iceland and Greenland has always, ever since Viking times, been given a particularly fearsome reputation for its 'gigantic triple waves' (*Tale of the Greenlanders*, in *The Olaf Sagas*, p.101, footnote), which on one occasion during the Second World War were even able to bend back the flight deck of an aircraft carrier. We should not therefore be astonished that supernatural forces were cited as the reason for poor navigation in those particular zones, any more than we find modern 'scientific' westerners looking for interference by Space Aliens in the Bermuda Triangle. For both malign and benign weather it was perhaps only to be expected that the Vikings should believe that they needed something more than good navigational skills to control their movements.

Their loss rate to accidental shipwreck certainly seems to have been very high, and we might not be quite as admiring of their navigational skills as we are, if we really knew how many of them were lost at sea. One telling statistic is that out of twenty-five boats from Iceland which set out for Greenland in 985, only fourteen (56%) arrived at their destination. The remaining eleven boats (44%) were turned back or lost, although unfortunately we do not know how many fell into each of those two categories. (Some manuscripts have thirty-five setting out, making a failure rate of 69%: *The Norse Atlantic Saga*, p.187.)

The sources for all this are very unreliable, although the remains of a few wrecked Viking boats have been found, as well as boats that were used in graves (Loyn, p.67: but note that the five well-preserved Skuldelev [Roskilde] boats were sunk deliberately, as blockships in a narrow channel, and were not wrecked by the weather). Nevertheless, it does at least seem to be a common theme in the sagas that very many boats were wrecked, and that this could sometimes obliterate an entire campaign.

Let us look at some examples:

- All 120 Viking boats at Swanage in 876 were lost in a great storm (*ASC*: Compare the annal entry for 1009, when a storm wrecked and blew ashore Aethelred's English fleet of eighty boats, commanded by Beorhtric, allowing them to be burnt by the enemy).

- A Viking fleet was destroyed in a storm at Nijmegen c.838 (Haywood, p.124, based on the Annals of St Bertin: *cf* his p.114 for the same fate overtaking an Arab fleet off Sardinia in 813). Note that in all four of the above cases the loss rate is reported as 100%.

- The *ASC* for 896 reports twenty ships wrecked on the south coast of England, presumably by a variety of accidents rather than all in one disaster.

- In less historical tales, we read that Göngu-Hrolf got his fleet of 100 boats through magical weather in the Baltic by roping them together and using his wizards to navigate: but one boat that became detached was sunk by a huge walrus, and nineteen others were later lost (*ie* a total of 20% were lost: *Göngu-Hrolf's Saga*, p.91).

- In *Bosni and Herraud's Tale*, also set in the Baltic, a storm dispersed three new boats from a fleet of eight, and sank all five of the older ones (*ie* 62.5% loss: *Seven Viking Romances*, p.201).

Sometimes a single shipwreck could kill an important individual, very much in the manner of Kitchener's death in 1916:

- Thor wrecks the Christian preacher Thangbrand's boat on an Icelandic beach: it shatters (*Njal*, pp.180–1).

- The hero Gisli dies in a fishing trip (*Gisli*, p.60).

- King Eystein of Vestfold is blown overboard (and drowned) by the magic of the warlock king Skjold (*Sagas of the Norse Kings*, p.40).

- Gudrod Ljome is lost at sea (*ibid*, p.76).

- Hallfred and most of his crew are drowned at Konunghella, on the way to Sweden (*Saga of Hallfred*, p.40).

There are also many other cases of lesser men being lost at sea, such as Skeggi in the *Tale of Scald Helgi* (p.63); Kari (in a cranky old tub, setting out from Norway, in *Njal*, p.330); Thorkel in *Laxdœla* (p.234), and Thorvald (on a lake) in the *Fljotsdale Saga* (p.16). More anonymous cases of boats being lost with all hands and all cargo are mentioned equally frequently, as in *Eyrbyggja Saga* (p.166); *Seven Viking Romances* (pp.146, 177); *Laxdœla*, (pp.79, where a huge seal presides over the catastrophe, 115, 180).

Other reported Viking shipwrecks are more benign, where the crew manage to escape and sometimes even to rescue some of the cargo and repair the boat itself. Examples may be found in *Njal* (p.329); *The Norse Atlantic Saga* (pp.188, 196); *Hrafnkel* (p.115); *Laxdœla* (p.52), and *Fljotsdale Saga* (p.7). One interesting story is that of a trading boat wrecked at Vik in Iceland which was repairable, but suffered badly from the local lack of timber. There were no forests to produce planks of sufficient size, and driftwood was at such a premium that too little could be obtained to make a very successful repair. The result was 'too narrow in the bow and stern and too broad amidships', thereby presumably making it a prime candidate for a second wrecking as soon as it put to sea (*Grettir*, p.21).

But the key feature of all this is that Viking sailing seems to have been (literally!) a very hit and miss affair, unless the way was short and well known – and even then we do not know how many boats were lost or mariners perished in the attempt to make a successful landfall. Even quite short passages between islands in, for example, the Hebrides, can still today be notorious for their treacherous tides, currents and wind traps.

The perils of the sea itself were not, of course, the only dangers that the sailor had to face. In *Hrolf Gautrekksson* (p.107) 'bad winds, fog and Vikings' are all equally warned against, and indeed we should remember that the original definition of the word 'Viking' was a pirate who attacked more law-abiding boats on the high seas. Such pirates did not merely ravage coastal provinces, but intercepted trade and killed or enslaved sailors for their wealth – which especially included their valuable boats. To this list we should add two other important hazards intrinsic to a mariner's life in Viking times: the risks of an unplanned landfall and of fighting in a naval battle.

A major danger in making a landfall was that you could never predict just what the attitude of the local population might be. At one extreme you might be murdered on the spot, perhaps by wreckers who simply wanted your cargo, your silver and your boat's timbers. At one point in his fantastic adventures (*Seven Viking Romances*, p.93) Arrow-Odd explains how he had acquired a particularly splendid knife in his youth: 'One day a ship was driven on to the rocks just where we were [making salt] and smashed to pieces. The crew were washed ashore very weak, so it didn't take us long to finish them off, and I got this knife as my share of the loot.' Again, in *Laxdæla Saga* (pp.90–1), Orn was dismayed when he was forced by bad weather to anchor in an Irish estuary, 'far from the harbours and market-towns where foreigners are supposed to have safe conduct. I think I'm right in saying that under Irish law they can confiscate all our goods, for they claim everything as flotsam even when the sea has ebbed less from a ship than it has here.'

Even where the local people did not want to plunder you, there was still always a risk that you might run into some past political opponent or vengeful distant relative who bitterly remembered an ancient family feud that you had (momentarily but fatally) forgotten about. Thus in *Orkneyinga Saga* (p.41) Eyvind Aurochs-Horn managed to make his way from Ireland to the Orkney area around the coasts, but he did not dare to make the next oceanic hop towards his home in Norway. He therefore put in to land, but found his old enemy Earl Einar awaiting him and was killed.

At the other extreme you might well be fêted as a man of substance and power, and embraced as a valuable potential ally by the local ruler. Somewhere between these extremes – and perhaps the most common experience for most travellers – lay the more ambiguous type of welcome in which one has to make some sort of payment for hospitality and a safe winter season before one can resume one's voyage. In *The Story of Burnt Njal* (p.315) Flosi loses his way and is wrecked in the Orkneys, but decides to give himself up to Earl Sigurd and ends up paying atonement for being spared and accepted into the earl's bodyguard. Something similar happens in *Egil's Saga* (p.151) when Egil voluntarily surrenders himself upon being wrecked in the Humber, then has to think up a panegyric poem at high-speed, in praise of his arch-enemy Eric Bloodaxe, in return for his life.

Clearly there was a notoriously difficult moment whenever a traveller was forced to put in at an unexpected port (or beach, or – even worse – exposed rocky coastline). He would have to present his credentials to the locals while he was still apparently in a posture of extreme weakness, and while they were still in an initial frenzy of greed and hope. Sometimes it could lead to a spontaneous battle, as in the case of Orn's beaching in Ireland in *Laxdœla Saga*, cited above, and sometimes it could lead to shipwreck and even execution. Even in the happiest circumstances it could often mean a delay of maybe half a year before the journey could be resumed. It was much better, therefore, to stick to predictable destinations and short passages.

When it came to participation in a set-piece naval battle, however, the risks to life and limb were obviously very much greater, and the owner of a valuable boat might easily find he had been deprived of it by the end of the day's fighting. Yet against this there is every indication that very few Viking boats were actually sunk in battle. In the first place, Viking naval combat often seems to have been conducted with a group of boats lashed closely together, side by side, to make a stable platform upon which the infantry (or 'marines') could fight almost as if they were on land. No naval captain would wish to become involved in such a tight and unmanoeuvrable formation unless the wind was very low and the sea was both calm and sheltered. Such manoeuvres as were needed would be made by oars rather than sail; in other words this would in essence amount to 'galley' warfare. A fjord or estuary in good weather would be an ideal battlefield; but even marginally gusty weather off an open coast could quickly make any battle entirely unthinkable. If the wind was at all fresh, then either side could probably show its opponent a clean pair of heels (under sail) if it wished to avoid combat. Even assuming an accurate interception of one individual boat by another – which in the open sea was itself surely a very big 'if' indeed – it would still have been very difficult for any grappling or boarding to be successful. If the sagas are to be believed at all, indeed, any sort of boarding was always likely to be very difficult even in set-piece battles in smooth water. In a serious swell it must have been all but impossible.

Even if both sides were anxious to fight, they would surely not have found it advisable or even possible to coalesce into a closely-lashed raft of shipping if the wind and waves were high. They would be buffeted too much by the weather to manoeuvre with precision, and the whole lot could only too easily find itself wrecked on a lee shore. The very concept of naval battle was thus incompatible with the type of high seas that might possibly endanger the safety of the boats themselves.

If conditions were calm and favourable, however, there seems to be no indication whatsoever that anyone ever tried to sink an enemy's boat in battle. The decisive weapon of naval combat was the boarder's sword, axe or thrusting spear, which would clear the enemy's decks of men while not affecting the boat itself. Boarding, however, was the 'heroic' option. A rather greater proportion of naval combat probably took place using longer-range or standoff missile weapons, such as arrows or throwing spears. Once again, these were designed exclusively for an anti-personnel role rather than an anti-shipping one. Sometimes we hear of quite heavy weights being hefted into an enemy's vessel – *eg* a thrown anvil that crushed a man in *The Olaf Sagas* (p.38), or a pile of big stones with which Onund Treefoot's ambush party pelted its opponents once it had lured their boats under a carefully pre-prepared rocky outcrop (*Grettir*, p.8). However, in neither of these cases does the intention appear to have been to penetrate the hull of the enemy boat or to hole it below the waterline, but only to kill its crew.

Everyone involved in Viking sea battles must have been only too well aware of the cash and prestige value of boats to their owners, quite apart from their precious ability to transport people and goods over long distances. They must have been seen as potential assets, rather than as threats to be destroyed or evil influences to be shunned. If they carried forbidding dragon-prows or hex-inducing magical paintwork, then those were status-enhancing features for the owner, to be envied and admired rather than feared. The real threat and evil came from the enemy crews of these boats, not from the gloriously, outrageously 'big bad' boats themselves. Unlike much modern user-specific and non-interoperable military equipment, they could be used equally well by friends and enemies alike. The trick was to get your hands on them and make them work for you, rather than to dispatch them uselessly to the ocean floor.

There seem to have been only three main exceptions to this rule. The first was when a force of landlubbers happened to capture a beached enemy fleet, as the result of a land battle, in which case the victors might not be able to sail off all their newly-acquired boats and might see them only as a potential threat for the future. In the *ASC* for the decade of the 890s, for example, there are several recorded cases of English forces from London capturing beached Viking fleets but not being immediately able to conduct all the boats away to safe keeping.

In those cases they deliberately wrecked or burnt the remainder.

Secondly, a strong anti-shipping instinct often seems to have arisen whenever a smaller naval force wished to make a hasty departure from the proximity of a moored larger one. It would wish to immobilise the latter's boats during the crucial moments of its own escape and so, by stealth, it might seek to bore clandestine gimlet holes in the enemy's hulls so that rapid pursuit would be impossible. Examples of this may be found in *Laxdœla Saga* (p.113), and in *The Olaf Sagas* (p.241). Note, however, that in both these cases the intention was to immobilise the boats in question and increase their baling problems, but not to destroy them beyond repair. An opposite form of clandestine boat tampering is mentioned in the *Saga of Gisli* (p.37), where Gisli strips his boat of its tackle and makes it look wrecked and awash, as a deception measure to suggest he has drowned while in reality he is making good his escape.

For the deliberate, unprovoked, unlamented and total destruction of a boat, the third case would have to arise: namely a particularly prestigious state funeral. When some great decedant was cremated or buried in an especially opulent boat such as no ordinary man could possibly afford to own, let alone cast recklessly aside, it sent a strong and solid message to all good Vikings which confirmed the exalted value of both the man and the boat. This type of conspicuous consumption was the single, paradoxical, exception to the general rule that 'good boats constitute the highest possible form of wealth, and that it is therefore criminal to "waste" them'.

Apart from the above three special circumstances, surely no Viking can have ever wanted to sink or otherwise destroy any boat, especially since they could so easily be captured intact once their crews had been killed or chased overboard. In this regard Viking boats seem to have represented a diametrically opposite type of military target to the shipping used in, for example, the Second World War. In the latter conflict the whole aim was to destroy absolutely anything that floated under the enemy's flag, while always doing one's best to spare his crews – who were generally considered to be relatively harmless, 'soft' and innocent. In the Viking era, by contrast, the boats themselves must surely have amounted to one of the absolutely primary forms of economic objective (or loot), while it was their crews who were seen as the real threat. The life and limb of the enemy leader was certainly considered to be the most important political target of all – and his personal treasure chests were doubtless always economically alluring – but what Viking could possibly resist the idea of winning a nice new undamaged boat for himself, and at no monetary cost? Besides, if you happened to choose the *right* boat to attack you might end up with not just the boat itself but also the enemy leader's head on a pike, and all his treasure chests in your own hold – and all three trophies finessed in the single self-same action!

In the French Revolutionary and Napoleonic Wars the Royal Navy lost 101 frigates or larger warships to accident or the elements, without any intervention by the enemy whatsoever. By comparison it had only ten ships sunk by enemy action, or 9% of the total major ships sunk (Michael Lewis, *Social History of the Navy, 1793–1815*, London 1960, p.345). Twenty-four more were captured (18% of the total lost to all causes), although that should be set against the much higher total of over 200 enemy ships captured by the British (including some recaptures). Something very similar seems to have happened in Viking times. Boats might very often be captured in battle, but they were very rarely sunk. Almost all of the boats that entered a naval battle would be likely to emerge from it in a perfectly sailable – or at least easily repairable – state. When boats were sunk or wrecked it would almost always be as a result of bad weather, bad navigation, or both.

An Essentially Coastal Navy

As already indicated, we should be wary of overstating the extent of the Vikings' success as sailors. In particular, we should remember that they often got lost and confused, sometimes leading to shipwreck. Seafaring was a very high-risk business. Nor was their change from inshore to ocean-going boats (in the 700s?) really quite as important to them as we sometimes like to imagine, since they did not often need to take advantage of this capability. It turns out that their military operations around and within Western Europe were not often dependent upon a specifically oceanic capability.

One advantage that the Vikings do seem to have enjoyed over their neighbours in Frisia, Saxony or Frankia was a slightly better ability to sail close to the wind. Haywood (p.69) makes a fascinating argument that the Viking boats were in theory superior in this, because of their T-shaped keels, compared to the more flat-bottomed Frankish, Frisian or Saxon boats of the same era. Yet he also argues that this capability was probably used only in exceptional circumstances, since sailing close to the wind imposes a disproportionately heavy strain on rigging, hulls and – perhaps most significantly of all – crews. He finds little need for a deep keel in most inshore or coastal operations – indeed it is a positive disadvantage in beaching – and sees it only as a sort of 'reserve booster' for oceanic travel in the wilder northern waters. The Franks, Frisians and Saxons therefore had the optimum vessels for their more southerly operations, while the Vikings tended to divide their boats between small inshore boats for local use only – skiffs, fishing boats and twelve-oar 'scooters' (see Foote & Wilson, p.234) – and bigger vessels that were adaptable to absolutely all conditions, even though this meant they were somewhat less than ideal for their major coastal operations in England and Normandy. One is strongly reminded of the contrast between von Tirpitz's single-mission fleet of heavy battleships that could not operate very much further afield than the North Sea, and Fisher's global-cruise navy of relatively light but much longer-range Dreadnoughts, supported by an exotic array of riverine gunboats for imperial policing.

Even so, we may still question the basic premise that any of the Viking boats were ever able to sail particularly close to the wind at all. Being square-rigged rather than lateen-rigged, they were surely incapable of very much manoeuvre within even 90° of the wind. We certainly often read literary accounts of Viking movements being delayed by contrary winds against which their supposedly wonderful boats simply could not make any headway. The T-keel was not, apparently, by any means a complete solution to the weather, any more than the mere possession of a gang of ferocious warriors could guarantee a meeting with the enemy in battle. Admittedly exactly the same considerations often remained frustratingly true for strategists even as late as Nelson's day, so we should not be particularly surprised to find it recorded for the 800s and 900s (although an important question-mark still hangs over just how close to the wind the Vikings would have sailed their boats by comparison with Nelson's ships).

It is certainly true that the longer Viking voyages could not have been undertaken on a regular basis without the perfected ocean-going sailing boats, and even then they would be largely dependent on the trade winds, since the Viking boats could not sail very close to the wind (at least by modern standards). Obviously ocean-going boats were needed for the heroic deep-sea passages directly from Western Norway to Iceland, as in Thorarin Nefiolfsson's alleged four-day voyage already cited. But the same is also true for journeys that are split up into more cautious and segmented oceanic hops from Norway to the Shetlands (200 miles) and Orkney; from Shetland to the Faroes (200 miles); from the Faroes to Iceland (240 miles), and even from Iceland to Greenland (200 miles to the nearest point, but 450 to the first area suitable for settlements). We must thus agree that if access to the Shetlands, Faroes, Iceland and Greenland was essential to the Viking Age, then the oceanic boat designs were also themselves essential to it. But just how essential, in fact, was access to these distant places? We should remember that Iceland was not even discovered until some eighty years after the Viking Age had begun, and the richest pickings found by the Vikings were usually far closer to home and located in or adjacent to waters that were accessible to coastal and riverine navigation – or even movement overland – rather than needing oceanic hops at all.

We will discuss the boats themselves in more detail in the next section; but it is worth stating here that relatively little of the Vikings' activity seemed to require boats of as high a technical standard as they actually possessed. Most of their movements were inshore, following coasts and rivers or hopping from one island to the next, in short daylight passages – rather than prolonged oceanic or deep sea voyages. Within Norway itself, for example, it was possible to move around the fjords only if one went by boat; but in this case the smallest and most primitive types of ferry boats or skiffs could easily suffice. For the coastal journey between fjords, furthermore, good protection from the weather was

Figure 10

Some of the 'vital statistics' of island-hopping

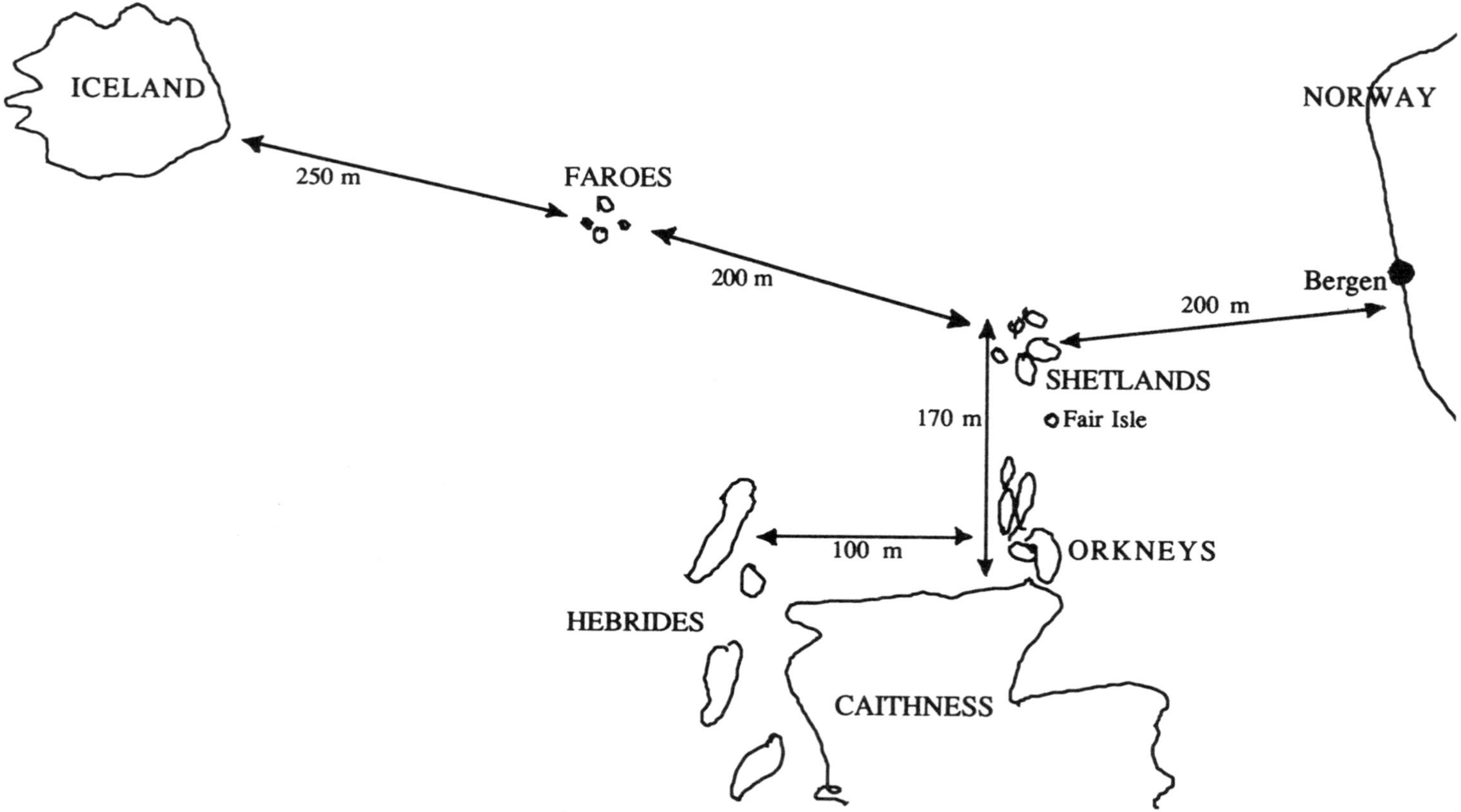

usually provided by some of the 16,000 offshore islands or skerries. The inshore Norwegian coast can often offer a peculiarly sheltered passage to the sailor and he can usually find a good overnight campsite on land, or for as many nights as he might need to shelter between storms. Therefore when Thore Hund escaped from Norway to join Canute in England in 1027, it was recorded as strange and exceptional that he travelled so far out to sea that the 'land is sunk' (*The Olaf Sagas*, p.291).

Further south there are not very different conditions in the Danish channels and round to Bornholm, Oland and Gotland. The Uppsala-Birka-Sigtuna region, which in so many respects became the centrepiece and showcase of Viking wealth, is absolutely honeycombed with small lakes, rivers and inlets. One certainly did not need a grand deep-sea galleon in order to ply one's trade in that particular zone. Further east in the Baltic there are admittedly some more extensive stretches of open water and some bad bald bare coastlines, but it remains true that the Baltic is still a relatively shallow inland sea, and moderately tideless, which gives it a certain amount of shelter from ocean swell. Land need never be far away if the weather threatens, although admittedly the local populations might not always be friendly.

South-west from Denmark the voyager does encounter a long open coastline off Frisia and the Netherlands, although it is once again in a relatively shallow sea, and the really interesting and rich places – just as in Poland or Russia – turn out to be located inland down the broad navigable rivers. To a Viking, the whole continent of Europe was magnificently accessible through the Dvina, Vistula, Oder, Elbe, Weser, Rhine, Meuse, Scheldt, Seine, Loire and Gironde, at least if the river mouths were not well defended. In every case he could find not only centres of trade, plunder or slaves ready for the plucking, but also time to rest for a while, in sheltered waters, between his hops from one of these rivers to the next. He did not usually have to make any heroic effort of oceanic seamanship, of the type that was required for more distant targets like the Orkneys, Faroes or Iceland.

All this leaves us with the British Isles, which can be considered as either a coastal target if they are approached from Calais into Kent, or an oceanic one if they are approached directly from Bergen to Caithness or Lindisfarne. In some of the recent literature it is stated that the shocking surprise power of the Vikings' raids against the British Isles lay in their direct deep-sea voyages across the North Sea to the Eastern coast of Scotland or England, and that the unexpectedly oceanic nature of such raids gave them their peculiarly new and horrible aspect in the minds of contemporaries. Unfortunately for this opinion, however, the evidence seems to point in a very different direction. The Shetland and Orkney staging posts were the first places to be reached by the Norwegians, by 780 or even earlier. If we include the fifty-mile stretch of open sea between the two – which is itself broken at the half-way point by Fair Isle –

these two archipelagoes represent a moderately dense line of islands almost 200 miles long, between which no oceanic sailing is needed at all, from Unst at the north-east tip of the Shetlands all the way down to John o'Groats on the Scottish mainland. It is only the initial 200-mile hop from Bergen to Unst which should be counted as anything other than coastal. In theory this might be crossed in only a very few days; but since its end points are well out of sight of each other it must still have represented an oceanic voyage to a Viking. In terms of total distance to be covered, however, it had the great advantage of being less than a quarter as long as the south-easterly coastal sea lane leading from Bergen to the Straits of Dover. Once the traveller had successfully arrived in the Shetlands, moreover, all the remaining navigation anywhere within the British Isles and Ireland was entirely coastal, inshore or riverine. From Orkney, Norwegian raiders might travel down the East Scottish coast to Lindisfarne, for example, or west to the Hebrides and then to Dublin or Man, or from Dublin to Chester, Anglesey or Bristol, without ever having to make anything like a serious oceanic voyage.

In 865 the Danes, coming south-about, surely started with only a twenty-five mile leap across the English Channel, which was scarcely a 'shockingly unexpected' or novel avenue of approach. Nevertheless, the *ASC* indicates that they may have surprised the men of Kent, and went on to sustain a whole series of shocking surprise attacks into places like York, Nottingham and Thetford. They may have achieved this by exploiting their numbers, military organisation, brutality or just low cunning – we will never know exactly what really happened – but at least we can be certain that long deep-sea journeys were not a factor in any of these surprises. The continuing shock power of the Danes seems to have lain in their ability to make surprise attacks merely from one English county into the next, rather than from anywhere as far away as 'Noroway o'er the foam'.

Scotland is little more than five miles from the Orkneys across the (admittedly treacherous) Pentland Firth, which is considerably closer than Dover is from Cap Gris Nez. You can certainly see Ireland from Scotland and the southern Hebrides, and from mid-crossing between Dublin and Holyhead, you can see both of the end-points very clearly (although ironically the same is also true of the five-times longer crossing between Iceland and Greenland – but only because the mountains on each side rise to such towering altitudes). There should at least be no doubt that all the pairs of islands in British waters are separated by no more than a single day's easy sailing in good weather. The main thing that might prevent a Viking boat from making such voyages would be bad weather, and a severe storm in any of these crossings can certainly be fatal even today. But it is always understood in the Icelandic literature that a navigator cannot be expected to venture forth until the wind is favourable, making for a set of powerfully restrictive safety regulations reminiscent of those that have governed most flying in the twentieth century.

Sometimes a sailor might wait for a fair wind during an entire season, although he would risk ridicule if he happened to get it wrong. For example, in *The Confederates* (p.86) Odd of Mel could laugh at all the Norwegian merchants who spent the summer waiting for a suitable wind in Thorgeirs Fjord, Iceland, as soon as he discovered that there was actually a good wind only a few miles further out to sea. He had his own boat rowed out into the better weather, and was then able to make the round trip to Orkney and back, under sail, in only seven weeks, during which time the other merchants had not even left the inland water. In this case Odd took a gamble and won, but the fact nevertheless remains that most of his contemporaries would set forth only if they could be absolutely certain that the weather was good. They would stay at home if they believed it was in any respect risky or unsettled; and we might add that in most normal cases they would be reluctant to sail at all if their destination was beyond direct visual range of their starting point.

It is noticeable that in the sagas about Iceland itself there is a convention that if a man sails abroad he is not expected to return for three years, and not expected to sail at all during the winters (mid-October to mid-April). This implies one summer for the outward journey, two winters and one summer for the core business of the trip, and one summer for the return journey. It is clear that a voyage to or from Iceland was still considered to be a very major undertaking indeed in the 1200s, and so surely not even the wonderful deep-ocean sailing ships of the 700s or 800s could have been relied upon to make more than one such voyage per year, or sometimes even to get much further than an intermediate stage in the Faroes, Shetlands or Orkneys during the first year of the attempt. Storms could halt the traveller at any of these places, so it seems to have been standard practice to proceed rather tentatively from one staging point to the next, rather than in a straight line as the crow (or raven?) flies. This did not necessarily mean that the mariner would need to make an actual landfall at the intermediate stages, if the weather was fair; but he would have to sail past at close enough range to confirm the identity of the land. This type of visual confirmation was made essential by the unsophisticated nature of the Vikings' navigational technique. Although they might not have needed to come ashore to identify which coast or island they had reached, they did at least have to approach quite close, if they were in unfamiliar waters.

The exceptional difficulty of the voyage from Norway to Iceland is vividly confirmed by the fact that although several invasion fleets of several hundred boats appear to have travelled from Scandinavia to Britain (presumably using the southern route via Kent, although that specific detail is not normally supplied), the fleets sailing from Scandinavia to Iceland are never recorded as containing more than a very small handful of boats. Iceland was surely off limits for any large scale Viking activity. It must have represented the Botany Bay or even the Christmas Islands of the Viking 'Empire', whereas Rouen, Dublin and York were surely much more like New York, Cairo and Dublin, respectively.

In *Audun's Story* the normal route from Denmark to Iceland is stated to include a landfall in Western Norway, but this could be dangerous if Norway and Denmark happened to be at war with each other (*Hrafnkel's Saga and Other Stories*, pp.126–8). In *Laxdœla Saga* (p.52) the route taken by Aud the Deep Minded from Caithness to her eventual shipwreck in Iceland was via Orkney and the Faroes, at both of which she made a landfall and conducted diplomacy with the natives. Indeed, the natives of such staging posts must often have seen their livelihood more in terms of extracting money from passing boats (by hook or by crook) than of working the land and shearing the sheep. The wealth of the Orkneys, in particular, was surely attributable in a very large degree to the fact that they lay at probably the most important of all the key crossroads between Norway and all points west.

Once again, therefore, we are reminded of the dangers that could be encountered by poorly-armed boats which made an unplanned landfall. One alleged means of avoiding these was to spend the entire year heroically at sea, over-wintering in the boats themselves, which would be used as a sort of floating hotel accommodation, and making landfalls only when the conditions were tactically favourable. However, such a feat was probably entirely mythological, and it is conventionally cited in the sagas merely to indicate that a particular leader was an especially bad and tough Viking, such as Eythjof in *Arrow-Odd*, the 'sea king' Olaf in *King Gautrek*, or St Olaf himself after the battle of the Helge river (respectively *Seven Viking Romances*, pp.78, 166; *The Olaf Sagas*, p.310). It is perhaps possible that small bands of landless pirates did sometimes over-winter on remote and deserted beaches, with only their boats for shelter against the elements: but surely they would not have been insane enough to contemplate literally staying afloat all year, if they could possibly help it. Even the hardiest mariner liked to draw up his boat onto dry land – for repairs and to dry it out – when it was not actually in use. Boat-houses designed specifically for this purpose were apparently common, and the remains of several have been discovered along the Norwegian coast.

Most of the Vikings' major operations seem to have been coastal, inshore or riverine. They might travel from Jutland to Dorestadt, from Dorestadt to Kent and from Kent up the Thames. They might follow the English east coast around Essex to East Anglia, and into the Wash or maybe up the Trent to Nottingham. This was surely the normal manner of their progress, rather than by bold, direct oceanic leaps from Bergen to York, or from Dublin to Reykjavik. The Vikings surely did not choose to wander over seas and oceans if they could possibly avoid it, but preferred to have *terra firma* always close at hand. The gradual spread of Viking power during the 800s should surely be understood in this way. They followed their noses, in effect, from one place to the next, stopping where they discovered weak defences or attractive winter quarters, and moving on where the resistance was found to be strong.

The Boats Themselves

When talking of Viking boats it is important to remember that there was not just one all-purpose type, but many different designs for many different tasks. This diversity is faithfully reflected among the multifarious boat-finds that have come down to us, although it remains possible that some common types are not represented by any actual specimen, just as some rare and exotic types are doubtless over-represented. The famous Oseberg boat of the early 800s, for example, is spectacular partly because it was originally designed as a 'royal yacht'; a prestigious show-piece in which some great notable would progress around his, or her (was it really Queen Asa, mother of Halfdan the Black?), local fjords. It does not represent the long distance work-horses of the wider Viking 'Empire', nor was it a warship. The equally-celebrated Gokstad boat, dated slightly later, is a *karfi*: far more suitable for oceanic sailing and general duties, but still relatively small. Its contemporary *karfi* from Tune is even smaller (see Muckelroy, *Archaeology Under Water*, p.73); and most Scandinavian burial boats are even smaller than that. Obviously one did not normally expend one's biggest and most useful vessels in funerals, although the elegant play-things of the deceased might be perfectly appropriate (and disposable) for this rather specialised purpose.

None of the three main boat-finds from the Oslo area are really representative of either the ordinary Viking merchant boat or the ordinary Viking warship. For these we can draw a better impression from the collection of five boats dated at about 1000 that were found at Skuldelev near Roskilde, which consists of a small sailing ferry, one small and one big warship (*snœkke* or snake), and one small and one big merchant boat (*knarr* or *hafskip*). This collection is almost tailor-made as a representative sample.

Two especially important facts emerge from the Skuldelev finds. The first is that although the 'typical' warship (Skuldelev #5, probably comparable with the Ladby boat) might be roughly similar in its dimensions to the Gokstad boat, it was probably less ocean-worthy, but intended to carry far more men. The same trend is still more marked in the case of the larger of the two Skuldelev warships (Skuldelev #2), which might easily have carried as many as 100 warriors. Such boats are sometimes called 'levy ships' to distinguish them from the smaller and lighter 'longships'; but it is clear that in neither case was the maximum loading of troops at all conducive to oceanic travel. Although the norm for a warship might have been fifteen benches of rowers (*The Olaf Sagas*, p.19), boats of 'twenty benches carrying ninety men' are quite common in the sagas which, even if a 'bench' is taken as implying two oars rather than one, still represents a very large multiplier of warriors per oar (see Foote & Wilson, pp.

Table M

Dimensions of some Viking boat finds

Place found	Date?	Purpose	Length (metres)	No. of oars	Comments
Kvalsund	c.725	Inshore whaler (?)	20	20	No mast-stepping
Oseberg	c.810	Royal barge	21	30	Especially rich ornament
Gokstad	c.875	General purpose	23	32	High sides, ocean-going
(also had 3 ship's boats, 7–10 m long, two with both sails and oars.)					
Ladby	c.950	Warship	22	'few'	Especially narrow and
shallow; *ie* intended for use in the Baltic and Russia, not the North Sea.					
Skuldelev 1	c.1000	*Knarr* or *hafskip*	17	'very few'	Ocean-going workhorse
Skuldelev 2	c.1000	Warship	29	52	Big and prestigious!
Skuldelev 3	c.1000	Baltic cargo boat	14	10	Inshore workhorse
Skuldelev 5	c.1000	Warship	18	24	A 'typical' warship?
Skuldelev 6	c.1000	Ferry/fishing boat	12	'very few'	For sailing, not rowing
Graveney	c.1050	Inshore trader	14	Not known	Found with its cargo

234–5, for a definition of 'oars', 'rooms' and 'benches', and the multiplier for men per oar). In *The Olaf Sagas* (p.131) Erling Skialgsson has a thirty-two-bench boat which carries 200 men; in *Halldor Snorrdson* (*Hrafnkel's Saga*, p.117) we hear of boats loaded with 'treble crews'; while in *Arrow-Odd* (*Seven Viking Romances*, pp.44–6, 59, 120) the assumption seems to be that each boat should carry 120 men for battle, but only forty for voyaging. When Thorfinn Karlsefni went to Vinland from Greenland he had three boats, but we are not sure whether he had 160 or just sixty men (Gwyn Jones, *A History of the Vikings*, p.301), though it was surely more likely to have been the latter than the former. His successor Freydis would take seventy-five souls in two boats (*Tale of the Greenlanders*, in *The Olaf Sagas*, p.112). It may well have been the case that warships would be loaded up to their maximum capacity in order to lumber from one fjord to the next, or up a river for a particular raid: but they would have to be considerably lightened and streamlined if they were to think of undertaking any serious deep-sea crossing, or even to participate in sustained operations near to shore. In those cases their crews might be cut back dramatically to something much nearer to one warrior per oar, or maybe even less than that.

In this context we are reminded of some of the most famous (or notorious) of the literary descriptions of great Viking battleships: the 'Crane' (thirty benches, *The Olaf Sagas*, p.65); the 'Short Serpent' (thirty benches, *ibid*, p.68); the 'Long Serpent' (thirty-four benches, thirty-seven metres long, *ibid*, p.76); the 'Bison'

(? considerably more than twenty-three benches, *ibid*, p.302); the 'Great Bison' (thirty benches, *Sagas of the Norse Kings*, p.141); or the sixty-bench 'Dragon' reputed to have been built by Canute, alongside Earl Hakon's forty-bench ship (*ibid*, p.305). In *Halfdan Eysteinsson* (*Seven Viking Romances*, p.181) we hear of a dragon-prowed boat of 140 oars, but since it comes only three pages after a crossbow contest it is surely anachronistic for the Viking Age. Nevertheless it is apparent that the Vikings did value big battleships, and that their tactical value lay in their great size, the numerical strength of their crews and the imposing height of their gunwales over those of their opponents. They acted as fortresses at the heart of a fighting line, and as painted and gilded symbols of their masters' prestige. However, it is equally clear that they were not best designed to venture out into the deep sea, especially not with the top-heavy crews that they took into combat. Such boats would not leap in one bound from Oslo to Lindisfarne with a full complement of troops on board, but at the very best might stagger laboriously around the Frisian and Belgian coasts and then make the short Channel crossing at Calais, provided the weather was fair.

The second very important fact to emerge from the Skuldelev finds is that the Vikings' serious working boats had very different lines from their warships and royal yachts, or even general purpose vessels like the Gokstad boat. The normal design for a cargo boat, whether intended for inshore (Skuldelev #3) or long range work (Skuldelev #1), was deeper in draft, higher in the gunwales and far less shallowly raked at stem and stern. It was a square box (or cog) whereas the warships were elegantly 'long' boats or cutters with aesthetically flowing 'snake-like' lines. They could not be beached as easily as a warship, and were correspondingly less well adapted to riverine movement. Nor were they very manoeuvrable under oars when there was no wind. Nevertheless, the merchantmen possessed two cardinal qualities which the battleships did not. In the first place they were intended to be propelled almost exclusively by sail, allowing them to carry almost skeleton crews by comparison. Between ten and thirty men would be more than enough to get a *knarr* from Norway to Greenland, and even then the crew might not have to do any rowing at all. Indeed, in long voyages any larger crew might well have been difficult to feed, and a shortage of rations is mentioned quite often in the saga literature with reference to such voyages. Secondly, the merchant boats could certainly carry heavy payloads (some fifteen to twenty tons, or almost the weight of the boat itself) over oceanic distances, which was not at all the *forte* of a longship. The nine-ton Gokstad boat is also reckoned to have been able to carry a payload that was equivalent to its own weight, but the total still amounted to only half of what a *knarr* could carry.

Despite its relatively spacious hold, however, not even the ocean-going *knarr* could be considered a big vessel by the standards even of Columbus' or Raleigh's day. At around twenty metres long, the space available for crew,

Figure 11

Merchantmen and warships

Merchant ship -- large hold, few crew or oars, dependence on sails

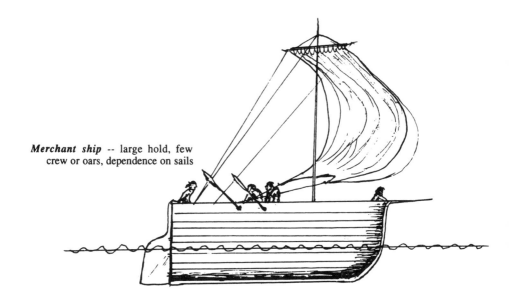

Warship -- large crew (especially in inshore operations) and many oars -- *ie* a true 'sailing galley'. Small decked areas at stem and stern

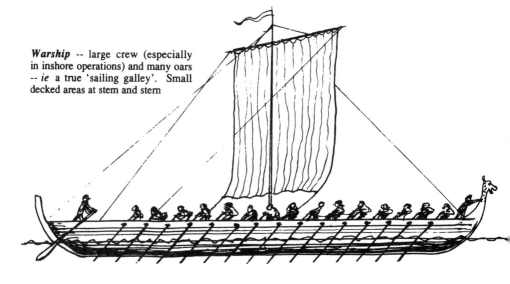

animals and camp-followers must have been appallingly constricted, and this could be doubly true of the over-manned battleships. Even with 'bad weather clothes' (mentioned *eg* in *The Olaf Sagas*, p.31; presumably made of oily skins), everyone must have been soaked through for most of any voyage. Comfort, sanitation and room to move at all must have been in terribly short supply, thereby making it doubly urgent to put ashore frequently and avoid heavy weather whenever possible.

Discipline must also have been absolutely ferocious and strictly hierarchical if any order or sense of purpose was to be maintained among a crew of thirty to 100 men crammed into such a small and dangerous space, especially since twenty metres makes an excessive distance for shouted messages to carry between the steersman in the stern and the lookout in the bows. There must have been some system of petty officers ready to repeat orders smartly down the length of the boat – and to enforce them by violent means if necessary – if intercommunication was to be achieved at all. The present author's experiences in both racing eights and narrow boats leaves him entirely awestruck that the Vikings were apparently able to cross open water in their tiny vessels, and survive, with the large sizes of crew that they seem to have deployed.

The transport of livestock makes a particularly problematic case for the student of Viking seamanship. It was always perfectly possible to put horses, cattle, pigs or sheep into the Viking boats, and even to carry them all the way to Greenland if required – modern experiments with reconstructed boats have shown how horses, for example, could easily be loaded and unloaded in exactly the way portrayed in the Bayeux tapestery (Sawyer, *The Age of the Vikings*, p.77, and photograph of a horse coming ashore). But what is far less clear is just how much valuable crew space such farmyard friends must have taken up, and how much inconvenience they must have caused to the sailors and to the general sailing properties of the boat.

For a relatively short and 'military' voyage, such as William the Conqueror's from Normandy to Pevensey in 1066, each armoured knight could presumably have found room on his boat for two or three horses which, from a fleet of perhaps 300–400 boats and with additional local procurement upon arrival, might allow quite a respectable force of mounted men to be assembled. Something similar probably applied to the Viking host of 250 boats that is reported in the *ASC* as sailing from Boulogne to Lympne in 892 'in one voyage, horses and all'. But such an invasion fleet would not, presumably, include much cattle or other livestock. It would be focused almost entirely upon immediate military necessities, and it would hope to seize most of its basic subsistence near the beach where it disembarked, by a process of living off the land. This was very much the type of expectation that the British Army was still taking along with it on most of its amphibious invasions during the Napoleonic Wars – although it must also be said that on such occasions the result was normally more likely to be a logistic disaster than a smooth transition from a seaborne force into a manoeuvrable land-based force. One is certainly tempted to believe that William the Conqueror happened to strike it rather lucky in his 1066 invasion, and it is quite possible that a number of comparable Viking expeditions came badly unstuck when their horses failed to survive the passage, or when their local procurement arrangements on a foreign shore turned out to be unexpectedly abortive.

In any voyage of more than a couple of days' duration, the Vikings surely had two additional factors to consider, neither of which may have troubled William the Conqueror in 1066. The first was that a balanced range of farm livestock might well be needed upon arrival, especially if a permanent colony was to be established in hitherto virgin lands. This meant that aggressive fighting bulls might have to be carried, no less than contented hens or complacent pigeons. When Grettir the Strong had to wrestle a fighting ox into his ten-oared boat, the boat started to disintegrate beneath him and it is likely that no one but the heroic Grettir himself could have successfully completed the very difficult journey home (*Grettir*, p.133). But secondly, the sheer weight of forage and fresh water needed to sustain each beast during a long passage would surely have mounted up rather dramatically, day by day, according to the length of the voyage. This might have seriously limited the number of other beasts that could reasonably be carried in any given vessel. Anything much more than two examples of a single species might have been entirely beyond the carrying capacity of each boat, so that a whole fleet would have been needed to carry even a basic set of all the farm animals necessary to establish a 'balanced' overseas colony – especially if one adds in the women, children and slaves that would be needed to run such a colony, but who perhaps could not be expected to do much towards helping to sail there in the first place. We are reminded of the twenty-five boats that set out together from Iceland to Greenland in 985, and can speculate that any smaller fleet would have been almost foredoomed to complete failure.

We must also remember that commercial slaving was itself an essential element in much of the Viking art of raiding. A really successful raid would surely be defined in terms of the number and quality of slaves captured quite as much as in the number of ounces of silver liberated, or the fine weaponry and mail salvaged from dead enemy soldiers. Silver and swords, however, could be transported relatively easily in a warrior's sea chest stowed securely below-decks; but slaves made a far more awkward type of cargo. They needed guarding, feeding and cleaning, and above all they occupied a lot of space. In 882 the Frankish annals (quoted in the article by Brooks) tell us that Hæsten was able to fill an entire convoy of 200 ships to send home his prisoners and booty from France to Scandinavia, and of this cargo by far the largest volume must surely have been taken up by the prisoners. All the pressures must therefore normally have been to drive slaves in overland convoys to the nearest slave market, and sell them off as quickly as possible, rather than to allow them to encumber working boats that were trying to collect still more of their kind. It was by their skills at managing this sort of 'human husbandry' that many Vikings must surely have measured their personal success or failure as pirates.

Even when the slaves were household servants rather than merely trade goods, they must still have made major inroads into the carrying capacity of a boat. In the story of Egil and Asmund, for example (*Seven Viking Romances*, p. 229), a crew is cited as 'thirty men, not including servants'. This makes us wonder just how many servants were considered necessary to service each 'man', and just how much space in the boat they occupied. If nineteenth century British Army norms are considered relevant – as well they may be – the answer might come out as something like 'half a servant per private soldier, and four per officer'. A boat with a crew stated as 'thirty' might therefore turn out to be carrying no less than sixty souls.

Another little-noticed aspect of Viking boats is that despite their normally effective caulking (with a mixture of tar, rope, and the generally finely-meshed planing of their clinker strakes), they nevertheless normally let in water, especially in heavy seas. For many Viking navigators, therefore, the art, science and sustained practice of baling was often absolutely a matter of life or death. In most of the early boats this meant that a bucket had to be filled in the bilges and then passed upwards through several different hands (and decks) until it could be emptied overboard (*Grettir*, pp.36–41; and see also the *Tale of Scald Helgi*, p.65 *ff*, and *Seven Viking Romances*, p.38). In later Viking times it seems that a more efficient centralised system of gutters, to channel waste water away, was often organised nearer to the boat's waterline (*Grettir*, p.241, footnote). But whichever of the two systems was used, the result was always a strain upon a minimum crew, requiring greater numbers of capable hands than were required merely to adjust the sails and navigate. Once again, in other words, it meant more crew were essential, and hence that there was less room for the payload.

A rather more familiar feature of the Viking boats was their shallow draught, at around three feet (the Gokstad example had 30–38 inches, or 74–95 cm, while the Oseberg had 36 inches or 90 cm). It was therefore relatively easy for them to be drawn up on a beach above the tideline for a night – or for a whole winter. The shallow draught was also essential for cross country movement, which for the Vikings meant movement up shallow waterways as much as it meant movement along roads.

The Vikings were capable of sailing on even quite small rivers, and the shallow draught of their boats even sometimes allowed them to dig tactical canals in a short space of time, for example to by-pass London Bridge in 1016 (as reported in *ASC*), or to burst out of Lake Maelare in heavy rain, avoiding the blocked main entrance at a time when the shallows were more passable than usual (*The Olaf Sagas*, p.120). The boats were also often portaged across an isthmus or around a cataract, without the help of a canal. A small boat with a flat keel and a small payload but a large crew (or slave population), would certainly be advantageous for this, and indeed we find some indications that just such boats were preferred in the Baltic, especially since it connected with the inland waterways of Russia. Some sort of portaging would always be required for a vessel to make its way down the lower Dnieper, where at least seven major sets of rapids (out of seventeen) still have names of Scandinavian origin. Still more portaging would be required to carry a boat across from the heads of the Baltic rivers (*eg* south-east from Novgorod, or south from Warsaw up the Vistula/Bug) to the heads of the river systems leading to the Black Sea (Dnieper, Dniester) or to the Caspian (Volga). Alternatively the cargo might be carried overland to a new boat on a new river while the original boat was sold, or left to await its owner's return at the end of the season. We certainly hear (from the Emperor Constantine VII, quoted by Blöndal, p.9) that the great convoy which left Kiev every June for Constantinople was built anew each year from timber sailed downstream to Kiev for that express purpose, and we wonder if the merchants ploughed their way back upstream with anything like the same number of boats. Boats – or at least their timbers – may well have been a major export of the Rus to the Greeks.

It is probable that all the difficulty and complexity of the portages involved in a voyage from the Baltic to either the Black or Caspian seas would have acted as a deterrent to many would-be Viking adventurers. In their own ways the fabulous cities of Bulghar (on the middle Volga) and Micklegard proved to be almost as geographically inaccessible to Vikings as the more fearsomely-named Giantland and Iceland. Nevertheless, unlike the last two (relatively poor and uninviting) target areas, these exceptionally rich eastern centres of trade and high culture do sometimes appear to have attracted large scale assaults from Viking Russia. Yet it was always the Rus armies that were defeated in these attacks. If Iceland was secure due solely to the difficulties of the oceanic crossing needed to reach it, then Micklegard and the Caspian were defended by a double defensive bulwark: firstly the difficult portaging and inland navigation needed for the long trip from Scandinavia across continental Russia; and secondly the very great strength, coherence and military experience of the local tribes or regular military garrisons within the target area itself. Against such obstacles the Vikings' expansion in the East proved to be far more successful if it was conducted by infiltration (*eg* in the guise of accommodating traders or mercenaries working within the local political structures and economies) rather than as death-dealing invaders who tried to overthrow everything and stamp it underfoot. Not even the 'Danelaws' established by the Rus within North Russia (*eg* in Staraja Ladoga, Novgorod and, especially, Kiev) appear to have been won by very large armies, but mainly by decisive political leadership working in

Figure 12

Viking routes across Russia

a) Via the Volga from Lake Ladoga to the Caspian Sea
b) Via the Dnieper from Lake Ladoga to the Black Sea
   (with alternative branches from the Baltic using
   the Western Dvina or the Niemen)

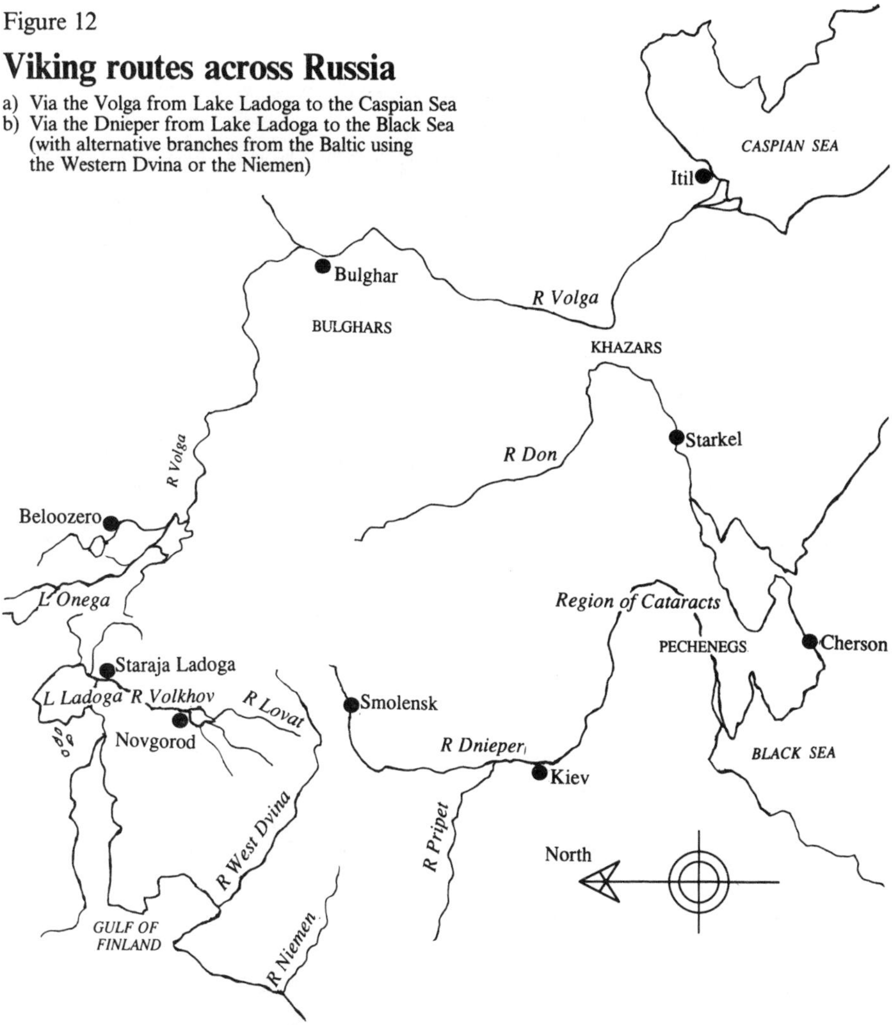

conjunction with local forces. In most of North-west Europe the diametrically opposite conditions often seem to have applied – but the key difference is perhaps that the Vikings' coastal navy could usually reach most of North-west Europe far more easily, and in far greater numbers, than it could ever hope to reach either the extreme eastern or the extreme western limits of its operational range.

As in so many of their operations, the navigation inland up a great (or not so great) river may often have been a somewhat tentative exploration, depending at best on merchants' tales or possibly unreliable native guides. The great explosion of Viking raiders into the rivers of England and France during the middle years of the 800s certainly suggests that they were exploring every estuary, creek and inlet they encountered along the coast, rather than necessarily knowing just what lay inland. Once this initial exploration had been done, however, they must have been better placed to assess the best routes and the most lucrative areas for operations, establishing preferences, set ways of doing things, and a pool of experienced navigators. Just as burglars are likely to return to a house that they have already burgled once, so the Vikings raided Noirmoutier four times between 819 and 843, and Rouen five times between 841 and 855. After that the lure of Paris seemed to become irresistible, and the Seine won the dubious honour of being the Vikings' first choice of inland waterway.

Overland Movement

The Vikings could reach deep into many parts of Europe by sailing up the rivers; but sooner or later the rivers would fade into trickles or the hills would make portaging too wearisome to contemplate. The watershed between one river and the next might occupy a much bigger area, and be far more difficult to cross, than was often true in the dense river grid that spread across the humid Russian plains. There was, in short, a very great deal of Europe that could *not* be reached by water.

In these circumstances the Vikings might not attempt to manoeuvre at all. They often visited distant Micklegard or Iceland by water; but they are not reputed to have been common visitors to the land-locked Alps or Carpathians, which lay very much closer to home. They might harry the mouths of the Elbe, Rhine and Loire; but they did not pester the hill peoples of the Harz, Jura or Auvergne. In part this was because such mountainous regions were usually far less rich or populous than more juicy targets located on coasts or great rivers (although the Harz did eventually become a great centre for silver-mining). We must remember that ease of access by water was itself a major reason why great towns might grow and civilisations thrive. There was also a military-political factor in play, in that the hard defensive potential of many countries tended to increase as one progressed successively inland from the mouth of a great river. The Carolingian Empire, in particular, was strong everywhere during the days of Charles the Great himself; but when it began to fragment it tended to do so from the peripheries. Its heartlands in central Germany and Eastern France were usually more strongly controlled than its more coastal provinces, and therefore they made more difficult targets for Viking attack.

However, whenever they encountered circumstances where the military and political situation allowed it, the Vikings would not be slow to leave their boats and continue their journeys overland. They often marched directly across the central keel of Scandinavia between Trondheim and Uppsala, or from West Gotland to Oslo. In *Orkneyinga Saga* (p.58), for example, we read of travellers from Novgorod who sailed across the Baltic to Sweden but then continued their journey to Norway overland. In *The Olaf Sagas* (p.314) the saint finds that he cannot push his fleet westwards from Sweden past Canute's well-defended

Danish straits, so takes his men out of their boats and walks them home to Norway. When he later makes a similar overland journey for his final Stickelstad campaign, he even takes some portable boats along with him (*ibid*, p.352). In Britain there also seems to have been a considerable overland commerce between York and the Irish Sea, across the keel of the Pennines; and in many of Alfred's wars the *ASC* suggests high intensity march-manoeuvres all across the interior of England, from Chester or Nottingham to Southampton or Thetford, and from Glastonbury or Exeter to London or Canterbury. In the later Viking Age there were also numerous intrusions into the Grampians, although Snowdonia probably managed to maintain its icy remoteness throughout this period.

Mountains may well have been unfamiliar to Danes, and even to Swedes who hailed from Uppsala or from Gotland Island. It would nevertheless plainly be ridiculous to imagine that mountains held any mystery at all for Norwegians, especially if the 'mountains' in question turned out to be puny little mole-hills like the Pennines. Such obstacles could easily be crossed, on foot or with horses and mules, provided only that the boats in which the Vikings originally arrived could be guarded and preserved at the beach-head from which the raiders decided to transfer from seafaring to overland transport.

We have already seen that his boat was a very valuable item to any Viking. To own one (or even a part share in one) might well be the culmination of a lifetime's ambition. Certainly ownership represented a major financial investment. Boats were given away by kings only to the most favoured of their courtiers, and they often changed hands commercially for entire farms or large purses of silver. Even quite rich men would sometimes be able to afford no more than a half or quarter share in one, and the sagas are full of deals in which such shares were bought and sold, just as they contain many references to the division of a boat's valuable timbers or cargo after a shipwreck.

Even a small boat required considerable labour and skill to build, although not necessarily a particularly long time. A single winter or even just a few weeks, apparently, could easily be enough to complete even a large boat, if the building team was sufficiently numerous, focused, disciplined and motivated. In terms of their building-time, therefore, there was a sense in which Viking boats could be seen as strategically expendable (*ie* easily replaceable) by any ruthless war leader who commanded plentiful resources; for example, Earl Hakon supposedly burnt his boats before going into battle in Gotland (*The Olaf Sagas*, p.27). However, in terms of financial outlay they must always have seemed entirely irreplaceable to most ordinary Vikings. Compare the case of the Sherman tank in 1944–5. From an Allied general's point of view, or from a logistician's, it was an overflowing commodity for which there were two or three available for every combat-ready crew that could be raised to run them. They were entirely expendable. But from the crew's own point of view their

Figure 13

The mountain ramparts of Central Europe – proof against Viking attack

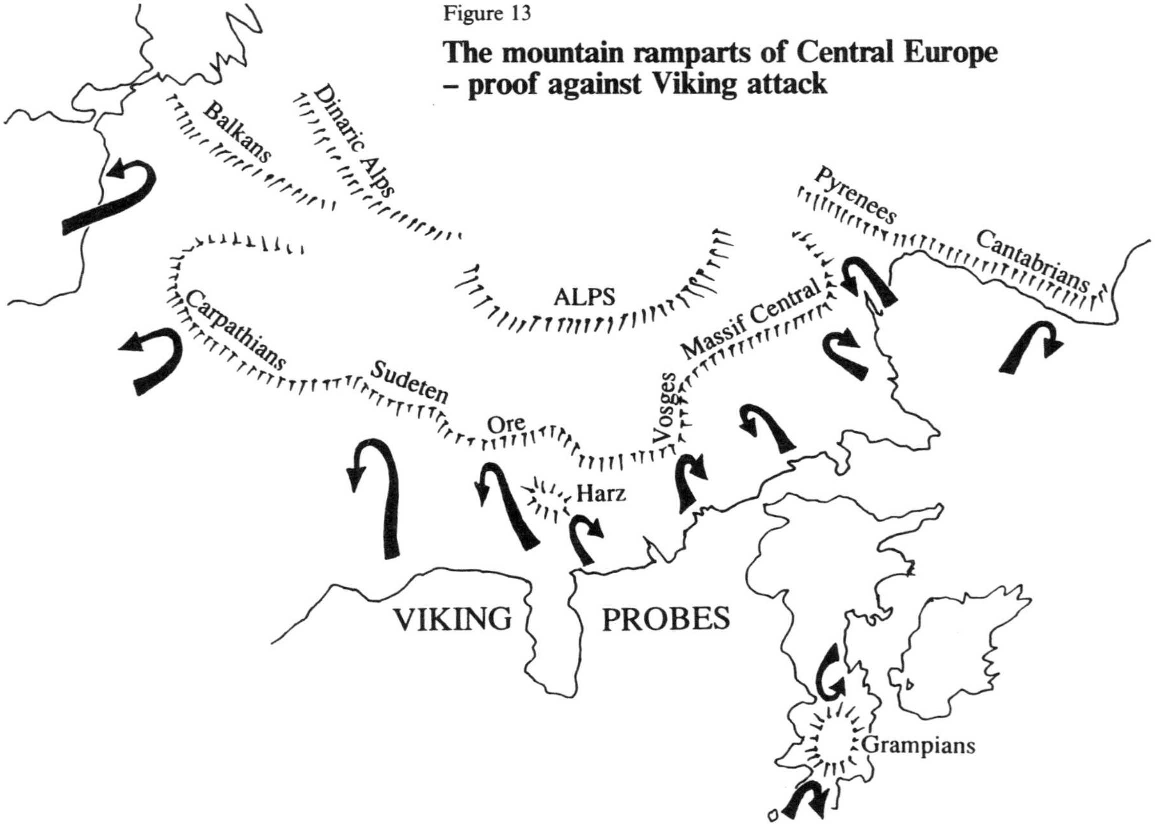

Cantabrians

Grampians

Pyrenees

Massif Central

Vosges

Harz

Ore

ALPS

Dinaric Alps

Sudeten

Balkans

Carpathians

VIKING PROBES

own particular example of this tank represented the only (highly uncertain) physical protection standing between them and a very sudden and nasty death. To lose that one particular tank would represent just about the most traumatic life-crisis that one could possibly imagine.

In these circumstances, surely, most Vikings must normally have felt that it was essential to make special provisions for their boats' security, whenever a major part of the crew departed to go swanning off overland. That meant leaving behind a very strong detachment to guard the boat – preferably on some relatively inaccessible island base or in a fortress – even though it might halve the number of men left available for the overland journey itself. In *The Olaf Sagas* for 1022 (p.247), for example, there is an account of how ten men from the crew of Asbiorn's boat stayed behind to watch it, while the other ten men went on shore to find the king of Rogaland. In the *Sagas of the Norse Kings* (pp. 222–32) Harald Hard-ruler leaves a third of his men to guard the boats during his drive on York in 1066, only to find that their late arrival for the battle of Stamford Bridge costs him both his life and the victory.

In the *ASC* for 892 the Danish fleet built a 'stronghold on the water' at Milton Royal to protect their boats and logistic echelon (including all the women and children), while raiding bands went inland to find booty. But the following year the Viking leader, Hæsten, moved this base to a new fort at Benfleet which was soon captured by the English while he was away on a plundering expedition. His boats were either destroyed or captured, along with his community's women and children, and it is even possible that exactly the same sequence of events was repeated very shortly afterwards, for a second time, in the same location. Then in 895 when the Danes took their boats up the River Lea, north of London, they drew them up on the river bank and protected them by building a new fort. This time, alas, their exit to the sea was speedily blocked by counter-fieldworks built by the English lower down the river. The Danish warriors thereupon rode off to the West in disgust, sending their women and children to safety in East Anglia, but once again allowing the Londoners to capture some of their boats and destroy all those that they could not move. This campaign finally seems to have broken the Vikings' resolution. Too many of their boats had been lost, so their raiding spearhead gradually despaired of victory and dispersed, thereby conceding to King Alfred his final and, in many ways, greatest triumph.

Clearly there was always an operational price to pay, whenever a Viking raider split his force by leaving one part with his boats while the other part struck inland. For both Hæsten and Harald Hard-ruler this price turned out to be decisive for their entire campaigns, although in many other cases it seems to have been quite acceptable and no more than an inconvenience. If we can assume that it does not take especially large numbers of warriors to ravage and pillage an undefended district, then even a small fleet might well be able to provide enough men for that job while still maintaining a stalwart defence of the boats left behind on the beach. Nevertheless, there must always have been a sense of risk, whenever a Viking left his boats behind him, just as it was a nervous moment when the British split their advance on Port Stanley in 1982, with one detachment going on foot and the other by sea.

From 850 onwards the *ASC* certainly has many references to Viking operations in England that break completely free from the coast or the river system, including over-wintering across relatively large areas of country. The account of these campaigns also often contains specific reference to the disembarkation, local purchase, seizure or acquisition by treaty of horses. In 891 the host that had been defeated at St Lô is reported to have taken horses 'before the ships came' and advanced into Eastern France. When it was defeated there it returned to Boulogne the next year, somehow procured 250 boats and then invaded Kent, taking its horses along with it. This seems to suggest that the fleet attached to the army had either failed to join up with it when it was originally needed in Western Normandy, or had been deliberately sent away to some place of safety. Then it had made a successful rendezvous at Boulogne. An alternative reading is that a host with no boats of its own had asked for some from other Vikings, perhaps as far away as Scandinavia, but that none had been sent. Then at Boulogne a new fleet had been improvised by seizing local shipping and perhaps building some new vessels for the purpose. The Calais–Boulogne–Quentovic area would surely have had far more shipping readily at hand than the Cotentin peninsula.

If our standard picture of a Viking warrior will, almost inevitably, include a boat somewhere within its frame, it will nevertheless be deficient unless it also has a horse. The Vikings used horses for overland transport whenever they could get hold of them, both as pack animals or to pull carts as much as for riding. The Oseberg boat-grave included not only a unique – albeit surely untypically ornamental – example of a Viking cart; but also a tapestry showing several others in actual use (photographs in *eg* Arbman, *The Vikings*, plate 47, and Jones, *A History of the Vikings*, plate 21). Transport based on horses was probably far less efficient than movement by boat, using up much more human and animal energy (and grazing-time!), and making only perhaps a quarter of the headway on a fine day (*eg* thirty miles rather than 120). At least there was no risk of shipwreck in storms, although horses did suffer from many other hazards of their own, such as disease, stampede or thieving. If we further calculate that each man in a 'crew' could handle only a very limited number of horses, then it is very likely that less cargo could be carried by the complete crew than they would expect to move in the hold of their boat – and this would be doubly true if half of them had to stay behind with the boat itself to protect it. In any case, most Viking operations using horses probably advanced at a considerably slower rate than could be achieved with a force of pure cavalry.

Not only were carts cumbersome and prone to bogging down, but a certain proportion of those accompanying them would almost inevitably be travelling on foot. There might simply not be enough horses to go round, and in any case the status of some of the travellers (perhaps as shepherds, mule-drivers, cattle drovers or slaves) might well disqualify them from riding. We should not think of a Viking force moving with horses as a particularly speedy strategic asset.

A horse-based Viking army did, nevertheless, enjoy certain advantages over Viking forces which moved by water. In the first place, following the general European fashion of the times, some or all of it might quite possibly remain mounted in battle as well as merely for strategic movement. Doubtless the Vikings did not charge in formation with lance in rest, as later medieval knights would try to do; but mounted skirmishers, bowmen, swordsmen or spear-stabbers would surely have been welcome within any Viking battle line, just as mounted police form a normal part of the (mainly infantry) security line outside football matches today. This may not have quite amounted to 'Viking cavalry': but it surely does go some way beyond the conventional idea of them being 'mounted infantry' who would automatically dismount before they ever entered combat. Dr Guy Halsall, in particular, has made this point tellingly to the author; and he has especially explained how at least some of the evidence normally used to portray troops of this era as 'fighting on foot' (*ie* as infantry) may in fact be a confusion for 'fighting on land' (*ie* not in boats). Whereas 'fighting on foot' clearly excludes mounted combat, 'fighting on land' obviously does not. Since the Carolingian Franks were well known for their deployment of mounted men in battle, it would be odd indeed if neither the Anglo-Saxons nor the Vikings had heard of such a practice, or tried to emulate it.

Table N

The (notional) ergonomics of different forms of transport

Type of transport	Average **miles travelled** per (good) day	Number needed to move a ton:		Daily 'fuel'/food needed per ton moved (in pounds)	
		Men	**Horses**	**For men**	**For horses**
Men on foot	15	50	–	150	–
Driven horses	15	10	20	30	200
Ridden horses	30	10	30	30	300
Carts	12	6	12	18	120
Sledges	30	12	24	36	240
Warships	120	5–10	–	15–30	–
Cargo boats	120	1	–	3	–

Secondly, there was always the possibility of finding a good road. Despite its close proximity to the pulsating sea lanes, one of the greatest Viking feats of civil engineering in Jutland turns out to have been a major inland 'ox road' which included a long bridge and a causeway – surely telling us that road transport was by no means something that the Vikings systematically ignored (see eg Foote & Wilson, p.436). Certainly the ASC indicates that in Britain the Roman roads must have continued in regular use throughout this period, alongside even earlier routes that were scarcely less well defined. As soon as a Viking hit such a highway, he might very well expect to double or even triple his mobility as compared to the speeds he could make on local tracks or cross-country. Even the walking portion of his group would accelerate dramatically, in much the same way that a modern motor car on a motorway can easily average two or three times its speed on country lanes or paths. A good road has a better surface, is wider and, apart from anything else, makes navigation far easier. One does not need to stop to ask the way at every village, but can simply follow the main carriageway.

Thirdly, and perhaps of use only in extreme circumstances, we must remember that an army based on boats could not eat its means of transport, whereas an army based on horses certainly could. For example, at the siege of Buttington, as reported in the ASC for 893, the Vikings extended their resistance for a very long time by this expedient. Not all Vikings, however, seem to have approved. There were some deep religious connotations and in the Sagas of the Norse Kings (p.94) the eating of horseflesh is viewed with great antipathy. We must conclude that the cultural opinions of the Vikings in this matter were probably little less polarised than are those of modern European society.

Finally, the Vikings do seem to have been fully conversant with overland movement under conditions of snow or frost. Skis, skates and sledges were all very well known to them, which is only to be expected if we remember that an important part of the Viking 'Empire' was located within or near to the Arctic Circle. They would doubtless have felt a little silly if they took their skis along with them to Noirmoutier or Seville, just as the French Chasseurs Alpins must have kicked themselves for forgetting their essential ski-boot clips when they arrived in Norway in 1940. But from such evidence as we have, it appears very likely that the Vikings could operate in snow just as effectively as anyone else in their time – although this definition probably does not include the overland movement of any large formation of warriors. Individuals, royalty, couriers or other special people could doubtless have moved from one part of snowbound Scandinavia to another; but armies must have been pretty much immobilised. A few guerrilla ski-troops are perfectly conceivable, but a ski-mounted 'great host' is surely not.

CHAPTER 4

The Viking Notion of Strategy

'A war,' wrote Sir G. Cathcart from Kaffirland in 1852, 'may be terminated by the surrender or capitulation of the hostile sovereign or chief, who answers for his people; but in the suppression of a rebellion the refractory subjects of the ruling power must all be chastised and subdued.'
– Colonel C.E. Callwell, *Small Wars*, p.41.

Four Types of Viking Warfare

In Carl von Clausewitz's classic post-Napoleonic work *On War*, it is clearly stated that war is meaningless unless it has a political objective. In Viking terms this objective would vary greatly according to the level and type of war being contemplated, since by no means every expedition fitted into Sven Asleifarson's twice yearly pattern, with one set of pillaging raids after sowing and one set after harvest. This particular pattern might be compared with the modern suburbanite's Easter or summer holidays, when he 'takes the caravan out for a few days', or 'goes for a fortnight's sailing'. However, there were plenty of other types of campaign that should also be considered.

For analytical convenience we can divide Viking warfare into four distinct types:

i) **'Saga Warfare'**, or the sort of thing that happened in Iceland during the 1200s when the sagas were being written, and which may well have happened throughout Scandinavia before and during the Viking Age. This is small-scale blood-feud stuff, ranging from formal duelling to clandestine nocturnal hall-burning. This last technique was especially popular, and became almost a military art form in its own right. One farmer and a few of his farm hands, neighbours and relatives might arrange a day to get together and attack another farmer, in order to expunge some dishonour or settle some dispute. Attack in the small hours after midnight was particularly favourable to the attacker since he could almost guarantee that his victim would have no sentries awake during the initial phases of the operation and then, when the target house was well ablaze, his gangs of men at each doorway could concentrate unequal force against each single and disorientated individual who tried to leave.

As in a good Western movie, 'saga warfare' might include ambushes, cattle rustling, declared semi-legal killings and secret undeclared murders. There are skirmishes with outlaws and spontaneous punch-ups in the law courts or in the drinking dens. None of it really amounts to 'warfare' in the full modern sense of the word; but because it *does* normally fall into the category of organised armed violence, it will get a mention here. In terms of political objectives, it was normally the aim of one family to exact justice or vengeance from another in circumstances where there was a code of laws but no formal police to enforce them. Every citizen of standing had to enforce the law for himself, with help given only by whoever happened to be his relatives and/or allies at the time.

ii) **'Royal Household Action'**, or the military activities of a king's immediate retinue as it accompanied him up and down the country. It was a major part of a king's function to progress around his subjects' halls with a royal household which doubled as tax collectors and conspicuous symbols of royal power. A glittering train of courtiers, politicians, poets, travellers and general enforcers went naturally with a great man's glittering treasure chest and set of nice boats, horses, hawks and dogs. Each year he would bring all this to each of his rich subjects' halls and demand hospitality for a few nights, thereby feeding the courtiers while demonstrating to the subject that he was really in control. He would collect as much tax and political support as he thought it prudent to demand, and might settle local disputes in between times. Alternatively, if the tax was not forthcoming or the legal dispute was beyond peaceful settlement, he would assert his will by using his household and courtiers as a loyal band of warriors or 'hearth troop'.

The incidents along the way might well be no bigger than those of 'saga warfare'; but sometimes it might be necessary to attack a particularly recalcitrant subject with a larger force, or even to fight a set-piece battle against a confederation of them. The long struggle by the two Olafs – Olaf Tryggvason and 'Saint' Olaf – to impose Christianity and central kingship upon Norway is a particularly well-documented example of this process that can be followed through the pages of *Heimskringla*. The details we have for Harald Finehair's similar operations in the previous century, which were so much resented by the Icelanders, are less reliable but add up to essentially the same sort of thing, and similar processes may be detected in Denmark and Sweden at around the same time.

iii) **'Going A-Viking'**, or the freelance plundering expeditions conducted by pirates on land or sea. Any individual farmer, petty lord or unreconstructed bandit was free to pursue this type of action at almost any time – provided he could gather a few companions and a relevant means of transport such as a boat or horses. Viking expeditions by a single boat's crew were apparently very common and Professor P.H. Sawyer has very pertinently pointed out just what an important effect even very small operations might have. You do not, after all, need more than a single boatload of villains to cause the international scandal of sacking a famous – albeit actually quite undefended – monastery, any more than you need more than a single car bomb to scandalise the world of culture by blowing up the Uffizi Gallery in Florence today. Even the *ASC*, which Sawyer sometimes criticises for wildly exaggerating the numbers of boats in any given force, often talks of groups of only three, six or nine boats. Small, speculative fleets of this sort of size were apparently very common on the sea lanes of the Baltic or between the islands of the North Sea and the Irish Sea. They also made a habit of pestering the coasts of England, Frisia and France. Against them the defending merchants might organise convoys of comparable size, or – on land – there might be defensive musters of the local 'Home Guard' or 'Territorial Army', and so the scale of combats might gradually tend to escalate to the point where the seaborne attackers became heavily outnumbered by the land-based defence. In theory, at least, Edward the Elder's Burgal Hidage implied there would be 27,071 men stationed in English garrisons at any time (article by Brooks, pp.18–20), or as many as would need about 1,000 boats to transport. This was far more than freelance Vikings could normally muster.

In the context of 'going a-viking' it may be useful to make a distinction between punitive raids, which have a mainly demonstrative and political purpose; and predatory raids, which are almost entirely for economic gain, or at least basic subsistence. Viking pirates were capable of both types. Sometimes they might have royal approval, as privateers commissioned to inflict punitive pressure and damage upon the king's enemies; but perhaps more often they would be acting entirely for their own ends in a predatory mode, and might easily have directed their action against the agents of their own nominal king. The 'punitive' aim of the Vikings might perhaps have been to seek some specific personal vengeance or some other particularly specific personal prize ('the hand of a fair princess' would spring to mind, had it not been so heavily romanticised down the ages as to appear totally ridiculous in cold modern print); but in general the aim was most likely to have been simply to get rich quick by whatever 'predatory' means, and regardless of who else had to suffer in the process (as long as it wasn't the pirates themselves!). Note, however, that for all their anarchic behaviour towards outsiders, the Viking bands may have been perfectly well organised within their own ranks, as constituting a small fleet or miniature army. They would be pursuing political ends insofar as they themselves were concerned, as a unit, albeit not necessarily in the interests of some higher concept of the state.

iv) 'Royal Army Campaigning', or the action of a specially-mustered host which included a major part of the military resources available to a king, either within one of his provinces or throughout the totality of his lands. In some cases, such as the famous Great Army which conquered the English Danelaw in

865–71 and then wandered round most of Northern France and Belgium until the early 900s, the 'kings' who were in command might have been landless (and self-appointed) 'sea kings', or merely a more grandiose type of pirate chief. Nevertheless, the significantly larger scale and duration of their operations clearly marked them out from the lesser groupings who would 'go a-viking'.

The aims of a 'royal army campaign' may well have been more sophisticated, and closer to what we would today understand as 'political', than those in any of the other three categories of warfare listed above. On many occasions the campaigns between the kings of Norway, Sweden and Denmark must have looked very like the normal dynastic wars that continued in Europe well into the nineteenth century. In some cases they might admittedly have been designed merely to extract tax or geld from some likely-looking victim; but in other cases they might have involved systematically harrying the lands of an enemy in order to increase pressure upon him so that he would see reason in possibly fairly subtle diplomatic negotiations. In other cases it might have been a purely punitive expedition. In all these cases the war would be less than 'total', in the sense that it was designed to make a point without necessarily committing the army to a decisive battle against the main enemy. Even a demand for Danegeld from a helpless victim was a sign of limitation and even weakness on the part of the Danes concerned, since the contract implied that they were prepared to stop fighting or devastating their enemy before he had been totally destroyed or subjugated. The Danes needed their victim to survive as a 'host nation' capable of paying again the next year, rather than as a depopulated wasteland.

In other cases, however, the strategic aim might have been to take over the enemy's lands completely, to burn his capital city, disperse his army, re-shuffle his government, and secure his unconditional surrender, his flight to distant parts or – most satisfactorily of all – the gruesome and public death of his king. In very many Viking campaigns it was certainly the death of the enemy leader, as an individual, which was the primary strategic objective of the entire operation. This should not, however, blind us to the fact that in many other campaigns the objective fell considerably short of that.

The nomadic and hence unseizable Great Army which was brought to England in 865 by the sons of Ragnar Lothbrok makes a rather special case. Constantly changing both its leaders and its rank and file, and apparently maintaining widespread international connections with the Viking community as a whole, its aim seems to have been less a matter of deposing Alfred than of constantly feeding itself from wherever it could, possibly dropping off colonies of settlers along its path, and then moving on. It eventually left England altogether for the continent in 879; but it returned around 892 and was finally mastered and dispersed by Alfred in 896. Hence it survived as a self-supporting strategic entity, territorially based only on the land it won by its own campaigning, for some thirty years. It had no homeland that one could counter-raid apart from the Danelaw of Eastern England, and even this could quite readily make a separate peace independently of the Great Army itself, if the Great Army happened to be absent at the time. The English commanders therefore found themselves frustrated and unable to establish any permanent settlement of law as between one sovereign power and another. The army of Sven Fork-beard a century later would operate in very much the same way and in a similar theatre, and it was only Canute's total triumph over the English that finally led to a definitive conclusion and regularisation of the Viking forces.

It is also worth noting that at certain times there were probably some similarly nomadic Viking armies operating in Russia, more or less according to the same basic ground rules, although we do not have any firm or sure details of their activities.

So much for the strategic aims in our four types of Viking warfare. Let us now turn to the general shape of the strategic principles which they required.

Some Principles of Strategy

The Vikings prized a number of military ideals. The strength and courage of Thor the Thunderer is an obvious example, just as skill at arms, in the sense of adroit personal weapon-handling, was obviously important to the up-bringing of anyone with the least pretention to nobility, and to many of the others besides. Skill in seafaring was also clearly an immensely useful attribute that could be learned by daily experience. But beyond such things there was also the more slippery ideal of Odin the wily war god, who was simultaneously the god of poetry, education, deceit and trickery. The association of all these qualities in a single figure surely tells us something important about the doctrinal back-ground to Viking warfare, insofar as it shows us that they would not always want to rush unthinkingly into a frontal attack. Cheating, and 'striking the enemy where he isn't' were both very central to the Viking art of war.

Yet this art was not laid down in any manuals of military doctrine, but only in advice, poetry and practical expertise passed down from one generation to the next by word of mouth and physical example. Chroniclers writing from outside the Vikings' own time or place did sometimes use Greek, Roman or later medieval terminolgy to describe Viking military activities (eg 'testudo' for an infantry phalanx, which may or may not refer to a 'shield wall'); but that is no evidence that the Vikings were themselves aware of the wider literature, or used methods drawn directly from it. However, they surely did often borrow methods, ideas and items of hardware from the enemies they encountered in their own time, such as Byzantine ideas about siege engines, or fine Frankish weapons – and perhaps the Byzantine and Frankish idea of fighting on horseback – not to mention the whole language and pantheon of gods that they held in common with other Germanic peoples. They often fought in alliance with non-Viking forces, whether for strategic reasons or merely for financial gain, so they must have been fully aware how other peoples fought. After all, the ability to assimilate themselves with alien cultures was one of the Vikings' more notable features.

But how did all this translate into a 'Viking way of doing things'? In 'saga warfare', and probably also in much of 'royal household action', the first recourse after a wrong had been committed would surely often be to diplomacy. What could be more wily and devious than winning your campaign in the courts or at the negotiating table rather than in the expensive and dangerous business of actual warfare? Accredited ambassadors (or something vaguely equivalent to them) would therefore probably be sent from one camp to the other, under more-or-less trustworthy safe conduct guarantees. Sometimes they were killed, if they carried a deeply unacceptable message or tried to exceed their diplomatic duties (eg Saxo Grammaticus, p.288; The Olaf Sagas, pp.161, 293, and compare p.264 for the tax-ships to the Faroes which failed to report home): but for the most part they seem to have been left free to do their business in a civilised manner. Their task might be to search for some form of peaceful reconciliation through such instruments as the payment of atonements, the conclusion of political marriages or the exchange of gifts, hostages or treaty obligations. If all this failed, then armed force would doubtless be resorted to.

As in 'going a-viking', the military tactics used would normally be those of small-unit terrorism or counter-terrorism, in which accurate, timely and detailed intelligence of the enemy would normally provide the key to success. Good intelligence alone could allow surgical raids or ambushes to be conducted where and when the enemy was weak and off guard. Such operations would enable the initiating force to achieve its aim while suffering only relatively light casualties, provided it possessed sufficient mobility and security to defeat the enemy's own intelligence antennae. As Colonel Callwell wrote in 1906 (Small Wars, pp.241–2), 'for carrying out such enterprises a good knowledge of the theatre of war, careful preparation and bold execution are essential ... [but] the most important point of all is to keep the plan secret.' In more Viking language the apocryphal Danish king Hring opined (Hrolf Gautreksson, p.31) that 'it seems a good idea to get the first blow in; as the saying goes, "the aggressor lands on top".'

Without good intelligence, security and 'bold execution', a raid might well fail; but even if it were a complete success there might still be no guarantee against subsequent reprisal raids by the outraged kinsmen (or the affronted lord) of the victims. A single raid does not make a strategy and, as in so many twentieth-century campaigns of terrorism or counter-terrorism, the feud might easily splutter on indecisively and unresolved, albeit still bloodily, for many years after the original assault. As such, its strategy should be characterised as

Figure 14 **The key factors for success in small-unit operations**

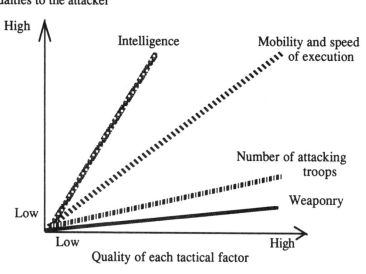

Chances that the operation
will succeed with low
casualties to the attacker

High

Intelligence

Mobility and speed
of execution

Number of attacking
troops

Weaponry

Low

Low   High

Quality of each tactical factor

endemic small scale guerrilla warfare, but despite its small scale it could not be dismissed lightly. Saxo Grammaticus (p.287), for example, suggests that it was the persistent pin-prick attacks by 'a tiny bunch of contemptible' Finnmark archers on skis, throughout a disease-ridden winter of 'magical' Permian weather, which brought his mythical hero Ragnar Lothbrok's forces every bit as near to defeat as had the whole proud array of Charlemagne's armies. However much this image derived from Saxo's imagination, or perhaps from Roman reports of unseizable Parthian horse archers, the fact remains that the concept of protracted guerrilla warfare already had a potent reputation some 700 years before Colonel Callwell (p.125 etc) warned his Edwardian readers that it was 'above all things to be avoided'. Its prevalence during the Age of the Sturlungs certainly seems to have led directly to the destruction of Icelandic independence in 1262–4, and the 'family sagas' written in that era are understandably full of cautionary tales of how feuds could turn very sour and ineradicable. *The Story of Burnt Njal* is just one of many examples, albeit perhaps the most poignant. Admittedly there must always have been plenty of similar feuds which soon petered out from a general lack of enthusiasm on the part of the families concerned; but that does not negate the key point that 'petering out' was by no means guaranteed.

Heimskringla itself is often concerned to show how slighted local Norwegian kings or earls might harbour deep grudges against domineering central kings, and pursue them down several generations through attempted murders or local uprisings. Such action would naturally incur retaliatory attacks, counter-murders and enforced conversions to Christianity along the way, the whole situation once again amounting to a state of endemic guerrilla warfare. The vicious cycle could be brought to an end only through an absolutely over-whelming victory of one side over the other.

In a more naval context the recurrent operations of small bands of pirates should also be seen in a similar light. They would operate as 'endemic guerrillas' within a particular area (which might be very extensive, eg all the Hebrides and the Irish Sea, or even the whole of the Baltic), while the coastal defence forces tried to make counter-attacks, either locally when the raiders were in their particular area, or by mounting more distant counter-raids against the Vikings' own home base. Once again, a lengthy exchange of unpleasantness might be ended only by an absolutely overwhelming victory of one side over the other.

But just how might such 'an absolutely overwhelming victory' be achieved, in these three types of guerrilla war? The most obvious solution, especially in small scale feuds, was the total disappearance of one of the warring families or Viking gangs. The specific line of kinsmen who were honour-bound to avenge their murdered relatives might simply die out in the normal cycle of mortality or, if external pressures were strong enough, they might quite possibly come to lose sympathy with their more distant clients and either emigrate to avoid doing their duty, or bluntly refuse to give help when it was needed. For example, Hrafnkel was able to finish off his long-term enemy Sam Bjarnison only after the latter's rich allies had finally and decisively decided to abandon his cause (*Hrafnkel*, p.70). Then again, there might be a heroic showdown in which one of the two sides was entirely wiped out. Thus Grettir the Strong was accorded particular fame and honour when he single-handedly (if entirely mythically) killed the notorious Halogaland bandit brothers Thorir Paunch and Ogmund the Bad, and all ten of their henchmen, when they tried to pursue a vendetta against his patron (*Grettir*, pp.47–54). More historically credible is St Olaf's pre-emptive surprise dawn attack against five conspiratorial Uppland kings while they slept at Ringsaker, before they had mustered their army. He rounded them all up, mutilated two, banished the remaining three, and then cashed in on the propaganda coup of being the only king who could defeat five other kings in a single morning (*The Olaf Sagas*, pp.180–2, 202).

A more diplomatic way to settle a running feud, however, would be the deployment of such a disproportionately superior force that it was sufficient to overawe its opponent on a long term basis. In the Icelandic 'family' context this meant that a small farmer might be dominated by an alliance of his neighbours who were loyal to a big farmer, and therefore always able to turn out a far larger posse whenever required. Elsewhere the gradual growth of centralisation meant that a central king would increasingly have his own powerful local agents laid out to 'mark' potentially troublesome local magnates, and act in the combined capacity of tax collectors, to reduce their wealth, and as an early warning system, to activate mobilisation against them if they should rebel (see Foote & Wilson, especially pp.123–44). In the case of coastal defence, once again, successful pacification meant that all key points would be organised and ready to react quickly in case of a raid, with beacons for early warning and strongholds to protect the essential items of wealth that might be the raiders' targets (see Haywood, especially pp.118–35). In all three of these cases the key to permanent pacification was seen as the improvement of local organisations directed towards a single goal and controlled by the central ruler. This idea would be strongly echoed in Callwell's precept (p.130) that 'experience shows that, if possible, the whole area of operations should be sub-divided into sections, each of which has its own military force'.

As for the logistic aspect of all these operations, it was probably very simple, since so few men would be involved. In 'saga warfare' a farmer would collect his own labourers and call on those of his relatives and allies. They would form a posse and take rations with them, from farm stores, for the two or three days that the raid might last. There might be only one or two such raids per season, so it would not impose a very great strain on the farming manpower or food stocks. With a royal household the logistic problem was solved even more easily, since the whole aim of a household's progress through the country was to assert the king's authority precisely by eating in the halls of the local magnates, and collecting taxes from them. Once again, any military operations would probably not take more than a few days to complete, so there would be no danger of starvation.

With pirate gangs 'going a-viking', the problem of subsistence was ostensibly more complicated. The raiding cruise might last for many weeks, and might be only partially sustainable from a boat's stores. If the main raid failed, there might be no inflow of plunder to feed the men on their return journey. This problem was nevertheless more apparent than real since, apart from legitimate recourse to local purchase, fishing and bird-catching, there was always the naughtily illicit tradition of the *strandhögg*, a small-scale beach landing to seize whatever livestock the coastal farmers might happen to have left grazing near the beach, regardless of whether these farmers were officially supposed to be your neighbours, your fellow citizens or your enemies; Rolf the Ganger, for example, was banished from Norway for conducting one there – ie on his home territory (*Sagas of the Norse Kings*, p.68). The *strandhögg* amounted to a sort of Viking raid in mini-miniature, without even necessarily involving any intrusion into populated areas or any loss of life on either side. Since the sort of Viking bands we are discussing here would by definition be relatively low in numbers, it would not require many sheep or cattle to keep them going for a few days until they felt they had to make their next *strandhögg*. Probably such mini-raids would often be economically bearable by the local population, although perhaps no less politically infuriating than a really major raid on a large town, and certainly a challenge to the local ruler. As the Viking Age progressed there was apparently a gradually-increasing crackdown on this particular form of populist criminality, with the law becoming ever more centralised and with freelance Vikings finding ever fewer places to hide.

With 'royal army campaigning', and even in some cases also with 'royal household action', the strategic framework shifts from the small and local to the big and nationally significant. With this size of force it is possible to fight proper battles and to pillage whole cities and provinces rather than merely hamlets and neighbourhoods – or at least to threaten such action unless a geld is paid. Once again, however, truly decisive battles and lasting peace treaties seem to have been rare. The Great Army that came to England in 865 stayed in the field for fifteen years and fought many battles (including allegedly nine in 871 alone) before it was finally tamed. Even then some of its members joined other Viking forces on the continent or in the English Danelaw, some of which were soon back harrassing the coasts of Wessex.

Campaigns which ended in the raising of Danegeld were especially notorious for their inconclusive outcomes, since a force that had profited from a geld one year would be only too tempted to come back for more the following year. Thus there was no final payment by the English to the Danes during the twenty years before Canute was made king, merely a succession of ever-mounting ones – and they subsided only very gradually even after he had achieved his main war aim of taking the throne itself. In other circumstances which might have been expected to lead to conclusive results – such as the death of a rapacious Viking leader – the outcome often seems to have been little happier. For example, after Weland was paid off (thrice over) by the Parisians in 861, he converted to Christianity, changed sides, and attacked other Vikings in the area, only to be killed in a duel soon afterwards; which left Paris no better protected than it had been before (Renaud, *Les Vikings et la Normandie*, p.42). The high mortality among Viking leaders could thus act to perpetuate hostilities as much as to dampen them down, and it is noticeable that some of the most successful peace-makers were the ones who lived long enough to see a single policy through to fruition over a period of many years.

Despite the probably inconclusive nature of its operations and treaties, a royal army could nevertheless certainly still deploy enough muscle to make an important mark upon the international scene – and upon the history books – although it was also correspondingly more cumbersome to move and more difficult to feed than a small raiding band or royal household. Such an army would normally be raised for only a relatively short period of time, to fulfill a specific task and then either retire to winter quarters or disperse. In that way its logistic needs could be limited to manageable proportions, especially since it would expect to feed itself mainly by a one-off raid to plunder the area in which it was operating. 'Living off the land' is a modern euphemism for what must have been a very cruel process inseparable from any army's movements. In campaigning far from home, however, the army might have to be maintained continuously for several years on end, so it would need to put its logistic arrangements on a more permanent footing. It would have to take winter quarters, which would mean staying in one place for many months on end, and therefore having to regulate the level of plunder in order not to exhaust the available resources too quickly. Winter quarters would normally be taken for one winter only, before the army launched its next spring or summer campaign designed to take it on to new quarters for the next winter.

This system implied that the army would always be consuming food grown by, and originally intended for, other people. However, if the same quarters were taken for two years running the Vikings would have a major problem. They would then themselves presumably have to take a hand in organising the sowing and harvesting of the second winter's supplies. Such a process could soon develop into a permanent settlement or colony as it did, for example, with Halfdan's army in Northumbria, 874–6 (when the troops were apparently

Table O

Winter quarters of the Great Army in England, 865–81
(From the *Anglo Saxon Chronicle*)

865–6	East Anglia (leaves ships and takes horses)
866–7	York
867–8	Nottingham
868–9	York
869–70	Thetford
870–1	Reading
871–2	London
872–3	Torksey
873–4	Repton
874–5	Halfdan's part to the Tyne, Guthrum's part to Cambridge
875–6	Halfdan settles Northumbria; Guthrum to Wareham
876–7	Guthrum at Exeter; a Viking fleet at Swanage
877–8	Guthrum at Chippenham: a Viking fleet in Devon
878–9	Cirencester (Guthrum signs treaty of Wedmore); a Viking fleet at Fulham
879–80	Guthrum in East Anglia
880–1	Guthrum settles East Anglia

ordered to set about ploughing, as a 'military operation': Sawyer, *Kings and Vikings*, p.105), and with Guthrum's in East Anglia, 879–81. Even then they might still find themselves in the same situation as Eric Bloodaxe's forces in Northumbria after 940 when, with 'little land and a large following he ran short of money, which is why he spent the summers plundering, while staying in his kingdom over winter.' (*Orkneyinga Saga*, p.32.) Something not too dissimilar may have afflicted Canute around 1020–30, when his demobilisation after the conquest of England seems to have left him with a surplus of warriors; and compare St Olaf's demobilisation in 1027 (*The Olaf Sagas*, p.317).

We must remember that in the Viking world the methods of producing and storing food were highly uncertain and inefficient when compared with those we enjoy today, and the effects of shortage could quickly become disastrous. There was much less of a safety net against starvation than there has been in Western Europe during the past 200 years – although even then there have still been many occasions of famine on a grandiose scale, especially in times of war. In Viking times a bad harvest could swiftly lead to famine, as noted in Norway for 974 (*The Olaf Sagas*, p.13 – the reason why Hardanger, or 'Hard-acre' was so named), for 1020 (leading to a pagan revival) and for 1022 (*ibid*, pp.232, 243). In England the *ASC* reports famines in 976 (associated with a comet); 1005 (when the Vikings evaded starvation by temporarily returning to Denmark); 1042 (cattle disease); 1044; 1047 (frost); and 1048 ('wildfire' and earthquakes). It is perhaps odd that more such instances were not noted, although that may be explained either by a different convention in reporting events before 976, or by the fact that the seat of warfare was usually confined to a single province at a time.

Quite often the winter quarters of an army are reported as only a small island near the mouth of a river; but this can be explained only if the 'army' is itself either very small – merely a Viking band – or if it is understood to be living off the products of a much wider coastal area, including pillaging the riverine trade, and using the island base as no more than a final refuge in case of a strong counter-attack. In 944 the Vikings' treaty with the Byzantine Empire specifically forbade them to over-winter on the Isle of Berezany, at the mouth of the Dnieper, since that would have given them too strong a fortress-base, too close to the Crimea. The implication was that if they had tried to settle on the mainland, instead of on an island, they would have been easy meat to the ravening Pecheneg tribesmen.

One of the more remarkable features of Viking strategy nevertheless seems to have been that even with their larger and more unwieldy armies it often proved possible to achieve surprise in offensive operations, at a level comparable to the surprises achieved in much smaller-scale ambuscades or hall burnings. In England between 865 and around 875, for example, the Viking host might lie quiescent in its winter quarters for a long period, lulling its Saxon neighbours into complacency; but it would then strike out rapidly and unexpectedly to seize a key strategic prize in a direction which no one had predicted. It would pop up in the middle of a particular territory, while the defenders were still peering outwards from its periphery. Whether they came by sea or by land, therefore, it was this ability to move armies with speed, surprise and precision which became an important feature of the Vikings' art of war. It was the 'pop-up' factor which gave them many of their best victories, and often avoided the necessity of fighting a set-piece battle at all.

With large armies in the field, however, a set-piece battle would always remain a possibility, and many were actually fought. Over sixty can be counted in the British Isles alone, during the Viking Age, and there were surely many more than that in the almost continuous Scandinavian civil wars. Such battles might perhaps be decisive, if key leaders were killed or disarmed when they had no immediate replacement at hand – although the casualties were not always those leaders originally tipped to lose. More often, however, set-piece battles may have decided only the temporary ownership of relatively small tracts of territory. Defeated armies usually managed to escape total annihilation, and lived to fight another day even though they might have been culled in the process.

There are few hints in the literature to suggest that armies liked to manoeuvre warily around each other for protracted periods, as was sometimes the case in both ancient warfare and that of the eighteenth and nineteenth centuries. Under Viking conditions such a prolonged concentration of troops in a single spot would surely have amounted to a recipe for starvation and misery, with both sides rapidly depleting whatever foraging-grounds were available. Instead, they seem to have preferred to close quickly with the enemy for a decisive test of strength, or, if one side felt it was markedly inferior, it would try to retire quickly from the area and await a happier opportunity in another season. Thus King Edward was brought to battle in his retreat from Cambridgeshire in 905, according to the *ASC*, only because his Kentish contingent ignored no less than seven messengers sent to pull them away from the path of a rapid Viking pursuit. Conversely the expected battle near Wilton in Wiltshire, 1003, failed to materialise purely because the English leader feigned illness once he had lined up his levies close enough to the Vikings to see them. This was perceived with disgust by his men as craven faint-heartedness, and they quickly dispersed.

The main exception to the apparent general rule that confrontations would tend to be relatively short-lived was the case of sieges, in which a large army remained concentrated around a much smaller fortified garrison for a long period of time. In such cases, however, the defenders would have had no opportunity to disrupt the besiegers' foraging, which could be pursued at leisure over a very wide area. The siege could therefore continue to be pressed to a successful conclusion unless some other factor forced the attackers to abandon it. It was either poor Wessex–Mercian political co-operation, or too short a term of levy-obligation among their forces, which seems to have caused the raising of the English siege of Nottingham in 867. Relief armies from outside the besieged area were rarely organised in time to break the strangle-hold, and even then the case of Paris in 886 seems to show that the besieger could still insist on a heavy geld before he would consent to raise his blockade.

Sieges have doubtless always contained a significant element of formality and stylised negotiation; but the literature, such as it is, frequently seems to suggest that set-piece battles were also seen as formal duels, fought at an agreed place and time, and even fenced around with hazel boughs like a boxing ring. Thus in *Egil's Saga* (p.119) the battle of Brunanburh, 937, is made an official fixture – and hazel-fenced – a week in advance, as a means of limiting the looting and depredations of the rival armies in the meantime; because they know they will have a formal test of strength on a set occasion, they will not expend their energies in gratuitous or premature violence elsewhere. Something similar is reported of Earl Hakon's victory at Sognefjord in 978 (*The Olaf Sagas*, p.18). At Clontarf in 1014 (*Njal*, p.320 *ff*) there was allegedly considerable discussion as to whether Palm Sunday or Good Friday was the most propitious day on which to fight. At Maldon in 991 (see Scragg, *passim*) the Essex side was defeated mainly because it had supposedly chivalrously allowed the Vikings to advance from a narrow frontage on the causeway to a larger and allegedly more fair battleground on the mainland.

There are many other examples of such formality and chivalry which might be cited from the literature, although ultimately few such stories really sound convincing. One exception, perhaps, was Sigurd of Orkney's set-piece 'duel' with forty men per side (*Orkneyinga Saga*, p.27): but a notable feature of that story was that Sigurd won the match only by cheating. Set-piece battles were surely not usually arranged with anything like a high level of formality or courtesy, but simply took place wherever and whenever the two sides happened to meet. However, one can certainly imagine situations in which two armies, having lined up facing one another, then found that neither side felt sufficiently confident to launch an assault. This type of 'non-battle' standoff might even last for several days on end: but it surely never amounted to quite the same thing as the 'formal duel' implied by the sagas.

The Vikings, of course, were above all amphibious warriors, so we should perhaps consider their operations mainly in the context of naval warfare. For this we must turn to Julian Corbett's classic 1911 work *Some Principles of Maritime Strategy*. In this book a key distinction is made between winning command of the sea and exercising that command once it has been won. In nineteenth century terms 'winning command' usually meant destroying the enemy's main battle fleet by the use of one's own, usually in a major clash of

Table P

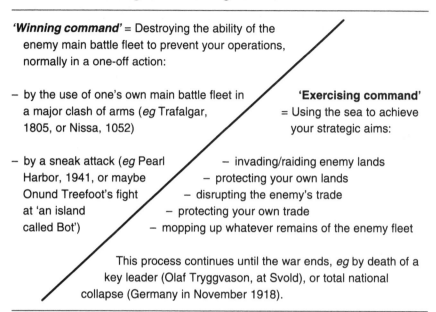

'Winning' and 'exercising' command of the sea

'Winning command' = Destroying the ability of the enemy main battle fleet to prevent your operations, normally in a one-off action:

– by the use of one's own main battle fleet in a major clash of arms (*eg* Trafalgar, 1805, or Nissa, 1052)

'Exercising command' = Using the sea to achieve your strategic aims:

– by a sneak attack (*eg* Pearl Harbor, 1941, or maybe Onund Treefoot's fight at 'an island called Bot')

– invading/raiding enemy lands
– protecting your own lands
– disrupting the enemy's trade
– protecting your own trade
– mopping up whatever remains of the enemy fleet

This process continues until the war ends, *eg* by death of a key leader (Olaf Tryggvason, at Svold), or total national collapse (Germany in November 1918).

arms such as Trafalgar. 'Exercising command', by contrast, meant doing all the useful things that superiority at sea could allow you to do, both defensively (*eg* protecting your homeland and colonies from invasion, or pursuing your own trade) and offensively (*eg* invading enemy lands, destroying whatever is left of his navy and capturing his trading vessels). Note that even if the enemy offers no resistance at all following his defeat in a decisive fleet action, the victor's task of exercising command will still require a very high level of maritime activity.

However, according to Corbett it was very rare indeed for any fleet to win complete command of the sea. Even after Trafalgar there were ten further years of sometimes quite dramatic naval action between Britain and the allies of Napoleon. Hence we should also consider a third state – 'disputing command' – which is the role of the side which has lost command of the sea but which refuses to submit and make peace. He can often continue to make life very difficult for the victor in all sorts of ways. He can maintain a 'fleet in being' in a protected harbour, thereby requiring his opponent to blockade it, or at least to budget for a superior counter-force held ready in home harbours. He can send off privateers in a 'guerrilla' role to harry the victor's trade and therefore force additional protection to be devoted to it. He can increase his own coastal defences on land, thereby increasing the task of any invader. Losing command of the sea, in other words, is not at all the same thing as losing the war. Indeed, Corbett assumed (contrary to the 'big battle' orthodoxy of his day) that an inferior navy would do best if it avoided a decisive battle right from the start, and accepted a 'disputing' rôle rather than trying to go through the motions of entering a main fleet contest that it was very likely to lose. The French fleet would surely have caused more problems to the British during the years 1806–15 if it had still been able to deploy all the ships it had lost at Trafalgar.

If we transfer this analytical framework from the nineteenth century to the Viking Age, we can still see many of the same patterns. Let us look at them in turn:

Winning Command of The Sea

There were in fact quite a number of Viking campaigns that quickly came to a decisive naval battle, particularly within Scandinavia itself. Corbett's perception must therefore be seen as somewhat less appropriate to Viking times than to the nineteenth century, insofar as the killing of a king in a decisive naval battle – like Eric of Hordaland at Hafrsfjord in c.880, or Olaf Tryggvason at Svold in 1000 – amounted to a total political victory for his killers, after which there could be no follow-on phase of resistance. At Trafalgar, by contrast, the killing of Lord Nelson was actually irrelevant both to the outcome of the battle and to the continuation of either the British monarchy or the British government. Nevertheless many of the supposedly decisive Viking naval battles still failed to kill the king or end the war, and allowed a subsequent reversion to revenge assassination attempts, low level harrassment or raiding modes of action. To that extent Corbett's model was indeed applicable even a millenium before he described it.

Exercising Command

In Viking times it was rarely possible to blockade an enemy's port, and only a few particularly narrow waterways could be controlled by a navy which wanted to prevent enemy movement by sea. The Sound of Denmark was an obvious example (eg in The Olaf Sagas, pp.311–14), although there were others in the Hebrides and along the Norwegian coast (eg Jederen, in The Olaf Sagas, p.277). The mouth of any river or fjord did admittedly make a natural choke-point for the control of an enemy's movements inland from the sea, while some of the more sophisticated anti-Viking measures on the Seine and on the Thames involved the building of solid 'bridges' (in reality barriers) to close the river to shipping – thereby denying the Viking armies access to the interior of the country. Closure of the Russian inland waterways could also have particularly dramatic effects on Swedish trade and prosperity, ultimately leading to the complete cessation of imports from the Middle East. Apart from cases like this, however, it was only the shipping already berthed in one's own home ports that one could be sure of preventing from moving. For example, the Norwegians were able to impose an embargo on salt and herrings upon Gotland (*The Olaf Sagas*, p.165), just as most of the trouble encountered by the Icelanders in Norway derived from restrictions placed upon their mercantile movements once they had landed in Norwegian ports. At times this almost amounted to a distant blockade of the whole of Iceland, since Norwegian ports were by far the most convenient ones for Icelandic traders to use (particularly with the trade winds blowing exclusively from the West except in Northern Norway). Their closure therefore represented a very significant act of economic warfare.

Apart from these special cases, however, it was usually very difficult for Viking fleets to deny use of the rivers or seas to their enemies' boats, short of destroying them at their home moorings – which has been a notoriously risky type of operation in almost every era of history that one can name. For the most part, therefore, anyone who wanted to sail a boat could normally do so, regardless of whether he had won or lost command of the sea, subject only to the natural hazards of weather and current. Without a close blockade and without such modern implements as mines, aircraft or radar, there was but little chance of restricting or monitoring an enemy's maritime movements. For example, the *ASC* for 992 reports an attempted interception in a sea battle which failed, except for one boat that was captured and its crew slaughtered. Thus boats carrying trade goods or invasion armies from one coast to another could not normally be intercepted with any certainty, even by a navy that had won a crushing Trafalgar-like main fleet action. In this context the abject defensive failure of Aethelred the Unready's magnificent navy is particularly worthy of study. He had all the necessary boats and crews, but he could not stop the invading Danes from using the sea in absolutely any way they wished.

In these circumstances exercising command of the sea often meant simply that a superior fleet would be able to plunder an enemy's coast on a bigger scale, more often, and more systematically than the enemy would be able to do in return. This would be a symbolic and demonstrative (or punitive) act as much as it was an economic (or predatory) one. The superior fleet would also presumably be better able to land larger numbers of men to invade the enemy's home territory, even if its own home territory could not be totally guaranteed against a counter-invasion. Exercising command of the sea, in other words, could often degenerate into a prolonged and unsatisfactory form of guerrilla warfare.

DISPUTING COMMAND

Not even in the works of Corbett was 'disputing command' ever seen as anything very different from guerrilla warfare or *guerre de corse*, since the whole aim of a defeated fleet must be to retain some form of vestigial existence and nuisance value for as long as possible. Just as a successful fleet in the Viking period was forced to use guerrilla tactics in order to exercise command, so the same must also have been true of its opponents who were disputing command. Since the sea-ways could not normally be blocked or blockaded, there was usually freedom to operate upon them in any way that seemed to be useful at the time. The nature of warfare could therefore easily turn into a painfully prolonged contest between two guerrilla navies (or amphibious forces) – one larger and one smaller – neither of which could decisively seize upon its opponent unless there was either a happy accident or a peace treaty.

Numbers Likely to be Engaged

As with most early medieval sources, it is not possible to establish the exact numbers of boats and men on any given occasion except when there are so few that they can be counted and named almost individually. We can know, for example, that just three people out of maybe 110 engaged were killed in the so-called 'battle' of Bitra in *Eyrbyggja Saga* (pp.183–5); but for the vastly bigger Great Army in England we have very few clues about numbers engaged.

Attempts have been made to count the boats mentioned in the *Anglo Saxon Chronicle*, but for large numbers such as sixty, 100 or 200 there is always a suspicion that the true number has been rounded up arbitrarily to make a more impressive total than the facts might actually warrant. This practice is certainly notorious in later medieval texts – for example the 30,000 men claimed for each army at Towton in 1461 is probably a tenfold exaggeration of the true numbers engaged – so similar exaggerations in the Viking period should be expected. There is also a suggestion that 'magic numbers' may be used systematically in the manuscripts, whereby the object is not to report the true number of boats at all, but to make a poetically and mathematically pleasing progression of numbers through the text, entirely irrespective of the facts. After all, what could a clerkly scribe, sitting in a distant monastery and fiddling with his pens and pigments several decades after the events he is reporting, possibly hope to know of such mundane military details as the number of boats in a fleet? How many of us today can remember just how many ships were in the Suez Task Force of 1956, the Falklands Task Force of 1982, or even how many ships are now regularly employed as cross-channel passenger ferries?

Having said all this, however, it does seem that there is a certain consistency and credibility about the general numbers quoted in such sources as the Icelandic sagas and the *ASC*. Figures of 200 boats are not at all impossible for the period, especially since we often read of a boat being built within a relatively few weeks, and sometimes continuing in use for many years. In the *ASC* entry for 896 it is even specified that the Vikings used 'warships they had built many years before', which are contrasted with the new and much bigger boats rapidly produced by Alfred to meet them. We can therefore follow N.P. Brooks when he argues against P.H. Sawyer's more sceptical approach to the *ASC*'s boat numbers. Even though we need not accept all entries as reasonable – for example, the entry for 836 (giving a victory to thirty-five Danish boats at Carhampton) is copied almost verbatim for 843 – we can still accept that the sagas and the *ASC* portray general orders of magnitude that are probably about right. A quoted round number like 100 need not be understood literally as 'precisely 100', and may be no more exact than perhaps '90 or 110' – or even '80 or 120'– but we can still agree that there were probably about 100 boats present.

Where we should not disagree with Sawyer, however, is where he points out that the Laws of Ine (written about 700) said that a body of more than thirty-six men was considered to constitute an army (or *here*), hence implying that an event could be classed as a 'battle' even if it involved a paltry handful of individuals. Hence we should accept the reality and importance of 'saga war-

Table Q

Some examples of boat numbers
deployed by the Vikings in their operations

(Sources – mainly Anglo-Saxon, Irish, Frankish and Russian chronicles as reported by Sawyer, Brooks etc)

Year	Place	No of boats	Year	Place	No of boats
789:	Portland	3	810:	Frisia	'200'
820:	Flanders/Normandy	13	836:	Ireland	60
836:	England	25 or 35	837:	Ireland	25 or 35
840:	Hamwih (and Portland?)	33 or 34	843:	Nantes	67
843:	England	35	844:	Corunna, Seville	70+80
845:	Paris	120	846:	Elbe	600
849:	Ireland	140	c.850(?):	Sweden	11+21
851:	Ireland	140	851:	England	350
852:	Frisia	252	859–62:	Spain/N. Africa etc	62
860:	Constantinople	200	860:	Seine	200+60
865:	Seine	50	870:	Ireland	200
875:	England	7	876:	Seine	100
877:	Swanage	120	878:	Devon	23
882:	Meuse to Scandinavia(?)	200	885:	Seine	700
885:	England	16+	892:	England (Great Army)	200, 250, or 350
893–4:	Devon	80 later 100	896:	Devon	6
907:	Constantinople	'2000'	912:	Caspian Sea	500
980:	Hamwih	7	982:	Portland	3
991:	England	93	1043:	Constantinople	400

fare', 'royal household action' or 'small scale Viking raiding' as much as we accept the reality of big royal armies and campaigns that were continued for many years at a stretch. Despite the fact that for most of the time it is more concerned with really big fleets and armies, the *ASC* itself sometimes talks of single boat actions, or battles between less than a dozen boats per side, and these must surely have had some sort of impact upon the general military picture. Apparently all four of the different types and scales of warfare could co-exist during most phases of 'the Viking era' ... although occasionally there might even have been intermissions of relative peace over quite wide areas.

The implication of all this is that the Vikings apparently had no general standard order of magnitude for an 'army' such as there may well have been, for example, within most of the nations fighting in Europe during the two world wars (where the 'army' was generally recognised as the command level which came between an 'army corps' and an 'army group'). We should not therefore seek to look for an average number of boats across all forces that the Vikings may have described as 'armies'. The best we can do is to look for a rough average within each of the four specific types of warfare that we have identified. The answer seems to be that in 'saga warfare' there may not have been more than one, two or three boats involved on either side, and in 'royal household action' or 'going-a-viking' the number may never have been many more than ten. It is only in the rather specialised area of 'royal army campaigning' that we find boat numbers rocketing to far higher figures.

In 'saga warfare' the upper limit to numbers was set by the resources upon which any given farmer could call. In many cases it might be less than a dozen men, although posses of sixty or eighty are not uncommon. 1,080 people are said to have attended Hoskuld's memorial feast in *Laxdœla Saga* (p.107), although that figure included women and children. In any case a warrior is doubtless easier persuaded to attend a feast than to go out on a hazardous night ambush.

In 'royal household action' the upper limit to numbers seems to have depended on the size of household that was conventionally acceptable to the king's allies upon whom he would billet himself. He needed enough people to make a lavish show and overawe his host, as well as ensuring his own personal security; but not so many that he would eat the host completely out of house and home. The aim was to win love and loyalty as well as food and taxes; so arriving with too large a household would be considered oppressive and poor kingship. Ninety may have been seen as a reasonable number (see Foote & Wilson pp.103–4), whereas hints in *Heimskringla* seem to suggest that the bounds of good taste were exceeded if the household became as big as 300 mouths – although far from all of these would be warriors, of course.

As for 'going-a-viking', there may have been no upper limit to numbers. A large pirate band might have been indistinguishable from a small royal army,

although doubtless there were some significant psychological thresholds that
had to be crossed along the way. The crew of a single boat, for example, made a
convenient and logical unit of command, especially if it was all drawn from the
farm and family of a single leader. Beyond that, there must have been some sort
of idea of a 'squadron' of boats that could still be commanded personally by a
powerful lord, and could sail relatively easily in company with each other,
within earshot or visual range of simple hand or flag signals. Perhaps ten or a
dozen boats would be the maximum that could fall within this definition. Any
force larger than that would surely have to be sub-divided into several
squadrons, and use a more far-ranging system of command and control, perhaps even with pinnaces to communicate between one squadron and another. If
it was to have any coherence at all – or any hope of arriving at a given destination as a unified force – such a fleet would need to be commanded by a 'sea
king' who was able and willing to trust an inner circle of subordinates and to
delegate important powers to them.

The larger the pirate fleet, the more cumbersome it would be and the longer
it might take for its cruises. That in turn must surely have implied a greater
need for 'support staff' in the shape of women, slaves and livestock, thereby
cutting back on the number of warriors that could be carried in each boat. It
would also doubtless have made a diverse mixture of boat types far more likely.
Whereas a small squadron might consist of warriors only, all sailing in warships, a large fleet would include many merchant boats and general purpose
karfi, together with smaller ferries and fishing boats as well (see eg the
description of Harald Hard-ruler's fleet of 240 boats in 1066, Sagas of the Norse
Kings, p.222). But then again, a small and ragged force of pirates may itself
have been pretty polyglot, and unable to afford the luxury of specialist warships.

As we have seen, it is likely that we can have reasonable confidence in the
general levels of boat numbers as reported in the sagas and the ASC; but a
possibly even more important question still remains. Which is: just how many
men should we assume were serving on each boat, and so by how many should
we multiply total boat numbers in order to find the total number of warriors
present in the army?

Here, once again, we find ourselves in Sawyer territory. He has argued
against the higher claims for boat crew size, in favour of lower orders of
magnitude. He dismisses repeated statements in the sources that 100, 150 or
200 men – and all their horses, cows, pigs, wives, girlfriends, children and slaves
– could normally be packed into a Viking boat. Instead, he sticks to the simple
idea that a boat of thirty oars would normally be operated by thirty-five men, or
maybe by many less in the case of a long distance cargo boat, or indeed any boat
that carried livestock or spare mouths. Alfred's special boats built in 896 were
stated in the ASC to have had sixty oars and to be twice as big as their Viking

opponents, thereby giving thirty oars each for the latter; and this does not appear to be too far off the mark from what we know of the Scandinavian boat finds of 'average' warships.

One may be pretty confident that the general size of these boats is well known, as discussed in the last chapter, although a question mark still remains over the size of crew that would actually have sailed in them, and over what distance. Surely the size of a crew would always have decreased quite dramatically in proportion as the distance and duration of the voyage increased. Where 100 warriors might be acceptable when hopping from one Danish island to another, even thirty may have been too many for a stab across the Bay of Biscay to Seville or Rome. The repeated inshore naval battles in Norwegian waters, as reported for example throughout *Heimskringla*, may well offer examples of promiscuous over-loading; but for long voyages in choppy seas we must surely think in terms of very much smaller crews.

If we follow the line of argument which offers '100 warriors on a big warship for inshore coastal operations; but twenty persons overall on a smaller oceanic boat', we may perhaps find our way towards a reasonable compromise between the persuasive 'small crew' reasoning of Professor Sawyer and the more expansive arguments made by others for much bigger crew sizes. Much of Viking warfare may well have been conducted as short-distance coastal raiding with big crews; but the alternative of long-distance oceanic trips with small crews must surely also remain a key element in their overall achievement.

With all the above in mind, we seem to arrive at a final conclusion which looks somewhat as follows:

Table R

Four types of Viking army

Purpose	Boats*	Mouths
'Saga warfare'	1–3 (?) Inshore	1–30 (up to 120?)
Royal household	1–5 (?) Inshore	60–150 (300 is considered impolite)
'Going a-viking'	1–10 All warships	20–500 (mostly men)
Royal armies	10–200 Assorted types	200–8000 (includes women, children and animals)

* Multiplier of 20–50 men per boat. Average = 30?

CHAPTER 5

The Composition of Armies

'Oh hell, it's the king wanting his taxes again'
– The perennial sigh of the early medieval farmer, as imagined by the late
Trevor Aston in conversation with the author.

'They weren't exactly the world's brightest people'
– Robert Griffith on Viking warriors, in conversation with the author.

The Classification of Troop Types

LEADERS

Having decided how many warriors there may have been in each army or on
each boat for each different type of warfare, we next have to decide just what
types of warrior may have been present. The single most important, richest and
probably also best equipped individual would obviously be the leader or
commanding officer, who might be:
– a king (whether national, local or 'sea-') in charge of a royal army
– an earl or *jarl* (in Norway he would probably also be the chief man of one of
   the sixteen provinces known as *fylke*), or a high *lenderman* (or 'Lord
   Lieutenant' of a *herred*) in charge of a major squadron
– or an individual clan chieftain, minor nobleman (*hersar* in Norway, of whom
   there were originally four per *fylke*; roughly comparable to an English
   'thane'), or just a plain pirate boss in charge of a single boat or small
   squadron. According to some codes of law the 'captain' of each boat would
   be an officially-appointed 'steersman', who might hold the office on a hereditary or even elective basis. Between one and four of them would be
   appointed per *herred*, depending on how many boats were to be raised from
   that particular territorial sector (see Foote & Wilson, p.124). Such a
   steersman might enjoy absolute control over operations if his ship happened
   to be sailing independently, but would be subordinate (and maybe even
   rather lowly) if a more senior leader was embarked with him, or even
   commanded him from afar within a squadron sailing together.

In some cases command at any given level might be divided equally between
two or more leaders, for example between two brothers with equivalent claims
to kingship, or between a confederation of several equally-important petty

127

kings or earls. The democratic (or anarchic) origins of Viking society doubtless meant that a formless and chaotic chain of command was rather more likely than it is normally supposed to be today, although it must be admitted that the military history of the twentieth century is itself littered with only too many examples of 'mismanagement by committee'.

Regardless of whether he was the sole leader or merely one among several, the prestige and leadership powers of a Viking commander would almost always depend to a considerable extent upon his personal physical behaviour – especially in battle, and particularly in its close-quarter climax. St Olaf, for example, was nicknamed 'The Thick' not because he was mentally dim, but because he was very solidly built and excelled at all sports as well as in combat. In an age when intellectual pursuits were as poorly regarded as they still are today (but when the rule of law was less well established), leadership tended to be violent, robust, deceitful and rude. There were, nevertheless, some exceptions. For example, noble leaders who had shown themselves to be clever diplomats, strategists, navigators and maybe poets or even chess players – despite being less adept at cleaving skulls than their heartier colleagues – would nevertheless still be able to earn a due measure of respect from their followers. Everyone also accepted that brutally despotic kings might eventually grow old and infirm without necessarily losing their personal charisma (although physical degeneration could also be the direct cause of regicide, which had been a venerable Scandinavian tradition in the pre-Viking age).

Active young warriors of high repute might certainly hope to mature through time into influential leaders, even though they might have suffered some tactically-disqualifying 'sports injuries', such as the loss of an eye or a leg, along the way (the comparable case of Lord Nelson once again springs to mind). In an extreme case even a helpless invalid might be allowed to command a Viking army, at least if we are to take literally the nickname of 'Ivar the Boneless' (or perhaps 'Spineless', in a physiological rather than a moral sense), who is thought to have been one of the sons of Ragnar Lothbrok who helped to invade England in 865. Perhaps he began life as a highly physical Viking and contracted some debilitating disease of the bones only later, after he had asserted sufficient authority over his army to remain at its head. Alternatively, his name might never have been intended as anything more than friendly irony, equivalent to the cognomen of short people who are called 'Lofty', or of tall people who are called 'Titch'.

Apart from personal physical or mental prowess, however, one of the most telling qualifications for Viking leadership was always noble breeding, even though that term might well cover a multitude of sins. It seems that in the Scandinavian 900s commoners were falsely able to posture as persons of noble lineage (and indeed as annointed bishops) no less easily than they routinely still do in supposedly sophisticated modern-day Western Europe. Even if their claim had to be justified by actual credentials, moreover, the title of an illegitimate younger son by a slave-born concubine may not necessarily have been considered inferior to that of a first son by a dazzlingly public royal marriage (and doubly so before the conversion to Christianity). A very great deal would always depend on the personal character and fighting prowess of the candidate in question, regardless of his family tree. It was a long-standing tradition in many Viking societies that leaders had to prove themselves, and be acclaimed by an assembly ('Thing') of their subjects, before their royal or noble status could be properly confirmed.

A leader would be expected to assert his status partly by indulging in conspicuous consumption. He would give feasts and valuable gifts freely to his followers, and would himself play with the very best dogs, horses and hawks. He would wear the richest available clothes, jewellery and armour. In many cases a boat's captain might be the only warrior in his crew who possessed a mail shirt, or one of the few who had a helmet. In the case of higher noblemen who were rich enough to surround themselves with a select band of fully armoured warriors, they would still make sure that their own helmet and mail were ostentatiously more distinctive, better gilded or otherwise ornamented, than those of their followers. At the Battle of Tarbat Ness, Earl Thorfin is noted for wearing a golden helmet and marching in front of his army (*Orkneyinga Saga*, p.54), while at Stickelstad the exceptionally tall and fair Arnliot Gelline is described as being 'well armed; [he] had a fine helmet, and ring armour; a red shield; a superb sword in his belt; and in his hand a gold-mounted spear, the shaft of it so thick that it was a handful to grasp.' (*The Olaf Sagas*, p.365). The spear, sword or axe which such prestigious warriors carried might be given a special name carrying mystical, magical or legendary connotations of its own, and such men would certainly try to sail in the best boat (also named and famous) of the fleet. If kings and noblemen owed their status as much to the sacred aura of their position as to their particular personal qualities, then their dress, ornament and armament could usually play an important part in the process.

ROYAL OFFICERS

Grouped around the leader would be a number of high ranking functionaries (see Foote & Wilson, p.103). Firstly there would be his private 'staff', which could include a marshal (*ie* a 'chief of staff' or 'regimental sergeant major', depending on the leader's social level) who might or might not be the same person(s) as administered his immediate household and/or supervised the care of his personal horses, hawks and hounds. In later medieval terminology such an officer might be called a steward, constable, or master of horse, etc, and doubtless the saga sources have sometimes been corrupted by the chivalric images that those names tend to conjour up. It seems highly unlikely that the

Table S

The chain of command in a 'royal army'

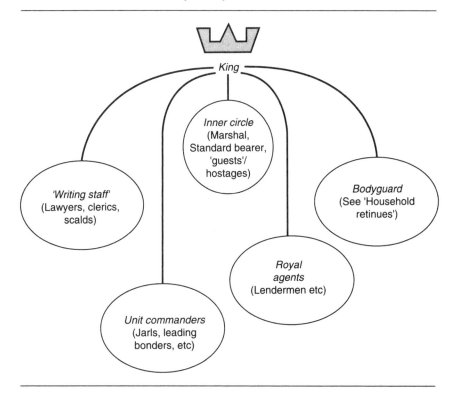

Vikings ever had formal court structures anything like as complex and exquisite as those of Chaucer's time; but they must nevertheless still have had some sort of primitive equivalent, however informal and unorganised it may seem from a modern perspective. No leader of more than a few handfuls of subordinates in any era can possibly operate effectively without some sort of foreman, bosun or (in modern terms) personal assistant to relieve him of the more trivial details of command, and the Vikings must surely have had their own equivalents.

A Viking leader would surely also have retained some equivalent of a trusty standard-bearer or shield-bearer to stand beside him in battle, whose loyalty and courage were unquestioned, even though he may not have been either a natural leader of men or any sort of intellectual. Loyalty has always been the primary military virtue in every age, rated higher than either cleverness or strength; and it was surely never any different for the Vikings. They would, nevertheless, also still have required an 'intellectual tail' or 'writing staff' (even before writing itself was a necessary attribute for the job), composed of such

Table T

Troop Types

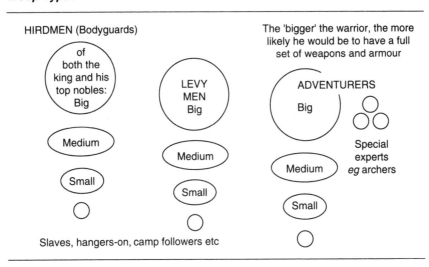

HIRDMEN (Bodyguards)

of both the king and his top nobles: Big

Medium

Small

○

Slaves, hangers-on, camp followers etc

LEVY MEN Big

Medium

Small

○

The 'bigger' the warrior, the more likely he would be to have a full set of weapons and armour

ADVENTURERS

Big

○○ ○○

Special experts *eg* archers

Medium

Small

○

people as lawyers, clerics and scalds. These officers would act not only as private advisers on matters of law and tradition within the leader's own household, but also as his mouthpieces and public relations agents outside. They might often also be used as diplomats representing his case to other rulers, or what in later medieval parlance might be called heralds. One other significant group that was surely present in most royal courts consisted of foreigners who were 'guests', and more or less hostages. They would be treated rather differently from the native courtiers, whether for good or ill depending on the case; although they would still be considered as a valuable and intrinsic part of the royal household (see Foote & Wilson, p.104).

Secondly, when he was touring his lands a king would pay especial attention to his agents, great and small, who acted as his representatives, stewards, sheriffs and/or tax collectors in each and every area. They came under many names, such as *bryti*, *armadr*, *hersir*, and especially *lendermen* ('land-men', or 'Lords Lieutenant', or alternatively 'men worthy of honour'). As time went by and kingship became increasingly centralised, there was a gradual decline in the independence of such officers throughout Scandinavia, and a corresponding rise in the king's power over them, none of which is to suggest that their own local social importance declined in any way. On the contrary: the more powerful the king became, the more respect would have to be paid to his immediate agents. When it came to overseas expeditions, however, there was no automatic obligation on these men to attend in person, and often they may have preferred to stay at home administering their estates – and the king's. But equally they may just as easily have believed that they could win additional favours by fighting at the king's side at his moments of greatest need. Promotion on the battlefield was doubtless a more normal expectation in Viking times than it has tended to be in most subsequent eras of history. Much would depend on the particular personal and politico-strategic relationships obtaining on each particular occasion.

The success or failure of any given royal call to arms would certainly depend to a very great extent upon the personal political willingness of the king's agents to show energy in his cause, and this in turn would depend on the popularity of the king at that particular moment. *Heimskringla*, for example, contains several cases where a popular king is able to raise all the forces he needs without any trouble, but an unpopular one encounters many delays and resistance to his mobilisations (*eg The Olaf Sagas*, pp.322–3). We should not therefore imagine that these agents were mere faceless bureaucrats in any modern sense. Throughout the Viking period it seems that mobilisation was far more a personal undertaking between individuals than an anonymous legal mechanism (see the article by Niels Lund).

ROYAL BODYGUARDS

Every Viking crofter or farmer retained a personal household retinue in the shape of his gang of farm labourers, who lived in his farmhouse and kept his farm running smoothly. In 'saga warfare' these men might occasionally be converted into an ambush team, an assassination squad or a boat's crew of raiders, without anyone noticing any particular clash of loyalties or even any 'rôle tensions'. They might also be reinforced by tenants and family members from other farms, and there were many types of artificial family membership, such as fostering or blood brotherhood, which might also have served to extend the natural limits of the clan.

At more elevated social levels, however, a leader's household retinue would be less closely associated with menial labour on any particular farm, and not necessarily part of his own particular clan. They might have been rather more noble in their origins, more specialised in their military skills, better armed, and might have followed their lord regularly as he toured around many different farms. They would have stuck close to him in battle and would have observed a code of personal loyalty in tactical affairs, as well as in the more general conditions of their employment. In some cases they might even have been worthy of the name 'professional soldiers' or 'mercenaries', although their social duties would normally have extended rather further afield than those that we associate with such men today.

It is within this group that we might perhaps look for the most military culture of the Viking world, and the purest ideal of how a warrior may have

Table U

Structure of a 'posse' for 'saga warfare' *(schematic)*

The FARMER (= the principal, in a feud)

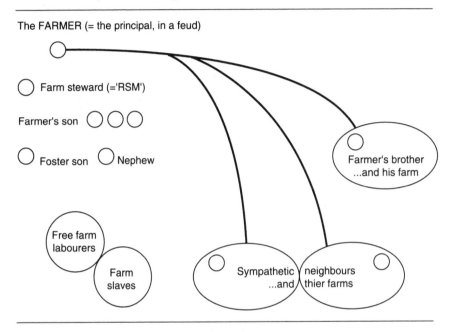

regarded himself. In a nutshell, he was trying to be strong, tough, well armed and mean. In physical terms this meant that he was muscular and adept at using bow, javelin, thrusting spear, sword, axe and (perhaps especially) shield. He could also pull out a sail shroud in a gale or pull at an oar effectively in calm water. He was not prone to sea-sickness or wasting away from nostalgia, and he was a keen sportsman. In mental terms he was no fading violet, but a strongly positive man who wanted to dominate his fellows, or at least enjoy their robust company, and make sure they all did their duty to their lord. Maybe he did not need to be especially bright or intellectual, and maybe he had a weakness for gossip and faction-forming such as is common among the members of any group of under-employed courtiers. He doubtless had a strong sense of his own status and dignity; but he did at least know his place in society and the importance of following accepted codes of conduct. (For the ideal of fighting to the death for one's lord, see Scragg, ed, *The Battle of Maldon*, pp.125, 201, 205.)

At the highest levels of kingship the household retinue could become something of a closed military guild, called a *Hird* or *Hired*. Its members might be called *Hirdmen* or *Housecarls* (see Foote & Wilson pp.100 *ff*), and they might have been subject to some strict household rules, or *hird* law, on the general basis that 'utter loyalty was the supreme virtue of the *hirdman*' (*ibid*, p.105) – which is, of course, very much the same sort of ideal as we see in such household troops as the Life Guards today. The Vederlov rules, for example, cited drinking penalties ('sconces') for bad behaviour in hall, as well as arrangements for booty-sharing and how men should be divided into companies, etc. In the *Saga of Hord* (p.54) the eighty outlawed Holm Dwellers adopt a monastic code of conduct, while the *Jomsviking Saga* (written c.1200) lays down a still more comprehensive code for the behaviour of a dedicated professional military force, although most of its supposed requirements are in all probability entirely fictitious.

In the Black Sea theatre of operations we hear from the Arab diplomat Ibn Fadlan that in 922 the 'King of the Rus has 400 loyal men, each with two slave girls' (Sawyer, *Kings and Vikings*, p.119), which is very probably a reference to Norse mercenaries and their 'perks'. There are certainly plenty of other references in the literature to Slavonic princes using *Druzhiny* (*ie* Norse 'friendly battalions'); but the really spectacular example of this type of mercenary must inevitably be the Varangian Guards that were employed by the Byzantine Emperor from at least the middle of the 900s until the 1100s and beyond. Not only did they become trusted bodyguards of the Emperor himself (although they probably had to pay for appointment to that privilege, maybe with as much as three years' wages in advance? – see Blöndal, p.26), but they were also widely used as shock troops well away from the royal court. Harald Hard-ruler seems to have served much of his military apprenticeship very successfully in this capacity, all around the Eastern Mediterranean, and came to serve at court in Constantinople only at the end of his Varangian career. When he did so, he scarcely behaved as an ideal bodyguard should, but it is probably true that the men he joined were actually a lot more like loyal retainers than he was.

Yet another example of a royal bodyguard may come with St Olaf (see his saga, p.161), who is supposed to have retained a dirty tricks department manned by 'pursuivants' (a highly anachronistic and suspect term) who were expected to do odd jobs such as assassinations or repossessions. More normally, however, such delicate tasks would surely have been entrusted to whichever strong men from the general bodyguard happened to be most in favour at the time.

Probably the military standards of royal household retinues were as variable as the personal characters of the kings themselves. There was surely no absolute level of proficiency to which they all had to conform, so they cannot all be lumped together as one particular troop type. Nevertheless, it seems likely that if anyone in the Viking world can be considered a professional soldier, it must be the royal bodyguards.

BERSERKS

In the *Sagas of the Norse Kings* (p.11 *ff*), and in many of the Icelandic family sagas, we find that the most highly-praised (or most highly-feared) and most warlike of fighting men were called either *berserkir* (berserks, or 'bearshirts') or less commonly *ulfhednar* ('wolfskins'). Many strange rumours have subsequently grown up around these 'troop types', and the odd thing is that these rumours still seem to be given widespread credence today. It has been alleged, for example, that berserks were liable to slip into lycanthropic fits, in which they could not be hurt by enemy weapons but believed themselves actually to be bears or wolves. They would fall into epileptic battle rages, possibly by consuming drugs or magic mushrooms, which would lead them to chew at their shields and behave in a generally frenzied psychotic manner, entirely reckless of their own personal safety. Alternatively, they might somehow have been related to the werewolves of Transylvanian mythology.

The propensity to act in a berserk manner has sometimes been asserted to have been hereditary, so that whole gangs of berserk brothers, and their sons, could be assembled. In other contexts they are often cited as being 'organised' (if such an idea is appropriate to such wild men) in units of twelve. Obviously a group of such men, if only their maximum enragements could all somehow be turned on at exactly the same moment, would make an absolutely wonderful spearhead assault force or shock troop. Thus in *Heimskringla* we hear of them being formed into regular bodies of twelve men and deployed on the bow or forecastle of a fighting boat (*eg* at the battle of Hafrsfjord, c.880), as the force specially chosen to make the initial strike against the enemy and to overwhelm him by the first shock of contact.

A more sober analysis, however, would tend to make a serious downsizing and downgrading of the whole idea of berserks (see the article by Bennett). They were probably no more exotic or peculiar than the red-coated 'bearskin guards' who still stand sentry outside Buckingham Palace (and, indeed, outside the Danish royal palace) today; and the fact that they were highly mortal is certainly very well attested in the sagas. Almost every great Icelandic hero in pagan times seems to kill at least one of them, in the course of making his reputation. There is, therefore, surely nothing at all supernatural or strange about these stalwart soldiers, apart from the general prestige and reputation that naturally attaches to any hand-picked military elite or royal bodyguard. At least some of the men described as berserks seem to have won fame only through their status as the chosen soldiers of their monarch, and not by any particular psychological condition.

Other berserks, however, may simply have been violent outlaws, and thus acting outside the normal conventions of civilised (and hence predictable) behaviour. The sagas often use the word berserk as a straight synonym for a Viking, in the sense of a pirate. In this context it may be worth noting the experience of the 1960s Glasgow street gangs, where academic research discovered that the 'leader aff' of each 'team' was usually the most psychotically violent and emotionally disturbed member (see James Patrick, *A Glasgow Gang*

Observed, London 1972). He won his position because he naturally and instinctively tended to take irrational behaviour to its furthest extreme: he was the one most liable to lash out blindly at any perceived insult, or in other words he was the one whose definition of his 'personal space', which he could not tolerate being invaded, was the widest. Normal people might start fighting if someone grabbed their tie and breathed threateningly into their faces – but a 'leader aff' would start if someone two yards away simply forgot to say 'good morning'. Interestingly, an alternative term for such a person was a 'psychie bass' (*ie* 'psychotic gang boss'). There was little evidence in the 1960s that any drugs beyond alcohol helped to enrage the Glasgow gang leaders, and indeed in those days the very idea of drugs was far more often associated with calmer moods like peace and love: but a particularly violent psychotic condition was nevertheless recognised as a natural state in certain individuals.

Whereas a Glasgow gang leader might like to clothe himself in threatening symbols like death's heads or Mötorhead badges, the symbolic equivalent in Viking times could well have been bearskins or wolfskins. Much of the remainder of the berserk legend is probably entirely mythological and spurious. For example, one suspects that their shields were 'bitten' by enemy swords and axes rather than by the shields' owners, and that the image was merely mis-translated or misunderstood at some point. As for the rest of the 'wolf like' behaviour, one is reminded of the howling of the Mountain Men in the old American West – or indeed of the Rebel Yell in the American Civil War. Men shout some pretty odd things in battle (or even at football matches); but this should not be taken as firm evidence that they believe themselves to be bears or wolves.

THE FREE: (i) PIRATE BANDS

Below the highly specialised level of royal household troops or berserks we reach the strata of the warriors who must have made up the great majority of the Viking forces. These men may generally be classified as 'the free', although in some cases that term might imply that they were 'outlaws who had not yet been caught' rather than that they were 'born as free men who recognised a legal obligation of military service in return for protection from a lord'. As was true for the leaders themselves, the exact legitimation of each warrior might often have been left a trifle hazy and imprecise, in the interests of providing raw numbers as much as for general harmony within the group. The men who were most eager to 'go a-viking' might not always have been free farmers with a stake in society and family responsibilities at home, but farm labourers or household slaves who had a very doubtful or menial status (see general dis-cussion of slaves in Foote & Wilson, p.65 *ff*). Such men might be used either to swell numbers, still under the personal supervision of their masters, if their masters felt the urge to go raiding; or they might be released and sent as substitutes if their masters acknowledged they had some family or other obligation to a particular pirate leader, but preferred the personal safety of staying at home. Escaping slaves might find the campaigning life a way of breaking free from the homestead altogether, especially if the expedition in question was a heavily unofficial one mounted by landless and lawless pirates, and the service of such 'brave slaughtering fellows' might well be seized upon by a major army on its way to battle (*eg The Olaf Sagas*, p.353, for just such an incident before Stickelstad). Ironically this process could well turn out to be very reversible, in that a free man who went into battle but was captured might well end up being sold into household servitude. Nor might a fine crew of *drengs*, for whom there was no further military employment, always be easy to settle on good land. For them, too, warfare might lead to a diminution of status.

THE FREE: (ii) BONDERS

In theory, however, it was the free farmers or 'bonders' (variously referred to as *bondi*, *drengs*, *hauldr*, *thegns* or yeomen) who were supposed to provide the mass of the troops for the genuinely royal armies. These were the men who formed the backbone of political society – the 'Thingmen' who manned the local political assemblies/courts and dominated local affairs under such laws as the Frostathing Law or the Gulathing Law. They were also responsible for passing round the 'war arrow' when it came to calling a muster and taking a lead, in their own persons, in giving military service. If the mobilisation worked well, each bonder might well go to war with a private retinue of his own clansmen, kinsmen, tenants or farm labourers, making 'distinct flocks or parcels' of men (*The Olaf Sagas*, p.356) – or what we might today call a miniature 'unit' (equivalent to a squad, a section or even a platoon) based upon the personal relationship between him and them. The bonders in turn might find themselves loosely grouped together in larger units (platoons or companies?) under a leading notable or the local royal agent. In any mobile operation, of course, this organisational structure would be further complicated by considerations of how many men could be fitted into each boat, and who owned the boat.

The actual scale of service on any given occasion might vary widely, based on the personal relationship between the person calling the muster and the people he was asking to respond. A distinction would also normally be made between a 'full' levy, for an urgent defensive operation, and a much more optional and voluntary 'half' levy, for offensive operations outside the local area. Most areas would nevertheless have some basic notional number of levy men that it would be expected to find per farm or per district, but always subject to the personalities of the people involved. In West Norway, for example, one man might notionally be demanded from every three (or later seven) farms. The Swedish *hund* (later converted into the English 'hundred') was supposed to provide four boats, each with twenty-four oars. The Danish *herred*, linked to both the local

'Thing' and to the local temple, was supposed to provide a levy of forty men (see Foote & Wilson pp.79, 105–7, 281–2). In other places the system might well be different, and today we do not really have any accurate means of knowing either how many men were theoretically liable to service in each area, or just how many might realistically be likely to turn up when a mobilisation was actually called.

Niels Lund has persuasively argued that there is very little good evidence for really large scale and compulsory Scandinavian levy systems, on the same basis as Charlemagne's Frankish model of about 800, before at least the early 1100s. Even as late as Canute, and even in generally better-developed Denmark, the Vikings always seem to have run a relatively haphazard system which fell far short of a total mobilisation. Sven Forkbeard's army was doubtless somewhat better organised and trained than Guthrum's a century earlier; but it still fell far short of a truly efficient force, because the centralised organisation of the state still left much to be desired. We might add that the history of nineteenth and twentieth century mobilisations would seem to indicate that even if they had enjoyed full 'Carolingian efficiency', the number of Viking warriors eventually turning up on the line of battle would normally have fallen very far short of the notional total liable for service. The influx of volunteers, adventurers, free-booters and other types of substitute for the legally-liable classes, on the other hand, would often have been correspondingly large.

The rank and file of a Viking royal army might thus have been drawn from a very diverse mixture of social classes, with very varied levels of military experience. Some would be wealthy tourists, unaccustomed to arms, while others would be indigent adventurers or scavengers who were accustomed to skulking round the edge of a major force, without ever needlessly risking their lives in the very front line. Some might be expert bowmen or swordsmen: others might be highly reluctant farmers who had been pushed into battle against their will.

The service to be had from local levy forces was certainly highly variable, and there are plenty of hints in the literature that they were viewed with suspicion by more experienced warriors. For example, the *ASC* attributes many of Aethelred the Unready's failures to the poor leadership of his levies (*eg* 993, 1001), while in *The Olaf Sagas* the bonders in 1021 ran away when the first spears were thrown (p.238), and in the following year 'they soon fell short, and took to flight' (p.243). In 1023 the bonder army lined up to defy St Olaf, but saw the true faith in the nick of time before he assaulted them (p.255). Then in 1025 the Swedish levy became homesick and sailed home, leaving nothing but the *hirdmen* to do the fighting (pp.310–11); while in 1029 'it went with the bonder army as is often seen, that the men, though many in numbers, know not what to do when they have experienced a check, have lost their chief, and are without leaders' (p.332).

Table V

Some levy systems – *a few of the possibilities*

Type of levy	Healthy males aged 14–65 called up?	Average troop quality?
Large and compulsory system (*eg* Charlemagne's c.800)	50%	Small
Scandinavian levy of bonders for a defensive operation (= similar to a normal English Fyrd muster?)	20%	Medium
Scandinavian levy of bonders for an offensive expedition (= similar to a small English Fyrd muster?)	10%	Medium
Royal bodyguard/retinue/hird	1%	Big
Adventurers, free-booters and other substitutes for those liable to call-up	3%	Medium

By the same token the quality and quantity of weapons and equipment would vary widely, ranging from the abundant to the minimal. We may assume that shields, spears and bows would have been plentiful, being made largely of wood, which was a cheap and readily available commodity; but more specialised items such as swords, helmets and especially mail shirts were probably much less common. Each man would bring whatever he or his immediate sponsor could afford or could scrounge on an individual basis: there would be no standardisation of units based on one particular type of weapon. Indeed, most warriors might expect to start a battle in the capacity of missile-men, using bows or throwing spears, and then to change over to close-quarter weapons for hand to hand fighting. Only a few specialists who were noted as archers – for example, Olaf Tryggvason's 'sniper' Einar Tambaeskelve (*The Olaf Sagas*, pp.94–5), or Atli's, who was named Asolf (*Njal*, p.9) – might be reserved exclusively for that service. Conversely the least well equipped might have only a thrusting spear and neither a sword nor a missile weapon (although even then there was still always the possibility of throwing stones).

The logistic echelon of a Viking army might surely sometimes have been composed merely of the humbler social classes in the fighting line itself, insofar as slaves and 'batmen' who fed and attended the free warriors in the morning might be called upon to do battle for them in the afternoon. In larger expeditions, however, there might well be many servants, women and children who had no such flexibility of role – even though female warriors or 'Amazons' are sometimes mentioned in the sagas. There would also be several classes of more specialised logistic personnel such as shepherds or cattle drovers, responsible for looking after the 'rations on the hoof'; smiths, armourers, sail-makers or carpenters, to keep the equipment in trim; and muleteers, carters or storekeepers – or, indeed, an entire flotilla of unwarlike storeships and their crews – charged with supervising the baggage.

In modern amphibious operations, such as Suez or the Falklands, a great deal of importance has necessarily been attached to the 'tactical loading' of stores – or in other words careful thought about the order in which key items will be loaded into cargo boats and then taken out of them when needed in battle. There are essentially two key principles. The first is that what will be needed first in encounters with the enemy should be loaded last and kept close at hand. In Viking terms this will imply some relatively straightforward things like keeping weapons ready for use at short notice, and fighting decks unencumbered by animals or other obstructions. The second principle is that the logistics of the whole force should not be compromised by the loss of a single vessel. Thus in Viking terms an army that relied on regular payment of cash wages would not be wise to carry its entire war chest in the same keel, even though that might make it easier for its owner to guard. Nor should an army expecting to make rapid movements on horses centralise all its stores of harness.

There would also surely have been a numerous ragtag of free-enterprise speculators who would hope to buy and sell almost any commodity around the fringes of the host, from silver to slave girls; from wine to walrus hide; and from scaldic verses to ship's stores. Armies are almost always great centres of commerce, since they have an enormous demand for food, entertainment and many types of specialist hardware, and they combine this with some unusual and interesting sources of supply that are not normally open to honest merchants. Not all pillage would be destined for immediate consumption by the pillager; but in order to sell it on he would always need a helpful middleman close at hand. In most periods of history the idea of a 'rolling bazaar' accompanying an army has therefore been inseparable from the very idea of an army itself.

Indeed, we have already mentioned that in many cases an entire Viking campaign might be designed entirely to feed this commerce, so that instead of an army being 'warriors with a few merchants tagging along', it might have

Table W

The 'tactical loading' of stores

Principle No 1
What is needed for battle first must be loaded last

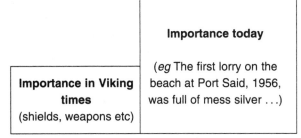

Importance today

(*eg* The first lorry on the beach at Port Said, 1956, was full of mess silver ...)

Importance in Viking times
(shields, weapons etc)

Principle No 2
Do not put all your eggs in one basket

Importance today

(*eg* The *Atlantic Conveyor*, Falklands 1982)

Importance in Viking times (= Low)

---

been exactly the other way round. The later Hanseatic League, in the Baltic, may be taken as perhaps the supreme example of such a development; but the Vikings already had their own (albeit less formal) groups of warrior-traders such as *felagi* or 'money-combining partnerships' and the *Væringjar* (from whom the 'Varangians' emerged in Russia and Byzantium), and even the beginnings of merchant guilds in towns, sometimes appearing as a seasonal phenomenon, but sometimes permanent (see Foote & Wilson p.97 *ff*).

Whenever a Viking army stopped moving and made a base, for example on an island or inside a fortification, its logistic tail might become settled, at least for a winter, and would presumably find or build houses as well as organising and storing whatever resources the country could provide. Given a favourable strategic situation it might not be a very big step from there to an extension of settlement into neighbouring lands, and hence the creation of a 'Danelaw' on a more permanent basis. Conversely, with active resistance and a bad season in a relatively sparsely-farmed region the logistics might run out altogether and the army be forced to move on. In 894, for example, the *ASC* tells us of a Viking force that could not sustain itself in the Wirral so had to move on to Wales and finally crossed Mercia to East Anglia to make its base on Mersea island. Another example was in 915 (or 917), when an army based on Flatholme island, in the West Country, was unable to fight its way ashore to forage for provisions, so was forced to move on to South Wales and eventually to Ireland. Such examples show how poor maintenance of the strategic aim could be imposed upon an army entirely by its tail and not by its teeth.

Viking C^3I

Having considered the types of people who made up the Viking armies, we may now look at how 'command, control, communications and intelligence' were conducted.

Viking commanders would be expected to lead from the front, setting a physical example of heroism. At least, this would be true after the initial skirmishing or 'missile action' phase had passed. Up to that point it seems to have been an acceptable convention for a leader to lurk within a 'shieldburg' or impenetrable hutch for all-round defence, made of overlapping shields held by his immediate circle of retainers (*eg* at the battle of Svold, in *The Olaf Sagas*, p.94, or in *Göngu-Hrolf*, p.106). A score of household troops might, for example hold up two or three shields to cover the front of the legs, two or three to cover body and face – and the same facing to the flanks and rear – with more to form a roof (see next page).

While he still remained in his shieldburg, whether at sea or on land, the leader would be practically invulnerable to the enemy's arrows, darts and thrown spears, but in consequence could probably not expect to control very much of the course of the battle. Only when he took the decision to emerge from the shieldburg for hand to hand fighting would he simultaneously increase both his power of charismatic leadership and his personal vulnerability. He might still keep some shield-bearers to cover him during his subsequent combats; but they would no longer be able to guarantee the same level of defence for his entire body. The eyes and ankles of even a fully armoured man were notoriously difficult to protect, if he was also fighting actively and trying to set an example to his followers.

The leader would wish to insult or challenge the enemy while urging on his own men, by shouting above the battle noise – and maybe even hitting shirkers. This was all very strenuous, especially when it was in the very front line. We do not think of Viking leaders as sitting back quietly on a hill – or on a horse – judiciously overseeing the action from a safe place behind the lines, monitoring developments and sending out terse memoranda to his lieutenants. Never-

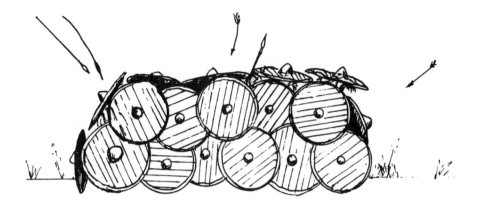

Figure 15

A shieldburg

The immediate retinue of a significant leader rallies around
him during the early phases of a battle to create a 'hutch'
that is proof against missile weapons. Later, when the time
is right for action at closer quarters, they may deploy their
standard and all advance together to attack with swords,
thrusting spears and battle axes.

theless, in battles involving more than a single boat's crew, whether by sea or
land, there must have been arrangements for long-distance communication,
beyond the range of shouted orders, if any sort of command was to be exercised
at all once combat had been joined. Maybe there was very little such communication by later standards, but there may well have been runners available
to commanders, or at least a general habit of taking up significant cries and
passing them along the line, thereby repeating the message for everyone.

Next to the leader would be planted his distinctive (and perhaps named)
banner or standard, which was always a vital symbol of leadership from ancient
times right up to at least the American Civil War. The banner demonstrated to
the rest of the army, which might well be fighting at some distance away from
the commander himself, just where he was and also that he was still in the fight.
Before the battle of Stickelstad training was given by the anti-Olaf *lendermen* so
that each man would know his place in the line (including the most resentful
being placed at the centre, where they were most likely to encounter him), and
would be able to recognise their own particular 'side men' and banner (*The Olaf
Sagas*, p.370). In this way it was hoped to articulate the entire army as a single
entity under flexible command. If the banner moved in a particular direction,
then the rest of the army might follow it, or at least take a cue for its general
tactical mood, depending on whether the banner was advancing proudly in the

attack or drooping shamefacedly in retreat. Olaf, for his part (p.373) was hoping to make a particular flourish at a key moment in the battle by suddenly raising his own banner at the decisive moment when he emerged from his shieldburg to get to grips with the enemy at close quarters. At the battle of Frædeberg, King Hakon's outnumbered men used banners and trumpets to create the impression that reinforcements were at hand (*Sagas of the Norse Kings*, p.102).

There were two important disadvantages associated with the use of banners. The first was that they could tell the enemy almost as much about your army and your posture as they could tell you. They scarcely constituted a 'secret' signal, unless they had first been invested with some mystical, magical or religious powers for your own men that inspired particular faith, loyalty and belief that was not shared by your opponents. Doubtless this was often the case, and one need look no further than our modern habit of hanging regimental colours in cathedral clerestories, in order to see the sacred connotations of these artefacts. Nevertheless, there has sometimes been an excessive enthusiasm to describe such alleged Viking exotica as the so-called 'raven banners' allegedly captured from the Danes in Devon, 878 (according to *ASC*), or carried by Orkneyers in the battles of Skitten and Clontarf (*Orkneyinga Saga*, pp.37–8). Just like the 'blood eagle', these were probably no more than the result of yet another confusion, by the early medieval chroniclers themselves, between real phenomena and the all-pervasive corvid imagery which dominates so much of Viking military poetry.

Secondly, no banner could possibly be erected in battle without immediately becoming a major target for the enemy's missiles and attacks. Standard-bearers have always been marked men in most periods of history, and it was surely no different in the Viking Age. Only the commander himself would be considered a more valuable prize, if only the enemy could cut him down.

We must constantly remember that individual leaders not only determined the course of Viking battles by their personal tactical direction, but they also usually formed a major part of the enemy's strategic objective. A Viking army might easily lay down its arms or melt away if it became known that its leader had been killed, just as it might continue to fight on, against all odds, if he continued to be active and visible at its head. There has been considerable literary discussion of the chivalric ideal of continuing loyalty to a leader even after he had been killed – for example, among Byrhtnoth's men at Maldon or Harald Hard-ruler's at Stamford Bridge (assuming that the saga account of that event is genuinely distinct from the story of Hastings) – but in realistic terms it is far more likely that a lord's retinue would fight on after his fall only if they were physically unable to make good their retreat.

Strategic, operational and tactical intelligence is usually of paramount importance in all warfare, and it does not seem to have been of any less significance during the Viking Age. Much of the Vikings' notorious ability to make devastating raids against soft targets, or to pop up in unexpected places with large armies, must surely be attributed to their care and concern for collecting good intelligence. Unfortunately, we do not really know exactly how they did it. It seems to be pretty well established that they had no maps or compasses by which to plot their theatres of operations, any more than they could expect timely news to reach them from distant parts. If it might take a whole season for any given ship to cross the North Sea, then the information it carried might well be distinctly stale upon arrival. There are many claims to the effect that 'news travelled like lightning' from one province to the next – often by mysterious means and far faster than an army could march or a fleet could sail – but in general these claims may be very deeply suspect. Surprise attacks always seem to have been an option open to any aggressor throughout the Viking Age, at short ranges as much as at long. They seem to have been common even after allowance is made for the normal tendency to report the occasional success more dramatically and vividly than the habitual failure. It therefore seems very probable that the Vikings managed to beat the gossip network, and achieve a genuine operational or tactical surprise, more often than they were defeated by a defender's intelligence. A manoeuvrable attacker could therefore, presumably, collect good general background information about his passive and immobile victim rather more easily that the latter could hope to obtain timely and useful tactical information about him.

Most kings or noblemen probably spent a very great deal of their time collecting general background information, largely by simply chatting about their relatives, their peers, and the wider world, with anyone – friend, enemy or neutral – who happened to arrive in their court. Even today it seems that generals spend much of their time gossiping about other generals, just as royalty passes its days discussing other members of its own class. It must surely have been the same in the court of any efficient Viking leader. Indeed, he might often have encouraged émigrés to attend his court specifically so they could be pumped for inside information about other courts and other countries. Thus the king of Norway might welcome Icelanders, Orkneyers, Swedes and Danes at his capital in Trondheim, just as the Danish king at Roskilde might entertain Swedes, Norwegians, Franks and Anglo-Saxons. Everyone, in other words, would make it their business to know as much as possible about their neighbours.

The study of genealogy and family history was certainly elevated almost to an art form, and took up a significant proportion of the attention of court poets. It was, after all, the key to all inherited wealth and even to the succession to whole kingdoms, especially since concubinage was widespread and any noted leader might well be running several different families simultaneously. Crucial geographical, navigational or other seafaring information was also surely relayed by means of verbally-transmitted formulæ that could be learned by rote. Details of a particular individual's jewels, pet animals and weapons would be stored in a similar way, especially since such items might be used not only as gifts but also to validate and accredit the missions of confidential ambassadors (eg Laxdœla, p.88). If Earl Eric of Møre was sent as King Harald's ambassador from Trondheim to King Sigurd of Gotland, for example, he would need to prove his identity and credentials by offering Sigurd a ring or a dagger that the latter happened to know was a part of Harald's treasure. In the days before the modern concept of documentation – and before even money was accepted at its face value rather than by its crude weight – such highly personal tokens were essential diplomatic bona fides (cf The Olaf Sagas, p. 178, for an alleged early use of letters instead of tokens).

Formal ambassadors apart, the use of spies, informers and tale-tellers appears to have been very widespread indeed. In the days before 'positive vetting' and the 'need to know' culture, rumours could spread very easily and quickly, and information was cheaply bought. Odin could get it simply by sending out his ravens, in rather the same way as Noah had used his doves. The 'kings' sagas' are certainly full of spying activity – for example, Hakon's merchant sent to spy on Olaf Tryggvason in Dublin, who later murdered Hakon himself (The Olaf Sagas, p.45); or the spy who betrayed the five Uppland kings to St Olaf (ibid, p.182). Also in St Olaf's Saga (p.270), St Olaf sends out his spies as soon as he hears that Canute is preparing to invade him in Norway, and there are other examples from some of his other campaigns (eg ibid, pp.328, 350). In Laxdœla Saga (p.146) Olaf Tryggvason spies on all the Icelanders in Norway, since they are suspected of running a fifth column, while in The Saga of Hallfred (p.24) it is the sons of Thorvald who use a spy to get into the Viking Sokki's room, where they murder him. As for counter-espionage measures, we sometimes hear of a systematic policy of executing anyone suspected of spying for the enemy (The Olaf Sagas, pp.358, 360), although the best policy usually seemed to be to get ahead of the enemy's news-gathering apparatus by sheer speed of movement (eg in Saga of Hord, p.63).

There seems little reason to doubt that any man of substance could keep himself well informed about the local politics of the next valley or fjord – and usually about many places that were very much further afield. In 865, for example, there are indications that the Great Army may have received intimate knowledge of Northumbrian political divisions before it had even left its starting positions in the Low Countries and/or Dublin. Rightly could it be said, therefore, that 'many are the ears of the king' (The Olaf Sagas, p.317).

Since the normal decision-making cycle for each campaign might extend through an entire winter season, there would usually be plenty of time to collect strategic intelligence and mull it over. The king could afford to discuss it with his advisers at length, and reach a carefully-considered appreciation before finally resorting to action. This phase might well include preparatory diplomatic feelers to foreign courts, the construction of any new ships that were required, the gathering of stores and the summoning of allies, as well as the crucial decision-making for the summer campaign itself.

When a Viking force was making an 'advance to contact' we can assume that it had specific ideas about the location and nature of its destination or target, or at least that it would be following the line of a river or coast to see what riches might turn up. It might have expert pilots, by sea, who knew the waters well; or on land it might recruit more or less willing local people to show the way. But for tactical security it would also require a screen of scouts advancing ahead of the main body to give early warning of any immediately impending threat from the enemy – or any unexpected booty that was slightly off the main line of advance.

Figure 16   **The decision-making cycle**

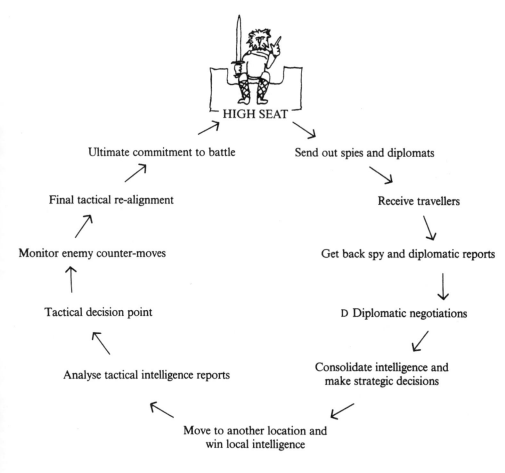

HIGH SEAT

Ultimate commitment to battle   Send out spies and diplomats

Final tactical re-alignment   Receive travellers

Monitor enemy counter-moves   Get back spy and diplomatic reports

Tactical decision point   D Diplomatic negotiations

Analyse tactical intelligence reports   Consolidate intelligence and
                                                              make strategic decisions

Move to another location and
win local intelligence

At sea this was probably less easy to arrange than on land, although local news might be sought whenever the fleet encountered other vessels – passing fishing boats or merchantmen, perhaps – or whenever it touched land. In general, however, a fleet might expect to receive warning of an enemy's proximity only when its own lookouts could see the hostile sails at the limit of vision. In *Orkneyinga Saga* (p.51) we hear of a stern chase across the Pentland Firth where the illumination worked in one direction only, so that the pursuers could see their quarry, but not *vice versa*.

On land an army would doubtless employ specialised scouts to fan out on horseback a few miles ahead and to the flanks, regardless of whether the main body was travelling on land or on a river. They might operate less as individuals than as troops strong enough to force any individual farm or hamlet to surrender its food, money and news, but not big enough to encumber rapid movement. Probably the leaders of these troops would be particularly trusted warriors who knew what to look for, what questions to ask and how to get what they wanted as efficiently as possible. They would also have a duty to report back their findings regularly, which is something that novices might easily forget in their enthusiasm for plunder.

When it came to defensive tactical intelligence, however, there seems to have been much less certainty. We may speculate that Viking Age sentries were similar to those described by Colonel Callwell in 1906 (p.240), who records that 'the forces which the regular troops are called upon to fight in these campaigns seldom protect themselves with outposts at night, and on that account early morning attacks on them frequently meet with brilliant success. A night march followed by an assault upon the hostile position at dawn is perhaps the most effectual means of carrying out a surprise.' A Scots dawn attack surprised Earl Thorfinn's local fleet at anchor in the battle of Deerness (*Orkneyinga Saga*, p.51); but he was soon able to get his revenge by travelling secretly through Caithness – where the population was 'faithful and loyal to him' – to Thurso, where he burned his opponent's hall before his presence had been suspected (p.53). Certainly there are very many cases of nocturnal hall-burning reported throughout all of the 'family', 'kings' and 'lying' sagas – and the impression we gain is that sentries were few and inattentive, so that there was very little defence against this type of assault. In *Gisli's Saga*, for example, there is already both a hall-burning and a counter-burning (with a total of thirty-two dead) before the reader gets even half way down the fifth page. In *The Saga of Hallfred* (p.22) the bullying Viking Sokki needs no excuse, apart from naked greed, when he burns out the innocent Thorvald in his hall in Halogaland. In *Hrafnkel's Saga* (p.57) Thorgeir batters down Hrafnkel's door at dawn and strings him up by his tendons to the roof beams, before anyone in the house has had time to wake up properly. Onund Treefoot burns out his enemy Grim the Hersir, and thirty of his men, in *The Saga of Grettir the Strong* (p.13), although

Figure 17

Scouts and guides

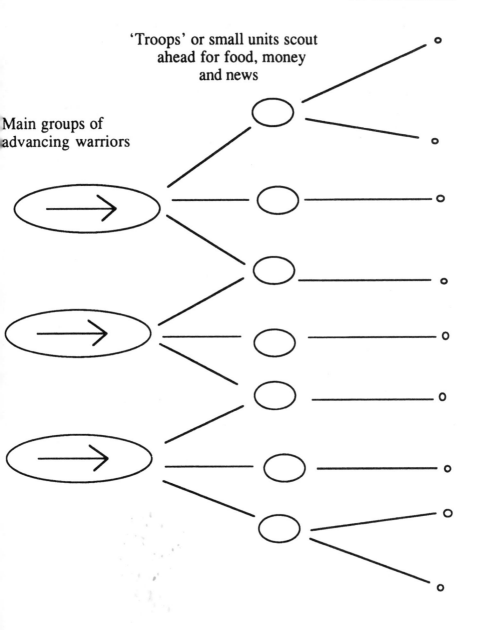

A few scouts and leaders
look ahead, over
the next horizon

'Troops' or small units scout
ahead for food, money
and news

Main groups of
advancing warriors

later in the same tale (p.106) Grettir himself accidentally burns down another hall where he is merely trying to borrow a light for his companions' fire. Ironically he is himself finally overwhelmed and killed when his own sentry falls asleep on watch (pp.208–12).

Attacks upon sleeping enemies in their halls did not, however, always go smoothly. Perhaps the most touchingly human reason recorded for a failure in this type of venture may be seen as the direct converse of a sleeping sentry, when Thorkel, in the *Saga of the Vopnafirthings* (p.54), could not be bothered to wake up in time to go out and burn his enemy Bjarni. His burning-posse therefore abandoned the operation and rode away in disgust, casting many insults at Thorkel as they went.

On many other occasions a hall's normal defences of sentries and guard dogs do appear to have been effective. In *The Story of Burnt Njal* (p.235), for example, Njal had been fully forewarned and was able to exchange many blows and missiles with his assailants before he finally felt he had to retreat into the building due to be burned. In this case there was no tactical surprise in the assault, although superior numbers prevailed and there was ultimately no mercy shown to the victims. When Thorolf's slaves were sent to burn Ulfar's house in *Eyrbyggja Saga* (p.106), by contrast, they were caught and hanged before they had a chance to do the deed. In *Hrolf Gautreksson* (p.119) the king beat off an attempt by two earls to burn his hall, as did Geir's intended victims in *Hord and the Holm Dwellers* (p.63), and Olaf Tryggvason himself in *Laxdœla Saga* (p.146). In *Hreidar the Fool* (p.104) there was even a complex hidden counter-ambush set out to sweep away an all-too-easily pre-dicted attempt at hall-burning, thereby neatly turning the tables on the would-be aggressor. Finally, in *The Olaf Sagas* (p. 149), it was the king's mounted sentries who successfully warned him, at midnight, that his lod-gings at Trondheim were about to be burned out by an enemy force of 2000 men, so he was able to escape with most of his household and treasure in his ships. That made a case of remarkably rapid decision-making, standing in clear contrast to the normally far more leisurely pace of royal strategic plan-ning.

Apart from sentries and dogs there were sometimes more elaborate early warning arrangements set up to give tactical notice of an enemy's approach, such as chains of beacons or bonfires. These could be used by the Vikings themselves no less than by the better organised Carolingians or Anglo-Saxons (*Sagas of the Norse Kings*, pp.99–100 for the Vikings; cf Haywood p.119 for the Carolingians), but they nevertheless made a very uncertain instrument, both because it was only too easy to start a false alarm, thereby wasting credibility as well as stocks of fuel, and also because it was only too easy for one of the watchers to miss a genuine threat by failing to ignite a key beacon in the chain at the right time. The maintenance of a chain of beacons implied a level of skill,

Figure 18
Hall-burning
(schematic plan view)

1) Attackers creep up at night to surround target hall, especially doors
2) Hall is set alight
3) Everyone trying to leave is killed or captured

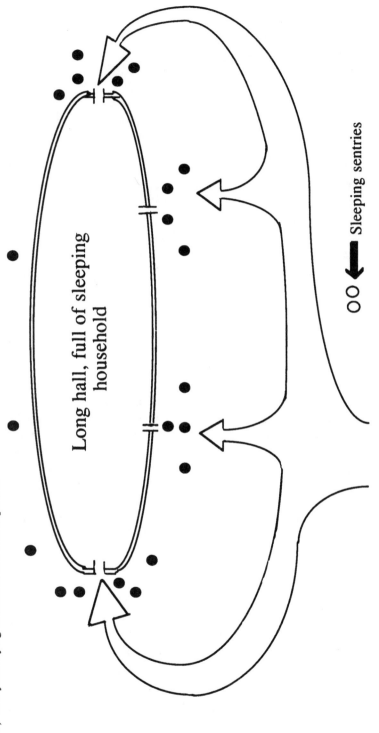

Long hall, full of sleeping household

OO ⬅ Sleeping sentries

professionalism and sustained alertness that was probably not easy to achieve on any widespread basis during the Viking Age.

A Viking commander might usually expect to hear about the noisy and cumbersome approach of an enemy army, if it came overland, from the reports of mounted scouts, couriers or even simple peasants. It might also take a considerable time for the two sides to form up in battle array, once they had come within sight of each other. In those circumstances there would probably be perfectly adequate time for tactical plans to be laid, the troops to take up their arms, and subordinate commanders to be fully briefed. With relatively small forces sailing quickly and quietly by water, however, there might be far less warning, especially if they were travelling at night. Picket boats would rarely be on patrol, and coast watchers might be positioned too close in to the target to be very useful. The first hint of an attacker's presence might not come until he was already at very close quarters indeed. Then it would be up to the defender's sentries and outposts to raise an alarm with shouts, loud noises and perhaps the blowing of their *lurs* or war horns (*eg The Olaf Sagas*, p.151, for *lur* calls at the battle of Nessie; p.308 for the battle of the River Helge). The war leader might then have very little time to make his dispositions against an amphibious or naval assault.

There would certainly be no time for leisurely decision-making once battle had been joined, since the tactical leader would himself probably be personally involved in the combat (emotionally as well as physically); would have a pretty limited vision of what was going on, and would not know just how much time he had to make decisions. In unannounced ambushes or 'pop-up' raiding, of course, the victim of surprise might have only seconds, rather than hours, to gather his wits, his personal equipment and a skeleton band of comrades ready to fight. In some protracted battles, by contrast, there might be hours spent in an indecisive exchange of missiles and insults before the close-quarter contest finally developed, if it ever did (*eg* at Møre, 977, it got no further than missile action: *The Olaf Sagas*, p.17). Nevertheless, on other occasions the key shock-troops of an outnumbered army might try to pre-empt a long fight by hewing their way decisively and rapidly through to kill the enemy leader before the majority of forces became engaged (*eg* at the battle of Utstein, 1028, in *The Olaf Sagas*, pp.329–30: battle of Stickelstad, 1030, p.363).

It seems that counter-measures were sometimes taken against this sort of tactic, in that a leader might employ a 'double' of himself, to draw the enemy's fire. Thus in *Halfdan Eysteinsson* there is a lot of clothes-changing to conceal the identity of the leader in battle (*Seven Viking Romances*, p.174), while in the *Olaf Sagas* (p.96) Olaf Tryggvason uses a double at Svold, and the wrong man is killed for St Olaf in poor light, in 1028 (p.323). In the *Saga of the Vopnafirthings* (p.53) a decoy is constructed out of a chopping block, to look like a rider (and see Scragg, ed, *The Battle of Maldon*, p.151, for leaders' look-alikes). Such artistry nevertheless runs directly against the need for charismatic front-line leaders in Viking warfare, who could not normally conceal their identity or delegate their decision-making to others. Unless very carefully handled, the use of a double could easily be seen as a cowardly act by the one person who could surely never afford to appear cowardly.

Engineering

We know that Iron Age peoples built many extensive hill-forts and that the Romans pushed forward siegecraft and fortification to a very advanced state. From the high middle ages we also have countless stone keeps and many references to complex siege engines designed to reduce them. But what came in between, during the Viking Age? We tend to think of the Vikings more as flamboyant adventurers than as scientific engineers, even though we know that quite a bit of cleverness must have gone into their navigation, and plenty of good practical carpentry into their boat-building and routine boat-main-tenance. Their boat portages, tactical canal-building and harbour-mouth boom-laying must have been organised in at least a rough equivalent to an 'engineering spirit', and must have involved a logical progression from sur-veying the site and conceptualising the operation to assembling the labour, tools and materials, and then pushing the whole thing through to completion. There must have been provision for logistics and security, as well as contingency plans against awkward physical obstacles such as bad weather or unexpected geology. None of this probably required any specially-trained engineer officers, since it would all come into the general fields of seamanship and command; but even on an improvised basis the job would still be done. Even if we look no further than the Vikings' boats and sailing skills, therefore, we are forced to admit that they must have known quite a lot about the basic principles of civil engineering. This is confirmed by Harald Bluetooth's impressive kilometre-long bridge at Ravning Enge south-west of Jelling (dated around 980) and the Kanhave canal across Sams island of about the same time (see discussion in Foote & Wilson, p.436).

When we turn to military engineering, moreover, we soon find many other striking examples of the Vikings' skills. Best known, and even most notorious, is the chain of precisely-planned circular fortresses that was also built by Harald Bluetooth for his wars against the Saxons around 955 – at Trelleborg (Sjaelland), Nonnebakken (Odense, on Fyn), Aggersborg and Fyrkat Mølle (both in North Jutland). All were built with moorings for ships, on waterways giving easy access to the Baltic and, in the case of Aggersborg, also to the North Sea. The rampart at Trelleborg had an internal diameter of 136 metres and within its perimeter there were sixteen identical long houses laid out in four symmetrical quad-rangles, with each house as big as a large warship and estimated to be capable of sleeping 100–200 men. Outside the main walls there were fifteen more such

Figure 19

The layout of Trelleborg-type forts

Aggersborg

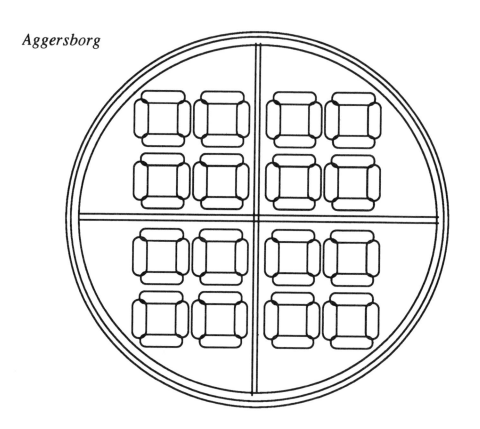

Trelleborg / Fyrkat / Nonnebakken type:

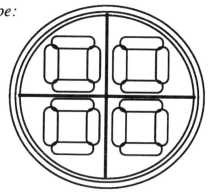

houses, which gave a potential total population that might have been as high as 6200 (but see chapters 3 and 4 for reasons why boats at sea might have carried lesser crews than their theoretical maximums). The Nonnebakken and Fyrkat fortresses were practically identical to Trelleborg, apart from their lack of the fifteen external houses. At Aggersborg the rampart had a greater diameter and contained forty-eight houses – barrack space for up to 9600 men – making for a theoretical total sleeping capacity in the four fortresses of something over 20,000 men, or a very respectable army in almost any era of history before the introduction of steam. Even if we accept the stingiest estimates of 4000 for the total, that was still quite a large army for the Viking Age.

These fortresses were built of thick earth banks interlaced with timbers and covered with turf, to a height of some twenty feet, upon the top of which were wooden pallisades. In front of them were ditches, beyond which there was perhaps a second, outer rampart and ditch. There were four gates placed symmetrically in the walls and strengthened with masonry, reminiscent of the arrangement of gates in the Romans' square camps. The likelihood of Roman influence is heightened by the consistent use of the Roman foot as the unit of measurement, although the circular design seems to have been less Roman than locally Baltic in origin. A similarly circular plan may be seen in earlier Scandinavian fortifications such as those on Oland from the Vendel Age, in some forts in Flanders (Haywood p.119), and in the Slav forts which are dotted around North Germany and Poland. Indeed, a deliberate imitation of Slav designs may have been especially appropriate for forts which are very likely to have been built with a Slav opponent in mind.

Mythology has somehow managed to associate these four uniform fortresses with the Danish colony at Jomsburg on the Oder (near Wolin), within Slav territory on the North German coast, where Sven Forkbeard is supposed to have run a training camp, on almost monastic lines, for a dedicated professional force of mysogenistic 'Jomsvikings'. These are supposed to have spent their summers raiding far afield in 300 ships, and to have returned each winter to a Jomsburg stronghold which boasted iron gates and stone towers. No actual trace of this fortress has been found and their saga, written in Iceland in the 1200s, is as fanciful, fantastic and improbable as any of the 'lying sagas' – or as the tales of King Arthur's knights of the round table. In the *Sagas of the Norse Kings* (p.145) we hear of a Danish counter-attack to retake Jomsburg from the Wends in 1042, although that might well refer to almost any Slav fortress in North Germany. Nevertheless, the myth of the Jomsvikings has rooted itself firmly in the popular imagination, to the extent that the ultra-disciplined Jomsvikings are supposed to have been a key element in Sven's eventual conquest of Aethelred's England. The additional assumption is also often made that they were joined in this mission by similar 'warrior monks' from the fortresses at Trelleborg, Nonnebakken, Fyrkat and Aggersborg.

Figure 20

Refuges, citadels and barracks

Fortification can be associated with populated areas in
    many different ways, including:

Completely open, undefended
    town, without fortification:

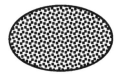

Open town with a citadel (or keep)
    for a few last-ditch defenders:

Open town with a temporary
    refuge for the population in
    their rôle as fugitives:

Walled town to protect entire
    population safe in their homes:

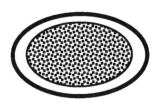

Walled town with
    strong inner citadel:

Purely military post or fortified
    barracks (as Trelleborg etc)

The uncompromising uniformity of the four fortresses that remain does certainly suggest centralised direction and a very high level of military organisation, although it is not necessarily clear that any offensive purpose was actually intended. The earthworks and pallisades may well have been intended only as refuges for the local communities, and the barracks merely an efficient means of housing them in moments of crisis. Their importance to the state may have lain only in the strategic geography of their positioning, in much the same way as was true of Charlemagne's coastal defences. It was supposedly contrary to the Jomsvikings' rules to allow women into their barracks – but copious archaeological evidence of female presence has been found within the walls of these fortresses. Nor can Sven Forkbeard be accorded the honour of having built them, since dendrochronolgy places the construction of most in the lifetime of his predecessor Harold Bluetooth, while the origins of Aggersborg may even date as far back as the Vendel Age. All in all, therefore, we cannot see these forts as amounting to a sort of 'Boulogne Camp' aimed at England, some 800 years before Napoleon, but rather as a defensive response to a growing threat of Wendish piracy within the Baltic. It is also notable that these fortresses, in common with the bridge at Ravning Enge and the Kanhave canal, seem to have been built in a frenzy of state-sponsored enthusiasm, but fell into disuse within a single generation. Hence they all represented a fleeting, flashy but expensive royal impulse, rather than a long-term solution to any particular problem.

More permanently and continuously significant, however, was the great earthwork built to defend the one and only front door to the Scandinavian world. This was the linear 'Danevirke', which was a rampart and ditch running overland across the base of the Jutland peninsula in a manner very reminiscent of Offa's Dyke or Hadrian's Wall (although both of those were far longer, and the latter was of stone construction rather than earth). The Danevirke was actually little more than a dozen miles long even though, due to the peculiar configuration of the local rivers and swamps, it still provided a complete strategic defence for Jutland against any land attack from the south. At its Baltic end lay the great trade centre of Hedeby, while towards the West – on the river Trene leading into the North Sea – was the smaller entrepôt of Hollingsted (see Gwyn Jones, *A History of the Vikings*, pp.99–105). The portage for ships or their cargoes may have been as little as eight miles between these two, performing very much the same function for the Danes as the Kiel Canal would do for the Kaiser in the nineteenth century.

The Danevirke was pierced by only a single gate, which was on the great north-south road running a couple of miles to the west of Hedeby. This channelled all overland trade between Denmark and the Carolingian Empire through a single customs post, which must have made for a highly manpower-efficient system of control. Equally, the walls themselves were in some places as high and as strong as the Trelleborg ramparts, and in front of some parts of

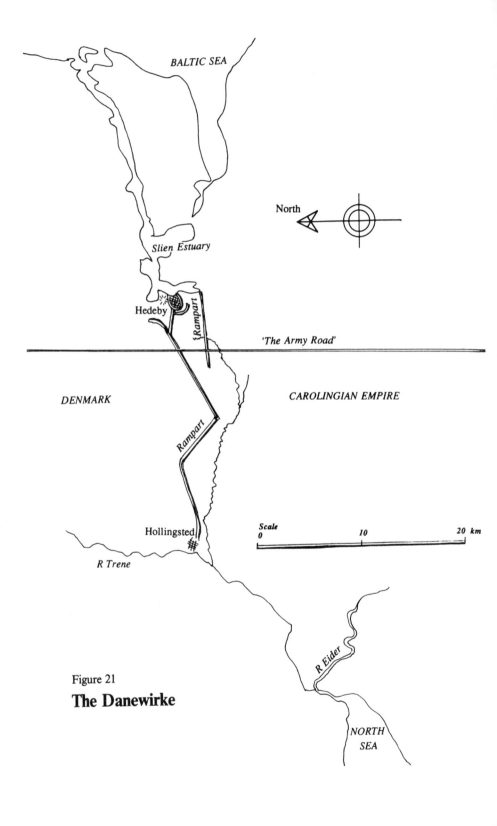

BALTIC SEA

North

Slien Estuary

Hedeby

Rampart

'The Army Road'

DENMARK

CAROLINGIAN EMPIRE

Rampart

Hollingsted

Scale
0   10   20 km

R Trene

R Eider

Figure 21

The Danewirke

NORTH
SEA

Hedeby there were as many as three lines of defence. In moments of crisis all this could surely have been manned, at least temporarily, with a very adequate size of garrison at an affordable cost. If we reckon one man per three metres of rampart, it would have needed something like 7000–10,000 men, which was certainly an achievable figure for a temporary defensive levy raised from a country as rich as Viking-Age Denmark. Once that garrison was in place, moreover, it could have quickly rectified any crumbling of the earth banks and pallisades that might have occurred since the previous mass muster.

When properly mobilised for war, therefore, the Danevirke must have represented a far more defensible military obstacle than many town walls in the same period – or, indeed, Offa's Dyke itself. Nevertheless, its significance should still ultimately be seen as symbolic and for peacetime purposes only, rather than as a really serious factor in Viking strategy. Its main purpose was doubtless to collect taxes in peacetime rather than to keep out invaders in wartime, and there are two main reasons which spring to mind. The first is that even if the garrison were fully mobilised it would still be too widely spread to resist a *coup de main* or surprise infiltration by an attacking army that was cleverly concentrated against a single sector of the works. It might well be able to resist a regular siege conducted along the whole length of the wall or a *coup de main* against the citadel (*ie* Hedeby); but it surely could not hope to guarantee the whole twelve miles against a mobile and aggressive opponent. The weakness of the linear Danevirke was that its whole length would necessarily fall – apart perhaps from Hedeby itself – as soon as its weakest point had been breached. Secondly, and still more fatal to its chances, it had no jurisdiction whatsoever over the seas which surrounded it. Any attacker who had a fleet – even if it was inferior to that of the defender – could probably bypass the land defences and sail on to ravage any Danish beach he chose. Indeed, the stronger the levies manning the Danevirke itself, the weaker would be the levies available for defence against such an amphibious descent on the coasts.

The Danevirke seems to have offered pitifully little resistance in 815, when Louis the Pious made an overland attack which apparently cut through it without difficulty. Some authorities believe his success was due to the fact that the work had not been built at that time – or even until the time of Harald Bluetooth in the mid-900s – but modern opinion tends to attribute its origins to the 700s. It is especially often credited to King Godfred (murdered in 810), which would mean that Louis the Pious would indeed have had to cross it. Having said that, however, it may not yet have been very strong at that time, and it seems to have been constantly repaired and improved right up to around 1170, in places on as many as ten different occasions, and sometimes with stone replacing the original earth and timber. Harald Bluetooth certainly did add to it; but so did his mother Thyre (wife of Gorm the Old) and doubtless many other rulers besides. This is clear testimony that it retained some sort of utility to Danish kings throughout the Viking period, even if it may never have won any wars, and it still stands as the biggest monument to their engineering skills.

The technical quality of Danish fortification and other engineering work seems to have improved gradually as the Viking Age progressed, even if the scale of their conception may have diminished from a grandiose twelve-mile Danevirke in the 700s to a more practical circumference of less than half a mile at Trelleborg in the 900s. The Danes, however, were probably more advanced in engineering skill than their Norwegian or Swedish comrades, who tended to occupy more mountainous defensive terrain and face somewhat less advanced opponents. Even the Danes themselves would try to cut corners where they could. In the English campaign of 865-79, for example, their Great Army usually took up its winter quarters in or around fortresses which already existed, and did little more than improve on earlier works. Only at Reading in 870–1 did they build a new rampart from scratch (Brooks' article, p.10), although they may perhaps be excused from the charge of laziness on the grounds that these one-winter-only fortresses should be seen as almost temporary in nature, even though they still usually needed over a mile of fortifications. Their task was to protect a large army against sometimes very violent assaults, as at York in 867, Nottingham in 868, and Wareham and Exeter in 876. In these circumstances the Danes' lack of new fortress building surely did not imply that they were in any way ignorant of the value and use of fortification, any more than the French and the English can be condemned for starting their own massive programmes of anti-Viking fortification only relatively late in the Great Army's career. The Maginot Line, after all, was begun only some time after the first Teutonic onslaught had been successfully beaten off in 1918 by mainly improvised fieldworks.

Wherever they went, the Vikings would always sooner or later arrive at a position they were forced to defend as a fortress, or would encounter a fortified target that they had to besiege in turn. It was only in very small-scale raiding that they could hope to keep on plundering undefended merchant ships, monasteries or 'hog strands' on an indefinite, irresponsible basis. Even then, the annals of saga warfare are full of heroic last stands by very small groups of bandits who find themselves besieged in natural (eg *Grettir*, p.184 *ff*) or man-made (eg *Eyrbyggja*, p.179 *ff*) strongholds, just as they contain some daring one-man assaults on enemy castles (eg some of Harald Hard-ruler's escapades against the Arabs, in *Sagas of the Norse Kings*, p.164 *ff*).

When it comes to the Vikings' art of besieging an enemy fortification, such meagre evidence as we have suggests that they very prudently preferred not to engage in protracted sieges if they could possibly help it. Their love of cunning and deception helped push them towards a strategy of *coups de main* and 'popping up' in the middle of enemy towns before the alarm had been raised, or making a secret night march to occupy a different attacking position from the one that was expected. If such ruses failed and the enemy town held out, a geld might be negotiated as the price of lifting the siege. It was only in cases when no negotiation was accepted, but the capture of the enemy town remained essential for the Vikings' further operations, that they would settle down to a regular siege.

Unfortunately we do not know anything at all about the level of sophistication which they brought to such operations. It is entirely possible that they could manage little more than a loose blockade – including all the laxity of sentries that we have already noted elsewhere. The twelve month duration of the siege of Paris in 885–6, for example, would suggest that active pressure on the defenders was left at a rather low level and that starvation was supposed to be the main weapon. Yet against this we have some colourful literary claims from Abbo of Fleury that this same siege included quite sophisticated Viking siege engines, such as covered battering rams and towers, not to mention fireships and fire carts. It may be significant, however, that even these descriptions concede that technology failed to make headway against the great fortified bridge, which was finally destroyed only by a natural rise in the river level rather than by any artificial means.

In *Hrolf Gautreksson* (p.56) we hear of some anachronistic-sounding catapults at Uppsala, as well as a siege tower (p.66); but there must be a deep suspicion that saga accounts written in the 1200s describe siege techniques of the latter period, or of Roman times, rather than those of the Viking Age. When we hear of Sven Forkbeard deploying mangonels at Trelleborg, or of the Rus using overland wind-ships (are these merely portages?) to outflank the walls of Constantinople in 907, we should take it all with a considerable pinch of salt, except perhaps insofar as the Varangians in Byzantine service would definitely have been familiar with the highest forms of artillery known at the time. In the *Sagas of the Norse Kings* (p.283) a 'slinging engine' was allegedly used by Varangians in Palestine c.1095, and we can accept this as probably true: but it is much harder to accept that Harald Hard-ruler burnt out an enemy stronghold in Sicily by sending sparrows attached to flaming material to roost under the eaves (p.164 *ff*), or that he used many other ruses to capture forts at other times, since in every case we can identify the tale as a commonplace of medieval mythology – if not of ancient literature (see discussions in Blöndal, p.71 *ff*). Equally, Olaf Tryggvason is supposed to have pulled down London Bridge by attaching ropes from his boats to its supporting timbers and then rowing hard downstream (*The Olaf Sagas*, p.124 – and some of the grappling irons from this operation have apparently been found at the site, along with Viking weapons). In all this there is a strong feeling of literary convention overtaking solid mechanical practicalities, and yet … and yet there is still always a slight, lingering suspicion that some small grains of truth may actually be hidden within such stories.

CHAPTER 6

Arms and Armour

'Une logique gagnante'
– General Noël Lhuissier in conversation with the author about the tendency of armoured warriors to do better against unarmoured ones rather than *vice versa*.

Missile Arms

When we think of Viking weaponry we tend to think mainly of close-quarter battleaxes and swords, but in reality most Vikings would doubtless have seen missile arms as equally important. Missiles were the inevitable preliminary to any fight (see *eg Njal*, p.124) – and on some occasions almost its only ingredient. Especially when troops were protected from their enemies by strong fortress walls or ships' bulwarks, an exchange of missiles might often have been the only mutually convenient way to express hostility. Viking battles which had no close quarter fighting at all were, therefore, very much a possibility ... and they had the very attractive additional feature that their casualties could be limited far more easily than was possible in a frenzied hand-to-hand mêlée. It is normally a lot more practicable to pull troops out of danger if they are doing their fighting one hundred yards away from the enemy than if they are only two feet away.

In terms of fighting with missiles, the average Viking warrior would think mainly of long-range archery and medium-range spear throwing. Both these skills may well have been prized very highly in sports or training (*eg The Olaf Sagas*, p.117) – albeit perhaps only because missile accuracy can be measured far more precisely in play, without hurting anyone, than can the ability to chop up one's opponent in an intimate axe-fight. Admittedly no missile action in real battle could ever be expected to inflict anything like as high a percentage of wounds per shot as could the deliberately aimed choppings of the close-quarter hackers – but the fact remains that standoff missile men could realistically expect to loose off far more shots in a battle than the hackers could expect to deliver heavy swipes. Quite a lot of the Viking heroes seem to have been killed by standoff shooting rather than by heroic blows from axes or swords (*eg* Harold Bluetooth, cited in Robert Hardy, *Longbow*, p.29; King Hakon, and Harold Hard-ruler, *Sagas of the Norse Kings*, pp.108, 232). We also read of noble warriors using missile weapons themselves, without suffering any loss of dignity. At the battle of Svold Olaf Tryggvason prided himself on his ability to throw spears with both hands at once, in between shooting arrows during 'the greater part of the day' (*The Olaf Sagas*, p.95). His son Trygve would repeat the feat at Soknasund in 1033 (*ibid*, p.394); Harald Hard-ruler would keep firing his bow throughout the battle of Nissa (*Sagas of the Norse Kings*, p.206), and Magnus Erlendsson would fight much of his battle of the Menai Strait with his bow (*Orkneyinga Saga*, p.84 – and compare Arrow-Odd's all-archery battle in *Seven Viking Romances*, p.114).

Against all this, however, we also have literary indications that the use of bows and throwing spears was somehow socially demeaning and 'not quite the thing' for noblemen (see Brooks in Scragg, ed., *The Battle of Maldon*, p.208). This probably reflects the tactical reality that missile action was indecisive, whereas close quarter action could be expected to leave clear winners and losers – and maybe not even at any higher cost in casualties. A leader willing to launch a bold onset therefore had many more tactical options open to him than one who believed in missile action alone. Hence the Viking ideal of leadership and nobility always had to stress a readiness to mix it at close quarters, and in literary sources this could easily become corrupted into a marginalisation of bows and throwing spears in favour of stabbing spears (as in the Maldon poem) or of swords (as in the Brunanburh poem). In the real world, however, missile weapons may actually have been a lot more important than this literary ideal would suggest.

Bows and Arrows

Archery was inseparable from Viking combat, and Saxo Grammaticus thought the Norwegians were especially famous bowmen (Foote & Wilson p.278). Late Viking levy laws in both Norway and Sweden specified bows as part of the armament the bonders were expected to bring to a muster. The bows themselves were of various types, both short and long, including some composites and 'self-composites' (*ie* exploiting the natural differences in texture within a single piece of yew wood: Hardy, pp.28–35). The arrowheads were also very varied in style, ranging from trefoil points to plain leaf-shape and barbed designs for hunting. Up to forty arrows could be carried in a quiver.

Crossbows are sometimes mentioned in the sagas (*eg Halfdan Eysteinsson*, in *Seven Viking Romances*, p.178); but such references are surely anachronistic since these weapons are not believed to have reached the Viking world until the 1100s. There are also occasional references to slings, but once again it is unlikely that this reflected a widespread Viking reality. Instead it may show familiarity with the biblical story of David and Goliath or, at most, with 'thonged spears' for throwing, used especially in hunting (mentioned *eg* in Saxo Grammaticus p.281 and *Fljotsdale Saga*, p.24). If stones were to be propelled against the enemy, they were more likely to have been simply thrown or dropped. In the sagas this normally happens when an otherwise unarmed fugitive turns against his pursuers (*eg Egil*, p.194; *Grettir*, p.202; *Njal*, p.112; *Gisli*, p.58). It was doubtless also common in sieges for the defenders to stockpile stones as a cheap form of ammunition.

Stones aside, proper archery must have been especially important in sieges, where the two sides were separated by earthworks but could still snipe at each other, including the use of indirect shots to reach behind a palisade. Much the same also applies to naval warfare, where we read of archers taking position in the stern of a boat to shoot over the heads of the close quarter warriors in the prow (*eg Sagas of the Norse Kings*, p.150). In a battle line on land the archers might also have been located to the rear of the swordsmen, although it was probably just as likely for the swordsmen themselves to have used bows during the early part of a combat and then to have laid them aside during the second, close-quarter phase. Horse-archers were also surely familiar to the Vikings, both from their intrinsic advantages in hunting as well as in warfare, and from encounters with other nations who had studied the literature of Roman wars against the Parthians.

THROWING SPEARS

Many different types of spearhead have survived from the Viking era. In general the lighter and more streamlined patterns were used for throwing while the heavier (and winged) spears were for stabbing; but many designs could be put to either use. This was the case with the broad bladed 'leaf' spears no less than with the narrow pointed javelins, although certain 'pilum' style javelins (or 'darts') could not be used for stabbing, and the Frankish 'southern spear' or *Angon* was also mainly for throwing.

An important tactical consideration with throwing spears was whether or not they could be returned by the enemy. With a pilum the whole head was designed to break off or bend round when it became embedded in a target, making the spear unthrowable until it had been repaired by a blacksmith. With a harpoon or barbed spearhead the intention was to make it difficult to extract the weapon from a victim's flesh, although presumably that would not prevent the return of spears that had failed to find a victim. Less elaborately, but probably more practically, it seems to have been common to remove the pin or nail which held the spearhead on its shaft. Thus the two parts would stay together while the spear was initially thrown forward, but would become separated by any attempt to pull the shaft backwards (see *eg Grettir* pp.127–8; *Fljotsdale Saga*, p.42).

It was apparently traditional to start a battle by throwing a spear right over the enemy army, to claim it for Odin (*Eyrbyggja Saga*, p.143). After that there might be a 'spear song' of thrown javelins, which could be parried to some extent by the deft use of shields or other protection, but which would still disorder and unsettle a formed line. If there was a very high volume of thrown

Figure 22

Throwing spears

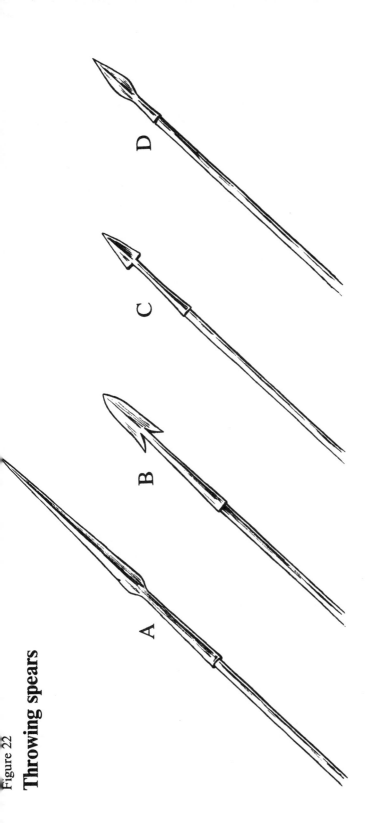

A = Pilum type designed to bend, once embedded in an enemy shield,
    to prevent immediate return.
B and C = Barbed javelins
D = Non-barbed throwing spear

spears all arriving at the same time, avoidance would not be possible and a high level of casualties might result. The thrown spear was certainly not a weapon to be ignored, as is reflected by the sagas' frequent reference to it. Thus in *Gisli's Saga* (pp.30, 42), a thrown spear is caught in flight and thrown back to kill a man, then Gisli himself is hit in the calf by another – as he is again later, while trying to swim away from his enemies. There are more deaths from thrown spears in *The Tale of Gunnar Thidrandi's Bane* (*Tales from the Eastfirths*, pp.71, 74), while in *Egil* (p.146) a thrown 'halberd' goes through a shield. Halberds came into Viking warfare only late in the day, and were certainly not designed for throwing, so this last example may be an anachronistic distortion, unless the reference is simply to a normal spear with a broad blade.

Defences

SHIELDS

By far the cheapest and commonest item in the Viking armoury was the shield, which was also the most useful item in battle. Rich or poor, young or old, no warrior could afford to be without a shield – and sometimes he might have more than one – regardless of whatever else he took with him. The shield was his main line of defence against all forms of attack, and if used correctly it could make helmets and mail shirts almost entirely superfluous.

The traditional Viking shield was circular, around a yard in diameter, with a metal boss at the centre to cover the hand grip. It would be made of relatively narrow strips of wood, possibly laminated and preferably lime, with some iron struts as its frame at the rear and a leather (rarely metal) reinforcement around the rim or even all over its face. In the 1000s this design was joined by the 'kite' shield as portrayed in the Bayeux tapestery and mentioned in some of the sagas (*eg Njal*, p.97; *Laxdœla* p.187), although its actual incidence among true Vikings – as opposed to Normans, or Scandinavians of a later age – must remain problematical. The kite was presumably optimised for mounted combat, covering the whole of the left leg of a horseman; but it was much less manoeuvrable and handy (especially on board ship) than a circular shield. It admittedly had the advantage that it could be stuck in the ground to make a 'pavise' covering a man who needed to use both his hands in some other task (*eg* archery); but all in all it cannot have been seen as much of an improvement except by the obsessively fashion-conscious. The Vikings may sometimes also have used rectangular and oval shields, as well as convex (or 'hollow') ones and smaller circular bucklers; but in none of these cases is the evidence particularly overwhelming. We are safe to assume that for most of the Viking Age it was the large circular shield which characterised most battles.

The shield was unlike most other items of Viking equipment insofar as it was supposed to be expendable. Its entire purpose and *raison d'être* was to be hacked to pieces by the enemy, in order to spare its owner the same fate. In the Gokstad boat burial there were two real shields for every putative oarsman, giving him a considerable margin of protection, while in Icelandic duelling the rules of combat specified no less than three shields for each contestant. Presumably the idea was that neither warrior in a duel would be left with enough energy to deal his opponent a really dangerous blow, if he first had to reduce three shields to matchwood.

The literature is certainly full of the idea that shields could shatter under the impact of the enemy's axes or swords. In *Fljotsdale Saga* (p.44) one warrior found that 'his shield had been hacked to pieces, so that not an inch was left except around the grip'. In the *Tale of Thorstein Rod-Stroke* (p.64) both players in a duel simultaneously destroy their enemy's shield. In *Gongu-Hrolf* (p.46) the shields shatter in battle and spearheads are cut off by enemy blows, while in *The Story of Burnt Njal* (p.289) the shields just fall apart and apparently serve no purpose at all.

Shields do not necessarily preserve their owners from harm. Apart from the incidents cited above, the sagas are full of examples of the man being cleaved as well as his shield – and even his mail shirt. Consider the following passage:

Hrolf struck at Orn, but as he tried to ward off the blow with his shield, the sword sliced through, and the point ripped open the whole of his belly so that his guts poured out. Next Hrolf ran Herkir through and cut both legs off Lifolf. Stefnir stabbed at Ulf with a spear; and, as Ulf thrust his shield against it, the spear pieced right through into his thigh, wounding him badly. Ulf cut the spearhead off the shaft. Har pounced on Hrolf and struck him on the helm with a nail-studded club, knocking him unconscious: yet still Hrolf managed to turn on Ulf and thrust at him with the sword. The mailcoat failed, and the sword went right through him. (*Göngu-Hrolf*, pp.99–100)

Something similar happens in the *Saga of Gunnlaug* (p.35), where a shield is cleaved in a duel, and in the *Saga of Grettir the Strong*, where a single blow goes through both the opponent's shield and his calf (p.116), and later through both his shield and his brain (p.128). Obviously a Viking shield did not make a perfect protection for its owner, any more than the armour on a modern tank can positively guarantee longevity to its crewmen. Nevertheless, a Viking shield was still a very great deal better than nothing, and its ubiquity in warfare was scarcely an accident.

Perhaps the most memorable visual image of Viking shields is the proud interlocked line of them that was often ranged along the bulwarks of a dragon boat. Apparently this was normal only when the boat was in harbour, just to make a show, although there does also seem to have been a solid tactical use for it in battle. By raising the effective height of the bulwark by a couple of feet with its shields, a crew could continue to row without exposing itself to arrows or thrown spears (see *eg Laxdœla*, p.91). However, when it came to close-quarter combat the shields would doubtless have been more useful if they were carried in the hands of each warrior rather than left inactive along the bulwarks.

The particular heraldry exposed on the shields may well have been significant to Vikings, even though the basic two-colour patterns themselves seem somewhat simplistic and random by comparison with later medieval designs. We do not, however, know much about this subject, and it is equally possible that most Viking shields may actually have been left plain. The saga references to specific patterns may certainly be dismissed as anachronistic and misleading, especially since they are often propagandistically linked to the (very late Viking) crusaders' cross (*eg* in *Laxdœla*, p.159; *The Olaf Sagas*, pp.152, 356).

HELMETS

In the case of (relatively cheaply manufactured) spears, shields and bows we can be reasonably confident that as many could be made available to Viking warriors as were needed for any given campaign. With helmets, however, we encounter a distinct problem of supply. Unlike the situation obtaining in the twentieth century, the Vikings could not mass produce this particular item, and the sheer skill and scale of metal-working required to make just one example must have made it an altogether more expensive proposition than a spearhead or shield boss. The iron itself, however, was probably not in short supply, since Scandinavia was rich in ore. For example, around 1000 the Møsstrond site near Telemark was producing about 4000 kg of iron per year (Sawyer, *Kings and Vikings*, p.63), while the Gokstad boat alone used some 80 kg of iron in its nails and fittings.

Since we have very few surviving helmets – about one from the Viking world itself (the Gjermundbu helmet, c.880), and only a handful more from its surrounding eras and territories (There are only about eighty, worldwide, for the whole period 500–1100) – we cannot be sure whether helmets were restricted to a very small privileged elite or spread more widely among the military classes in general. Obviously no one who went to war would feel entirely safe without one, and no one would pass up the chance of grabbing one if he possibly could. There is no doubt that possession of a helmet was considered to be a mark of high status for a Viking warrior, showing not only that he was wealthy but also that he was better protected in battle. Helmets were ostentatious as well as practical, and a very great deal of social envy and one-upmanship tended to be invested in them. They were often gilded or otherwise decorated; they made particularly suitable gifts for persons whom one wanted to impress (*eg* in *King Gautrek; Seven Viking Romances*, p.166), and they often had a place in rich burial hoards. Some idea of the overall effect that rich armour was intended to produce may be gained from such exaggerated passages as the following:

King Hreggvid's armour was the only set of its kind. The helmet was covered with precious stones, and so strong it was impossible to destroy. His mailcoat was of the hardest steel, treble-plated, and it shone like silver. The shield was far too broad and thick for any iron to bite and the lance which went with it was hard and tough ... (*Göngu-Hrolf*, p.29)

Or again:

Olaf ... was wearing a coat of mail, and had a gilded helmet on his head. He was girded with a sword whose pommel and guard were embossed with gold, and in his hand he held a barbed spear, chased and beautifully engraved. Before him he carried a red shield on which a lion was chased in gold. (*Laxdœla*, p.91)

Nevertheless there is still considerable doubt about just how widespread helmets may have been when it came to battle. In the Maldon poem there is no mention of them at all – and they appear on English coins only after the date of that battle, leading to the view that they were sadly rare in England around 991 and hence that the Viking invaders had a decisive technological edge over their opponents. Against this there are some contemporary pictures in which the entire crews of Viking warships are portrayed as being fully armoured from head to foot; yet in view of the scarcity of surviving helmets we cannot be sure that this reflected anything more than a wistful ideal (*cf* if one believed the images peddled by Hollywood today, one would be tempted to think that every combat soldier of the 1990s had a miniature Vulcan cannon slung around his hips).

Men who lacked a helmet could probably have got along well enough without, relying upon either their shield or a strong hat (made of leather or other resistant material) in its place. In common with Second World War commandos, they might even have made a cult of 'doing without' and opting for the Viking equivalent of the cap comforter or beret. Even those who did have helmets were apparently sensitive to the changing demands of fashion, and there seem to be grounds for believing that 'the most modern style' changed relatively often. The civilian decorative arts evolved about once every half-century, and we may take military items like helmets to have evolved about once every one or two hundred years. Thus the European 'spangenhelm' of around 500 AD was made up of a series of essentially triangular plates, held together at the base with a circular headband (with or without a protective piece for nose or eye), and at the top with some sort of spike or ornament. This basic design continued to influence helmet construction for about half a millenium thereafter, but in its details it kept changing. In the Vendel era c.600 (about the same time as the highly decorated Sutton Hoo and Benty Grange helmets from England) the headband was high (extended downwards by

Figure 23
Helmets

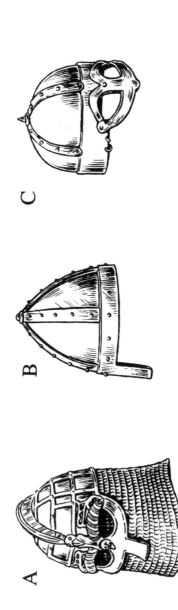

A   B   C   D

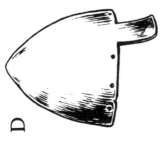

A = The elaborately decorated pre-Viking Valsgärde funerary helmet, comparable to the Sutton Hoo and Benty Grange helmets of a similar era.

B = A 'Spangenhelm' constructed from many small decorated plates. This general design, albeit with many local variations, continued in use throughout northern Europe from the 400s to the 1000s.

C = The Gjermundbu helmet (late 800s); one of the very few genuinely Viking helmets to survive. Constructed by the Spangenhelm technique.

D = A typical one-piece helmet of the 900s and 1000s, with nasal. The Olmütz, Poznan and Prague 'Wenceslas' helmets are particularly famous, although many similar pieces appear in the Bayeux Tapestery.

'spectacle' type eye guards) and the plates could be rectangular rather than triangular. There was also a pronounced 'comb' running from front to rear across the top. Later the headband came further down, the top became flatter, and the whole construction was less elaborate – as in the York helmet of c.750 and the Gjermundbu helmet of c.880; but this trend was followed from the late 800s by taller and sharper basic 'Norman' style conical helmets with one-piece nasal guards in place of the 'spectacles'. Some of these helmets continued the spangenhelm method of construction by plates, but they were later joined by others ('Olmutz', 'Wenceslas' or 'Poznam' type, from the 1000s) which were made from a single piece of metal.

MAIL SHIRTS

As with helmets, there is considerable doubt as to how many Viking warriors had access to mail. A mail shirt was still harder to manufacture than a helmet, and involved even more advanced metalwork. Not many more examples have been discovered by archaeology than in the case of helmets, and it is likely that many warriors had to go without – perhaps using leather coats as substitutes, although the evidence for these is scanty. We can at least be certain that there was no plate armour in use in the Viking period, despite occasional anachronistic references in the sagas (eg *Laxdœla*, p.205).

Also as with helmets, ownership of a mail shirt was a matter of high prestige, and it might be passed down from one generation to the next over a considerable period of time. A requirement for men liable to levy service to possess a mail shirt is stipulated in various laws (eg *ASC* for 1008), while rulers might demonstrate their authority in part by keeping stores of mail to be lent out to their retainers whenever there was a muster. On a more personal plane there was great pride associated with mail – for example, Hjalmar in *Arrow-Odd* was very pleased with his 'mail coat with fourfold rings' (*Seven Viking Romances*, p.64), whereas in 1066 Harald Hard-ruler's was so long it looked like a skirt and so his men nicknamed him 'Emma'. The mail shirt 'reached almost to the middle of his leg, and [was] so strong that no weapon ever pierced it' (*Sagas of the Norse Kings*, pp.230–1).

It might appear axiomatic that a mail shirt could not be pierced, although this was not necessarily so. There is some evidence that the Vikings distinguished between thick and thin mail, or mail made from relatively softer or harder metals. There are also some spectacularly poetic reports of mail shirts – and helmets too – being cleaved asunder by powerful blows. For example, at the battle of Fitjar

> The body-coats of linked steel,
> The woven iron coats of mail
> Like water fly before the swing

Of Hakon's sword – the champion-king.
About each Gotland war-man's head
Helm splits, like ice beneath the tread,
Cloven by the axe or sharp sword-blade.
(*Sagas of the Norse Kings*, p.107)

Or again, King Olaf 'hewed from the Danes, in armour dressed, the iron bark off mail-clad chest' (*The Olaf Sagas*, p.28).

More realistically, as Harald Hard-ruler seems to have been aware, there were two specific weak spots in a fully-armoured man's protection. The first was the leg below both the shield and mail shirt. On the late-medieval battlefield of Visby in Sweden most of the bodies discovered by modern archaeologists had been either shot with crossbows (possibly executed after action) or wounded in the legs (probably in the heat of combat: see Christopher Gravett, 'The Face of Medieval Warfare', in *Military Illustrated*, no.6, April–May 1987, pp.17–21). From the Viking Age itself we certainly often hear of heroes who are wounded in the leg, from Onund Tree-foot (so named after the wooden leg that he used after his ankle had been hewn off at Hafrsfjord: *Grettir*, p.3) to the Ulfkel who lost a big toe to Halfdan Eysteinsson's sword and then three more toes soon afterwards to a tall stranger who split his shield with the self-same blow (*Seven Viking Romances*, pp.182–3). In a duel Gisli (p.4) broke his opponent's shield and took off his leg with a halberd, once again creating the need for a wooden leg, while in another duel both combatants are reported to have wounded the other in the leg almost simultaneously (*Droplaugarsons*, p.103). In *The Story of Burnt Njal* (p.98) Gunnar avoids a sword-cut at his legs by making a particularly athletic leap which is doubly impressive since he has just killed three men. In these circumstances it is certainly not surprising that a favourite name for a Viking sword was 'Leg biter' (*eg* in *Laxdœla*, p.208; *Sagas of the Norse Kings*, p.273, etc).

The second vulnerable point was the eye, since it could not be covered. Once again the anecdotes are numerous, from Harold Godwinsson at Hastings in 1066 to Earl Hugo 'The Proud' of Anglesey in 1098 (*Sagas of the Norse Kings*, p.265 and *Orkneyinga*, p.84). In *Göngu-Hrolf* (p.101) Mondul shot a barbed arrow 'so deep into Tjosnir's eye that it went in right to the end of the shaft'. However, we should not perhaps take this last case as showing that eye wounds were particularly frequent, since there are many descriptions of men being killed by every other conceivable type of wound on the same page of the saga. Helmets, shields and mail coats are apparently cleaved just as easily as unarmoured hands are cut off or unarmoured throats are pierced. It would indeed seem that a Viking combat was a very dangerous place to be. Even outside combat there were dangers from sly murderers who might bypass their victim's mail by stabbing them 'up under the corselet' (*Göngu-Hrolf*, p.33) or 'under his mail shirt' (*Saga of Hallfred*, p.24).

Despite all these ways in which mail could be outflanked, its value was generally recognised by the Vikings, and its availability doubtless increased as time went on. At a guess, perhaps a half of all Viking warriors had mail by 1000, with an even greater proportion having it by 1066. Yet there are also numerous reports of Vikings who deliberately cast it aside even when it was available – either through bravado, or because it was too hot and heavy and odious, or for some other reason. Thus Magnus the Good threw off his mail at the battle of Lyrskog Heath (*Sagas of the Norse Kings*, p.147), and Harald Hard-ruler left his mail with his fleet when he went ashore in 1066 (*ibid*, pp. 222–32). In *Egil's Saga* (p.123) neither Egil nor Thorolf wore mail at the battle of Brunanburh, although the reason is not stated. One would have expected warriors to use all the protection they could get in a big battle, whereas they might not have worried about it so much in a 'saga skirmish' where man-oeuvrability was at a premium. Perhaps they simply did not possess mail at Brunanburh, since they were not true nobles.

Close Quarter Arms

SWORDS

If helmets and mail were prestigious items, the same was also true of swords, although they were generally more widely available and many more have come down to us as grave goods or deposits in rivers and lakes (some 2000 from Scandinavia). They were made by quite sophisticated forging techniques to give hard, carbon-steel blades (the process known as 'pattern welding', which was also sometimes used for spearheads), although individual hardened blades were sometimes welded onto softer but more pliable steel cores. Swords tended to have a better finish and decoration than spearheads, with ivory or precious metals being incorporated in the hilts of the richer examples. They were also more likely to be named, as a symbolic or mystical dedication of both the sword itself and its relationship to its owner, and they seem to have gone out of fashion rather less quickly than helmets. They may therefore have had a longer 'shelf life' than some other arms, and so it may not have been at all an unusual case when Grettir's great grandfather's sword was handed down to him as a highly useful family heirloom (*Grettir*, p.37).

The best swords were reputed to be those made by Frankish smiths – notably the Rhenish Ulfberht who left his name on his blades, only to have it copied in many imitations all over Europe (see the explanation of damascened blades in *Gisli*, pp. 70, 130). The Vikings certainly imported many swords from Frankish lands (although Charlemagne had tried to prohibit exports), as well as from England – and in fact from anywhere else they could buy, steal or otherwise wrest them from their neighbours. We should remember that, as in almost every other era of military history before the present century, any battle represented a wonderful opportunity for the survivors to re-equip themselves at the expense of the fallen. A large volume of arms and armour, as well as money and jewellery, would normally change ownership during a few hectic minutes of scavenging and murder immediately after the honest killing had abated. This is rarely described in the literature, but the *ASC*'s account of the aftermath of a battle near Luton in 916 is eloquent for the salvage of horses and weapons in a way that we can certainly take as typical for the whole era.

Often the Vikings imported a basic blade (*ie* the most difficult part to manufacture) and had their own Scandinavian craftsmen add a suitably 'localised' hilt. Nevertheless, they did also make complete weapons themselves, and even exported some (whether voluntarily or not remains an open question). Their smithing techniques seem to have improved gradually throughout this period, in step with the increasing sophistication of their strategic outreach and contacts with foreigners.

The basic sword was straight, single-handed but double-edged, and about 35 inches (90 cm) long. It was normally kept in a sheepskin-lined, leather-covered scabbard held on a belt or slung at the hip on a baldric and, because it was intended for chopping rather than thrusting, it often lacked a sharp point. The impression we get of Viking 'fencing' is therefore that they must have used their swords in rather the same way that they used their axes – in a series of heroic great swings with the full weight of the whole man and his weapon behind each. The weapons' edges were kept sharp, but they would probably not have had very much less effect even if they had been blunt. They were for cleaving shields, or skulls, or arms, or legs rather than for any delicate finesse of rapier-play. The tempo of action would therefore have been slow and deliberate – a forester's 'chop … chop … chop' rather than a chef's rapid and fluid 'swish-wish-wish …' as he sharpens his carving knife. In these circumstances it is not surprising that the saga literature contains many examples of warriors who meet their end as a result of swinging their weapon so hard that it misses its mark but embeds itself into the ground or into the woodwork of a boat (*eg* the sword embedded in the mast in the *Saga of Hord*, p.44, or the axe in the roadway in *Grettir*, p.62), so that they are effectively disarmed and present a helpless target to their enemy's next blow.

There seems to have been a certain ponderousness about Viking combat with sword or axe, to the extent that the saga writers were often tempted to record each individual blow as a distinct and major act, rather equivalent to each separate argument that was put forward in a court of law. The narrative would progress with one side laying down its forceful 'argument', and then the other side retaliating with an equally forceful 'counter-argument' of its own (see *eg Seven Viking Sagas*, pp. 225, 237; *Laxdæla*, pp. 187, 174; *Njal*, pp. 289, 312). It all adds up to excellent value for the reader, quite equivalent in its way to the artistic choreography of *The Gunfight at the OK Corral*, although probably rather

Figure 24   **Swords**

A selection of Viking swords

more firmly based in the essential realities of combat. It also lends a certain credibility to the recurrent idea that a potent tactic in saga warfare was to throw clothes or other heavy fabrics over an enemy's sword at a moment of crisis (*eg Saga of Hallfred*, p.43; *Saga of the Vopnafirthings*, p.55; or, for a similar use of foliage thrown on the enemy's weapons at Clontarf, see *Njal*, p.324). Because the enemy was taking mighty swings rather than darting about with clever stabs, he would be badly poised to disentangle himself and could be slowed down badly.

Nor did the sword itself always perform to specification, which indicates that high quality in the initial forging of the steel was more than a purely academic consideration. There are tales of swords which kept bending in both *Laxdœla* (p.174) and *Eyrbyggja* (p.143) sagas. In *Gunnlaug* (p.47) a sword is broken by the very force of its blow against a shield. As with helmets and mail shirts, in other words, the sword was not everywhere accepted as having yet reached a perfect level of technology.

Before leaving swords we should note that there were certain variants that appeared from time to time, notably the one-edged 'long-sax' that was quite common at the start of the Viking era but which seems to have largely disappeared by around 900. Shorter saxes were also quite widely used as daggers or small machetes, and there were many still smaller knives for use as eating implements or as 'penknives'. In *The Tale of Thorstein Rod-Stroke* (*Tales from the Eastfirths*, p.63) we hear of two men being killed with a sax, although in general it was always the sword that was accorded more noble status, while the smaller sort of knife was disparaged. 'He who has a little knife needs a long arm,' quoth Geitir in the *Saga of the Vopnafirthings* (*ibid*, p.42).

A XES

Almost as much as the warship, the battleaxe became something of an inseparable hallmark of Viking identity. It was a weapon that seems to have been almost as common as the sword and, like the sword, was often given elaborate decoration and a personal name to individualise it – for example 'Hel' ('Death') for St Olaf's and then Magnus the Good's axe (*Sagas of the Norse Kings*, p.148), or 'Ogress of War', which epically cleaved Thrain on the ice before he could put on his helmet (*Njal*, p.171). In common with the sword, or perhaps even more so, the battleaxe was custom-built for heavy, deliberate blows designed to split shield, helm, limb or torso. It was a highly uncompromising weapon which maybe epitomises the whole essence of Viking combat.

The battleaxe had been well known to the later Romans, who had apparently taken it from the Persians; but in post-Roman times it seems to have persisted longer among the Scandinavians than among most other peoples, and hence became a distinctive *motif* for them. In essence there were three main types:

– The first, and by far the most common, was the single-handed and relatively light axe, which underwent many varied configurations but which was always valued as much as the sword as a close-quarter shock weapon in the fighting line. Indeed, in *The Olaf Sagas* (p. 31) it seems to have been proved that axes could beat swords in a stand-up fight. Note that these weapons were in many respects indistinguishable from agricultural axes, and must have helped the Viking raiders to cut firewood – or break through an enemy's front door – as often as they helped slaughter their opponents.

– Secondly there is a distant possibility that the Vikings had throwing axes, which could be lighter still but were often indistinguishable from the ordinary hacking axe in everything but the method of utilisation (see *eg Laxdœla*, p.208).

– Thirdly and finally there was the two-handed, long-handled smiting axe from the 'time of the Huscarles' or of the King's Thegns, *ie* the 900s in Scandinavia or the 1000s in England. This was a highly specialised weapon which may have had little utility in a shield wall, since it took up so much space to wield and completely exposed its user's belly to stabs. If normal axes and swords were cumbersome, then the double-handed axe was doubly so. Its victims, however, would certainly be killed outright if it managed to reach them.

One troublesome variant of the axe (or perhaps of the spear?) was the 'halberd' or 'billhook', which is often mentioned in the sagas (*eg Egil*, p.123;

Figure 25
Axes

A = Bearded axe
B and C = Broad-bladed axe
D = The richly-decorated Mammen axe-head

Laxdœla, p.134), but which in reality appears to have been a much later medieval weapon. Its claimed presence in the Viking Age is not supported by archaeology before the 1100s, and so we should discount it and read 'axe' or 'spear' instead of 'halberd' whenever it occurs in the literature.

As with shields, helmets and mail coats, there is anecdotal evidence that axes were not always as robust as they might have been. Thus a wonderful axe with a 'huge crescent-shaped' blade inlaid with gold, and with a silver-inlaid shaft, was sent to Egil Skallagrim by (the appropriately named!) Eric Bloodaxe. Egil tested it by decapitating two oxen; but its steel edge broke on the stone slab under their necks, 'shattering the tempered part of the blade'. It had to be thrown away quietly, without telling Eric (*Egil*, pp.90–1). In his heroic last stand, Gisli used his axe so energetically against an enemy's spearhead that it broke the spear but itself shattered on a stone and had to be discarded (p.57). Obviously the problem of shoddy goods is not a uniquely modern phenomenon.

The techniques of axe-fighting have always tended to be studied less extensively than those of sword- or spear-fighting, since they were always somewhat more localised and specialised. Yet (partly for that very reason) they must surely have represented a particularly fearsome method of assault which could be highly disorientating to any opponent who had not been trained to counter it. The Vikings would seem to have enjoyed a distinct advantage in this department, simply because their culture happens to have placed a rather greater emphasis on axe-fighting than did others.

Stabbing or Thrusting Spears

The poor man's assault weapon tended to be the spear rather than the axe or sword, since it was cheaper to manufacture and more readily available, although among some peoples (*eg* the English at Maldon, 991) the spear was actually elevated to aristocratic status in its own right. It had the great advantage that if used in a disciplined way by a number of warriors working in concert it could keep an enemy beyond sword range. Unlike the Vikings' main hacking or chopping weapons, moreover, the spear was designed for more precise and pin-point stabs. It depended on an entirely different concept of close-quarter combat, although it was probably best used in conjunction with axes and swords rather than in separate units. By thus multiplying the tactical problems facing the enemy, such a mixture would increase the chance that he would make a mistake and fall.

The spearhead was mounted on an ash staff which might perhaps be bound with iron for protection in a mêlée. The length seems to have shrunk a little as the Viking Age progressed, from an average of 8–11.5 feet in the Nydam boat find of the Migration period, to something like 6–8 feet by the time of the Bayeux tapestery (Brooks in Scragg, ed, *The Battle of Maldon*, p.211). The spearhead itself would usually be a leaf shape, and it might well have 'wings' to

Figure 26

Stabbing spears

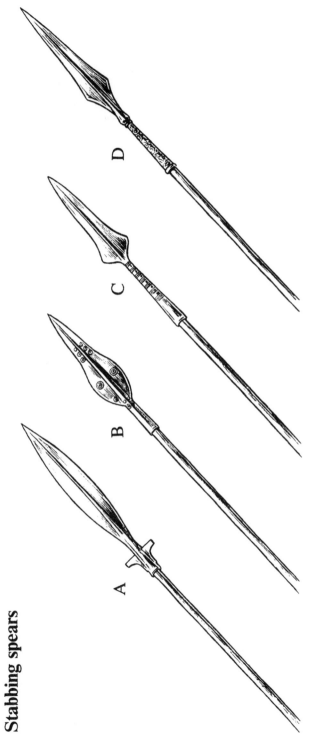

A = 'Winged' spear for easier extrication, imported from Frankia
B = Broad-bladed Swedish spear with runic decorations
C and D = Two common Scandinavian designs

prevent it becoming too deeply embedded in its victim to be easily extracted, since that would disarm the spearman. Both of these features are associated with Frankish models, and as with all other weapons the Vikings imported plenty of their material – although they were still able to produce their own.

A skilled warrior like Grettir the Strong could hope to impale two enemies with a single spear thrust (eg on p.52 he disposes of both Thorir and Ogmund the Bad in one quick movement); although more normally a hedge of spears might lead to a much less decisive form of action. The spears themselves might then become the target for enemy chops with sword or axe, in the hope of disarming the spearmen by breaking the shafts. There are references to this practice in, for example, *The Story of Burnt Njal* (p.80) and *Grettir* (p.210).

HORSES IN COMBAT

Mention of spears brings us logically to the idea of mounted 'knights' charging into battle with lances levelled, in the manner that would soon become stereotypical of medieval warfare as a whole, and which was already supposedly spreading from the Franks to the Normans during the Viking Age. It is even mentioned in some of the sagas (eg 'jousting' in *Göngu-Hrolf*, p.51), although in that context it is surely anachronistic and far from Icelandic practice.

Nevertheless, there may still be more than a grain of truth in the idea that the Vikings sometimes fought from horseback in their major campaigns in Scandinavia, the British Isles or France. It is very well documented that they often tried to get hold of horses, at least for transport, and we know they had both stirrups and high saddles – so why did they not fight from them? Conventional wisdom has it that the horses themselves were too small and puny for this use, as we can tell from the skeletons that survive; and there is precious little in the documentary record to support the idea of Viking cavalry. Yet by the same token there is little to rule it out, either. At the battle of Hereford in 1055 the *ASC* blames the panic flight of the English (at the hands of the Welsh and Irish) to the fact that they had been told to fight on horseback; but this rather begs the question of how common such a directive might have been. The fact that the cavalry ran away on this occasion is hardly conclusive proof that the English did not normally fight as cavalry, although Florence of Worcester added that it was 'not according to their custom' (the author is indebted to Dr Guy Halsall for this information). Whatever the truth of the matter, the record is probably deeply corrupted by the virulent nationalistic tradition that likes to have Anglo-Saxon yeomen fighting on foot like honest freemen, but Norman knights prancing around on horseback using fancy and suspect 'foreign' tactics (and this stereotype would be repeated at both Agincourt and Waterloo) – although just why fighting as cavalry should somehow be 'dishonest' is hard to understand.

In any case the English were not actually Vikings, and we know that they had subtly different military and naval equipment and tactics from the Vikings; so even if the English did not fight as cavalry it may not necessarily mean that the Vikings followed suit. Unlike the English, the Vikings often encountered Frankish armies in France and the Netherlands, quite apart from whatever exotic horse armies they might have found in the plains of Russia. There is even, apparently, some evidence of Viking cavalry at the battles of Montfaucon in France in 888 and at Sulcoit in Ireland in 968 (Heath, p.32), although once again it does not seem to be particularly conclusive.

What probably happened was that the Vikings did not move across country as all-mounted forces, but as mixed forces of horse and foot. When they came to battle the same principle applied, and some of them continued on horseback even though many others – quite probably the majority – fought as infantry. Hence the mounted fighting should be seen as 'skirmishing' rather than as heavy charging, which would not become the fashion – even for the Franks – until after the Viking Age had ended (Abels in Scragg, *The Battle of Maldon*, p.149 and notes). As for the weapons used by mounted warriors, they might include absolutely any weapon in the Viking armoury, from bow or javelin to sword, axe or thrusting spear.

The social position of the men who fought mounted is entirely conjectural. There is a strong tradition that horses – in common with falcons or hounds – were a mark of nobility and, according to the Old English maxim, 'a nobleman ought to be on a horse's back' (quoted in Scragg's *Maldon*, p.229). Yet in a battle where the majority were on foot and the cavalry were seen merely as skirmishers, there are some grounds for supposing that a leader would prefer to stay on foot, surrounded by his own shield-wall of personal retainers, rather than standing out on horseback as a prominent target. A leader had to be wherever he could most effectively lead his men. A horse might enhance this by its mobility, but it might also degrade it by removing the leader from the centre of his responsibilities. Probably the Vikings used different solutions on different occasions, depending on the local circumstances.

CHAPTER 7

Battle

'... as so often happens, it was the home army that won the day'
– Hrolf Gautreksson, A Viking Romance, p.128.

'The old saying was borne out again, "Numbers always tell"'
– ibid, p.129.

Land Battle

SAGA WARFARE AND 'VIKING'

In 'Saga Warfare' there were a number of recognised techniques open to any Icelandic citizen who believed himself to have been wronged, and he perhaps saw them as little more than the physical counterparts to the equally-important verbal stratagems of legal pleading at the *Thing*. Duelling, for example, had its own rigid rules and regulations, even if it seems to have attracted rather a bad reputation as a result of its abuse by 'Berserks and Vikings' who made a living by challenging honest men to fight for their money or their womenfolk. In a formal duel the 'ring' was supposed to be seven and a half feet square, ditched and hazel-fenced, and if either contestant put a foot outside it, he was deemed to have 'retreated'. If he put two feet outside it he was considered to have 'fled'. Each man could use up to three shields, until they shattered, and in some cases he might also have had a 'second' to hover around holding one of them as his protection during the fight itself. The fight went on until the first shedding of blood, after which the worsted contestant could buy himself out (see editorial note in *Gisli*, p.66).

Hall burnings and ambushes also had their own 'standard operating procedures' (see chapter five, above), just as did less common types of bloodwipe such as Whale Fights (*eg* in *Eyrbyggja Saga*, p.175), human fights resulting from Horse Fights (*eg* in *Njal*, p.106; *Grettir*, p.79), or even the strange and rare spectacle of a Porridge Fight (*Eyrbyggja Saga*, p.127). Most politically significant of all, perhaps, was the mobilisation of enough men at a *Thing* to influence its deliberations, and there are many saga accounts of how such gangs could jostle the judges or descend into fisticuffs against supporters of the opposition. Apparently the convention was to restrict such violence to a moderately limited level, and not to cross the lethal threshold into murder – but there were naturally some notable exceptions to that rule.

Small-unit 'viking' against rich but essentially undefended abbeys or villages must also have followed a somewhat standard set of procedures. First the abbey would have to be located by a navigator and the assault teams set ashore as near to it as possible – preferably under cover of darkness, if this was not too inconsistent with the need to find the way accurately (nocturnal operations have often been mistrusted by warriors, and no less a hero than Grettir the Strong was specifically afraid of the dark). The trick was to pop up in the middle of the target before its inhabitants had received warning or had had time to depart with, or to conceal, their wealth. Since the inhabitants themselves might also represent wealth in their own persons – if they were to be ransomed or sold as slaves – some sort of cordon around the target would normally have been indicated as a preliminary measure. With one group of Vikings holding the main exits from the site and another group rampaging through it, the victims could be rounded up and classified. Anyone who seemed to be saleable would be secured and taken back to the boats: anyone else might well be killed out of hand. There could then be a systematic search back through the site for valuable items, livestock and other comestibles – and digging under floors or in back gardens where treasure hoards might be buried – until such time as the expedition's leader thought he should depart. Probably some of the less disciplined spirits would commit acts of random arson in the course of this process, although the fact that some abbeys could be raided many times over, within the course of a few years, would seem to suggest that they tended to lack centralised purpose in that particular type of work. (Note Sawyer, *Kings and Vikings*, pp.94, 96–7, is amazed at how light the attacks on monasteries were.)

Whatever his particular form of combat, each warrior would doubtless have been aware of certain essential background factors that might have tended to help or hinder him. In spiritual terms he might well have gained a moral boost by believing that either Odin or Christ was on his side (St Olaf seems to have committed most of his worst atrocities in the name of Jesus, and indeed to have won his eventual beatification as a direct result of those acts). In legal terms legitimation might have come from the technical fact that his opponent was a foreigner or an outlaw, or in a state of unrequited blood feud against the warrior's family, while he himself was 'a good dreng' and still free. In mystical terms the discrete powers of some named banner, sword, helmet or mail shirt might have made all the difference between passivity and activity, while acts of communal yelling or shield-beating might have helped to bolster team confidence at crucial moments. In purely tactical terms the actual levels of strength, armour, armament, mental aggression and general intelligence must have been as important in the Viking Age as in every other age. Also as in every other age, it was important for warriors to be well rested and fed, and not to be in a state of internal dissension or mutiny, at the moment when they went into action. Genuinely good leadership by their commanding officer would

Figure 27   **Cordon and loot**   Schematic plan view of a Viking attack on an abbey

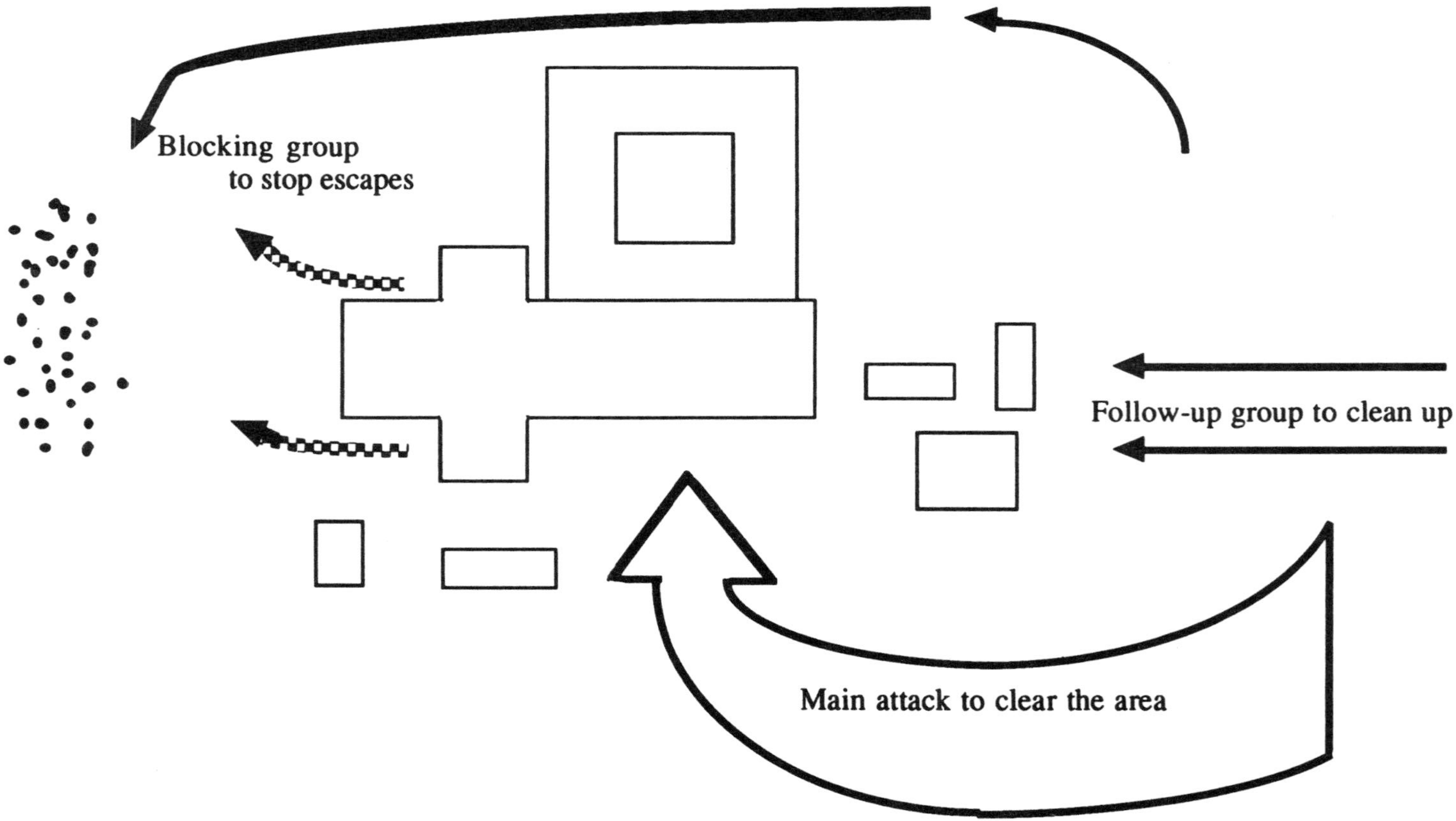

Follow-up group to clean up

Main attack to clear the area

Blocking group
to stop escapes

obviously have been important, although that particular quality must surely have been as rare among Vikings as it has been in every other era of military history.

Having made all these conventional provisos, however, we are left to ask about the basic mechanics of just how the Vikings would have fought battles that were larger in scale than 'saga warfare'. We may first discount the notion that battles were pre-ordained to take place like duels at particular times or in 'hazel-fenced' sites, since the action of large bodies of men surely cannot have been governed by such formality when very high stakes were at risk (see discussion in chapter one, and *cf* claimed examples of hazel-fenced battlefields at Frædeberg [around 960?] in *Sagas of the Norse Kings*, p.101; and Sogn, c.978, in *The Olaf Sagas*, p.18).

Normally one might have expected the larger (or otherwise more powerful, better trained or better motivated) army to seek out its opponent and present it with a choice between battle at a disadvantage, abject flight, or retreat into some walled citadel. However, the perception of relative strengths as between the two sides might well have been wildly inaccurate, so that an inferior force might easily have blundered into initiating a battle against a superior one, or a larger army might have retreated cravenly in front of what was actually a relatively minor threat. As we will shortly discover, many Viking battles seem to have been fought between distinctly unequal opponents. Much would have depended upon the quality of scouting and intelligence available to the two sides (see chapter five), and the underlying expectations in the minds of the two opposing leaders. Most probably a commander who had spent most of the summer raising an army and bringing it into action would feel honour-bound to go through with the fight itself, even if the odds looked unpromising. In many circumstances the alternative might have involved an unacceptable loss of face in intangible terms, not to mention a highly tangible loss of troops and political support for a leader perceived as unwilling to take his business through to its logical conclusion.

It was always quite possible that an encounter battle could develop as a result of clashes between extended foraging parties or scouting screens, which were then successively reinforced to make for a scrappy sort of contest in which the winner would be the side who could arrive at the key spot 'fastest with the mostest'. Some of the combats around Reading in 870–1 may have had this character, since a number of skirmishes seem to have built up gradually into a bigger battle. In these circumstances much would have depended on quick initiatives by relatively junior commanders who would have helped the general cause if they marched swiftly to the centre of action, or hindered it if they did not.

Figure 28

The 'suction effect' of encounter battles

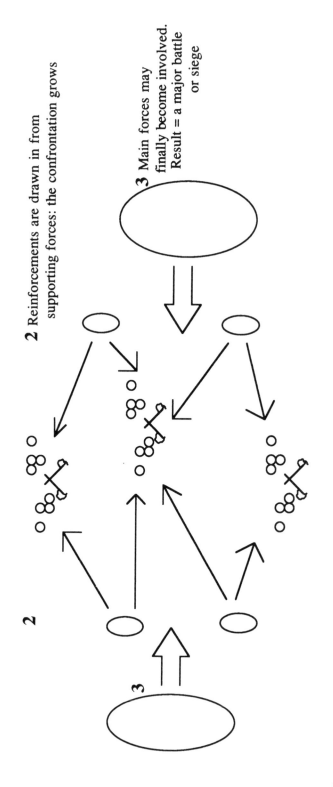

1 Accidental encounters between extended groups of foragers or scouts

2 Reinforcements are drawn in from supporting forces: the confrontation grows

3 Main forces may finally become involved. Result = a major battle or siege

Assuming that both sides succeeded in bringing their main army into the enemy's presence, there would doubtless have been some jockeying for position, as each side tried to occupy the best terrain. The theoretically ideal position was narrow and flankless but – as was seen in the preliminaries to Maldon in 991, where the English controlled the causeway with a frontage of just three men – an army which really did hold an ideal position was actually entirely unassailable. It spoiled the game for everyone, and converted a 'potentially exciting battle' into an 'unavoidably boring siege'. Hence at Maldon – and doubtless also at many other unrecorded places besides – the unassailable army seems to have been willing to give concessions to the enemy by making itself just a little bit more assailable than it strictly needed to.

The truly ideal battlefield would therefore have been moderately open and broad, but with a gentle slope (not too steep) falling away in front of whichever army had managed to get to it first, and perhaps a small obstacle (not too deep) like a stream or a ditch running across its front. Throughout military history it has always been a remarkable fact that generals have tended to see such trivial terrain features as 'insignificant obstacles' (von Schlieffen's immortal phrase) in their grandiose plans, yet common soldiers have tended to be unduly terrorised if there has been an active enemy defending them on the far side (even a two foot field drain can suddenly look like a major obstacle, if you have to fight your way up its far bank against determined opposition). Both the generals and the common soldiers have usually had a good point, of course – although they have both also been wrong whenever they have ignored the other's perspective. Generals really ought to see that even small folds in the ground can have a major influence on combat psychology, just as ordinary soldiers should understand that generals cannot always be expected to smooth out every battlefield into a flat billiard table. Ultimately, however, the inner subtlety of this game lies in the ability of a general to choose a battlefield that will not put his opponent at such an obvious disadvantage that he will refuse to make an attack, but will still mess up his men more than he expects, once he has been tempted into launching the attack itself.

By the same token an army's flanks should be anchored on a wood or a stream or a marsh – all of which can be crossed by skirmishers *in extremis*, but not by formed bodies of men. The flanks – or at least one of them – should not be made so entirely impregnable (*eg* by a cliff or by the sea) that no enemy at all can get through to make a demonstration. The aim is to lull the enemy into thinking he still has a fighting chance, even if you know that he hasn't.

While the armies manoeuvre for position in relation to the terrain, there will also probably be some long delays while everyone prepares themselves for the ordeal of battle itself. Diplomacy may be attempted, perhaps descending into proud boasts and challenges. Prudent leaders will try to ensure that their men are fed, have sharpened their weapons, and have left their baggage in a safe place to the rear. There will be pep talks, last-minute tactical advice, and reminders about who is to stay next to which companion or rally to what banner. There will probably be religious observances designed to give the troops confidence, legitimacy and luck. Cunning spirits may secretly send off flanking parties to seize key hills or buildings, or to conceal themselves in woods to one side of the expected battlefield. Most important of all, the leaders will want to set out their main battle arrays in the formations in which they are supposed to fight. This was perhaps the single most important task that a Viking leader could discharge in the running of a battle, outside the purely physical and charismatic business of personally behaving well at the forefront of the fighting. Once his troops had been put in line and pointed at the enemy, there would normally be little more that a commander could do to influence the course of events, apart from issuing the simple order to 'begin shooting' or to 'charge'.

The missile or 'shooting' phase of the battle was normally very important, as has been discussed in the previous chapter. It could sometimes determine the whole outcome and make any further action unnecessary, or it might create particular points of difficulty for the enemy against which an assault force would try to channel its efforts. Even in its least effective mode, missile action would still inevitably cause a certain level of attrition and grief to the enemy, unless he chose to stop it by launching a direct assault against the missile men themselves.

All this means that the time taken up by missile action could be highly variable. It might take only a few shots (lasting perhaps a couple of minutes) to goad the enemy into making an immediate attack, or in other circumstances the shooting might go on for hours or even days. Everything would depend on the time, place and national character of the troops involved. We cannot really lay down any generalisations about the likely duration of the missile phase, except to hazard a guess that the normal expectation may have been as long as it took to loose off twenty or thirty arrows (and maybe return twenty or thirty of the enemy's), making perhaps twenty or thirty minutes at the very longest. After that there might come an order to charge, and it is in this second phase of combat that formations would surely have started to become especially important.

FORMATIONS

Here once again we are faced with the basic difficulty that we simply do not know what the Vikings did or what types of formation they used. All we can say from first principles is that they probably did not march in step or use any modern definition of drill to take up their combat positions, but they probably preferred to fight in reasonably close order rather than in wide open order, so that every man could keep in close touch and communication with his neighbours and the shields could overlap to some extent for mutual protection. In *Eyrbyggja Saga* (p.47), for example, we hear of warriors 'closed up ready to defend themselves', and this is not untypical.

If we take a boat's crew as thirty men, we could imagine it forming a 'close column' or 'square' for all-round defence with a frontage of six men and a depth of five, occupying no more than five yards square. Most of the thirty shields would be ranged around this group to cover all points of the compass, and the weapons would be ready to strike down any opponent who came close.

This arrangement is not actually dissimilar to the assault formation known as the 'swine wedge' or *svinfylkja*, which was perhaps descended from the late Roman *porcinum capet* 'swine head' formation. Among other references we hear of a 'wedge shaped column' in *King Gautrek* (*Seven Viking Romances*, p.152). One Icelandic source suggests that this would have had two men in the front rank – presumably the wildest and most psychotic men in the army – then three in the second rank, five in the third and so on (quoted in Heath, p.32). However, this description does smack of academicism, and we must remember that it was written at a time and place remote from the battlefields it purports to describe. It would surely be safest to imagine no more than that assaults took place in a 'closely packed gang' (*ie* an offensive version of the defensive 'square') rather than attempting to impose a more complex structure like the swine wedge upon them. Besides, all semblance of rigid formation would doubtless have disappeared immediately after the first contact with the enemy, so even the most perfect swine wedge would have been an extremely transitory phenomenon.

However that may be, there is still a major uncertainty hanging over the battle formation normally adopted by units larger than a single boat's crew. Would an army form up in a line (*ie* still about five men deep, but with a total length depending on the total number of troops available), or in a column (*ie* maintaining a generally square overall outline)? In favour of the column we have numerous suggestions that the Vikings liked to fight in close order, and that their first line of shields was intended to be merely the outer skin of a rather deep formation. But in favour of the line formation we have equally numerous references to a linear-sounding 'shield wall', or *skjaldborg*, which was probably composed of a single row of overlapping shields without necessarily very much behind it. What purpose could a shield possibly serve in the second line, since its bearer was already fully covered by the shields of the first line? Nor, probably, would there have been any provision for a second or 'lower' deck of shields covering the legs of the men in front, except in the rather specialised case of an immobile 'shieldburg' or *testudo* designed to resist missiles but not to engage in close-quarter combat. Such an arrangement would surely have been too unwieldy and unmanoeuvrable for the rough and tumble of a genuine mêlée, and must have been intended for standoff action only.

Figure 29

Square and swine wedge

a) A thirty-man square (ie a boat's crew)

5--6 metres

4--5 metres

b) A 'swine wedge'

6--7 metres

3--4 metres

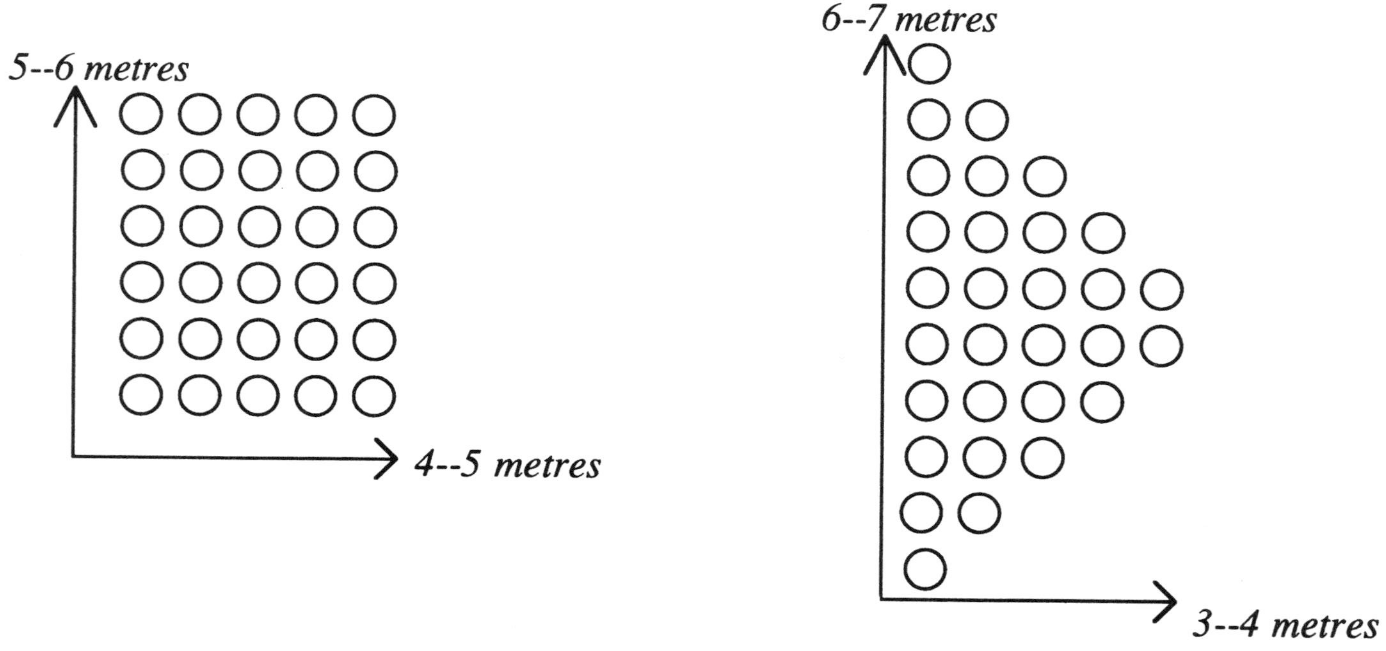

There is absolutely no way of telling whether the line or the column was normally preferred, and such evidence as we have – which in any case is very poor in quality, quantity and reliability – seems to be pretty fairly divided between the two. At first sight the sagas and other sources seem to offer us an alluringly large number of detailed references to tactical formations; but on closer examination they really do not add up to conclusive evidence for anything very much at all (and it may be worth remembering that the same claim can also be made for wars as recent as Napoleon's). Let us peep at a few of the more obvious examples:

– In St Olaf's fatal final battle at **Stickelstad, 1030** (*The Olaf Sagas*, p.350 *ff*), the king has about 3600 warriors ranged in three 'battles': Swedes on the left, Dag Ringsson's men on the right and the king's personal retainers and local men in the centre. The enemy host is described as also forming three battles along a similar pattern, although each of them is numerically much stronger. A psychologically telling detail which rings true (although it is rather suspiciously echoed for the enemy, as well as for St Olaf's men) is that the king wanted everyone to belong to 'distinct flocks or parcels' where they would know their comrades and exact places in the fight. However, the only hint we receive about the tactical formation itself is that the soldiers are arranged in a thinner formation than normal, to prevent them being outflanked by the enemy's superior numbers. This presumably indicates that the formation was somewhat more 'linear' than normal – but it scarcely tells us whether the norm itself was a line or a column. Perhaps it was a column, insofar as St Olaf's tactics are to make a violent headlong charge designed to throw the enemy's front ranks into confusion from the outset, and thereby come to a rapid decision – hence avoiding a protracted battle of attrition in which his inferior numbers would be at a distinct disadvantage. This would seem to suggest that the enemy (using a 'normal' formation) was arrayed in considerable depth, and the king hoped that the enemy's rearward ranks would never have a chance to come into action at all. Yet against this we are given a detail (on p.373) that the enemy had swordsmen in his front rank, spearmen in the second and missile men in the third. That would indicate a very thin and linear formation, just three ranks deep, although admittedly it is supposed to apply only to the second phase of the battle, after St Olaf has made his opening charge and the enemy is starting to counter-attack. By that time it was likely that the initial formations of both sides would have completely fallen to pieces.

– The description of Harold Hard-ruler's own fatal final battle at **Stamford Bridge, 1066** (*Sagas of the Norse Kings*, pp.226–32), looks suspiciously similar to the battle of Hastings, except that the king is eventually shot through the throat rather than the eye. We should not, perhaps, attach much credence to any part of this battle narrative; but for what it's worth it also contains an echo of Stickelstad, in that the king decides to adopt a formation that is 'long but not deep' (*ie* more linear than normal) because he is outnumbered. This repeats his successful linear assault formation at Gate Fulford shortly beforehand, when he had been able to secure his flanks on difficult terrain. As a refinement, however, at Stamford Bridge the king retains his personal party at a distance from the main body, but bends the main line round on itself to form a circle which cannot be outflanked. This sounds cumbersome and restrictive of mobility, but it may well reflect a very important reality of Viking warfare, in that the flanks of any formation were recognised as being both vulnerable and vital. In this case, however, it is supposedly a measure designed to counter the 'English cavalry' (which itself may have been either mythical or real: we have no way of telling). It does at least seem difficult to distinguish an army formed in a 'circular line' from an army that is formed in a 'mass column'. What is here presented as linear may thus in actuality have been columnar, and may even indicate almost a 'siege mentality'.

– In his battle of **Frædeberg (around 960?)** Hakon the Good is stated to have been outnumbered by over twenty ships' crews against nine (*Sagas of the Norse Kings*, p.102), or perhaps 600–1000 men against 270–450. He therefore adopted two complementary strategems. In the first place he said 'Let us draw up in a long line, that they may not surround us, as they have the most men'; and secondly he arranged for ten banners to be waved around behind a nearby hill in order to make the enemy believe that reinforcements were on the way. This was sufficient to scare off at least a part of the enemy army, allowing the king to defeat the portion that remained. As in the two earlier examples, however, it is noteworthy that the saga implies that a linear formation was accepted only under the hard pressure of circumstances, even though it was thought to be inferior to the more normal thicker formation.

– At the battle of **Brunanburh, 937** (*Egil*, p.122 *ff*, and compare the *ASC*), the opposed arrays are described as being just as symmetrical as those at Stickelstad, although in this case there were only two 'battles', formed in columns, on each side – ranging Mercians against Vikings and Saxons against Scots. Despite the all-round defence that was presumably to be gained from the columnar formation, the accounts still make considerable play with the idea that features of the terrain – a river or the edge of a forest – can add significantly to the soldiers' protection. Egil's final victory came when he made an attack against the unguarded flank of an enemy column, which would seem to indicate that the men posted towards the outer edge of such a formation were looking more to their front than to their sides.

– At **Clontarf, 1014** (*Njal*, p.322 *ff*), there were supposedly three 'battles' on each side, although the Irish King Brian was apparently posted behind the centre of his men's line, huddling in a 'shieldburg' (which did not, as it happens, manage to save his life). Beyond that, however, very little is said about the tactics.

Figure 30

Some battle formations

'Ideal' formation of a single 'battle' (3--5 men deep?) in line:

'Ideal' formation of two battles in line, one to feed reserves where needed:

More 'realistic' formation, of multiple groups, in depth:

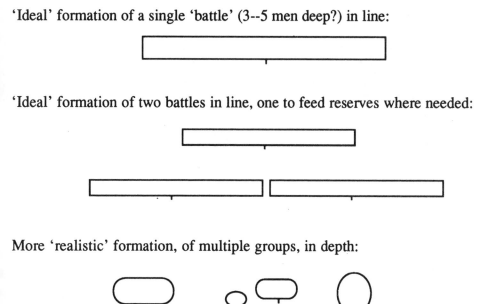

Two still more realistic formations, showing concern for the flanks:

(a) Refused flanks

(b) Flanks bent right round
(as at Stamford Bridge)

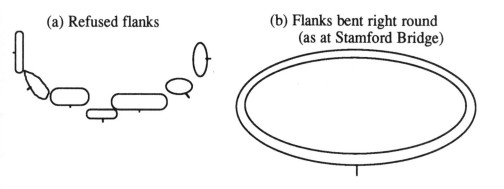

– At **Ashingdon**, 1016, the array was once again supposedly in three 'battles' (*Göngu-Hrolf*, p.116), although no further details about tactics are forthcoming beyond anecdotes of the swordplay displayed by particular heroes.

– In two other English battles, at **Ashdown** and **Meretun**, 871, the *ASC* specifically mentions two 'battles' on each side although – as in all the other cases cited above – there must remain a deep lingering suspicion that the mathematical symmetry claimed for the dispositions is actually nothing more than a literary convention.

There seems to be absolutely no certainty that one half of each army really did square off against a half of the enemy army – or one third against one third in some of the other examples – and indeed why should it ever have been expected to do so? It was surely far more likely that each army would have lined up according to its own internal structure and normal command arrangements, with each boat's crew or 'squadron' holding together in its own compact group, around its own leader and maybe even its own banner, regardless of the way the enemy was chosing to arrange his own ranks. The reality of all these battles must therefore surely have been a great deal scrappier and less formal than the simple 'two battle' or 'three battle' formations suggested by chroniclers and saga writers. And we must always remember that at the end of the day not even the sagas really try to tell us anything at all about whether the troops were supposed to be arranged in column or line.

Modern opinion – as generated most notably by the re-enactment fraternity – seems to suggest that a Viking army would normally begin a battle in a rather dispersed formation, optimised for missile action, and that in certain conditions of terrain, diplomacy or weather that in itself would be the end of the matter. The missile men would demonstrate their hostility by both taunting and shooting, and then everyone would go home. If the battle was doomed to continue, however, the troops would then close up together to make a solid shield-wall in which each shield might overlap its neighbour to as much as a half of its width (*ie* eighteen inches rather than three feet).

The warriors on each side would draw courage and confidence from their proximity to other obviously warlike and well-armed neighbours, and so they would advance together into the fray. With their dense shield-wall providing a solid protection, they would hope to keep aligned with their neighbours right up to the final moment when blows started to be exchanged with the enemy. At that point, however, it could well be expected that all formation would be lost, and total chaos would ensue (see *eg* Abels in Scragg, *The Battle of Maldon*, p.149; Heath, p.32). Chopping, hacking, hewing and smiting would be the work of the warrior's strong right arm, while pushing, dodging, barring and covering would be that of his left. No fixed or formal formation could possibly survive the demands of such athletic convolutions, and the entire battle array of both of the engaged armies would surely have dissolved within seconds into a pretty loose mêlée, as soon as they came into close-quarter combat with each other.

Once the battle had been fairly joined, the Vikings would surely have been fighting as individuals or small groups rather than as a solid formation. They would have shaken out far enough to give themselves space to wield their cleavers and manoeuvre their shields, although the very existence of those shields – and of supporting lines of warriors in rear – must also have given them a surprisingly high degree of protection. We should not necessarily imagine that a Viking axe-fight in the middle of a major battle would necessarily have been an occasion for particularly high casualties, however energetically the troops threw themselves into it, and however spectacularly gruesome the saga accounts of combat may sound to modern readers. There was probably a great deal of tiring but relatively harmless pushing and shoving with shields in these battles – and probably relatively few truly telling swings with lethal weapons like swords and axes were actually landed.

It is impossible to know how long the 'typical' clash of shield-walls would have lasted, since on each occasion much would have depended on local circumstances such as the balance of terrain, numbers, morale and training between the two sides. On some occasions it could all have been finished within a few seconds, if a well-formed assault shattered a poorly-prepared defence. On most occasions, however, it would probably have lasted a lot longer than that, as the two opposing lines jostled into each other without immediately achieving a breakthrough. If this did happen, then the fight could have been expected to continue until the front lines began to tire, which might have taken something between five and fifteen minutes. Once fatigue had begun to take its toll, there would obviously be an increased risk of carelessness, accidents and telling blows landing decisively on their targets. The warriors would start to fall, and once again there would be a distinct risk of a breakthrough by determined attackers who happened to face weak defences.

Against this, it was probably more likely that any reasonably well-organised defender would manage to insert fresh warriors (*vigfuss* or 'eager for battle': *Sturlunga Saga*, vol.1 p.475n.) from his second line into his first, to renew the contest until they too grew tired. Depending on the number of reserve lines he had available, a commander who was under attack could thus hope to keep postponing the moment when the mêlée would end. Once all his ranks had been used up, moreover, he might be able to send back some of the men who had already fought, for a second spell of front-line action.

A great deal of the 'tactics' in all this probably revolved around the willingness (or otherwise) of your friends to risk their all in covering your exposed side or pulling you out of a dangerous corner. In other words it was all based on small-group cohesion, rather than on any higher or more complicated tactical theory. Once the mêlée had started, it could not be limited or manoeuvred in any way by any commander, but was doomed to run its natural course until one side or the other broke and fled, or until both sides called a halt out of sheer exhaustion. If there were uncommitted troops waiting on the immediate flanks, they would inexorably be drawn in unless there was some distinct physical obstacle preventing them. Hence apart from setting a personal example in the front line, the only way a commander could hope to influence events would have been to hold back a reserve in rear, to make a decisive assault once the initial lines had fought themselves to a standstill.

One important feature of tactics which has not received the attention it deserves was yelling. It could powerfully demoralise an opponent, just as much as it could keep up the spirits of friendly forces. Thus in one of his battles Göngu-Hrolf (p.66) saw 'with horns blaring, the columns began to move against each other, both sides yelling out the war cry'. In a second battle in Russia (which, incidentally, is reported as having included 'troops of cavalry' on each side, p.95) the two armies 'shouted the war-cry, and the columns closed in on each other'. On another occasion Arrow-Odd (*Seven Viking Romances*, p.47) attempted to 'yell' an enemy out of his position before any physical contact had taken place. This was not actually an unreasonable expectation, and there are documented examples of the same thing being effective as late as the American Civil War.

Sea Battle

When we turn from the land to the sea we find, perhaps surprisingly, that the Vikings seem to have left us a lot more details about their higher battle-handling. Maybe this was because in a sea fight the commander could order precise manoeuvres by each ship, as a distinct unit, in a way that he could not do with shambling bodies of undrilled men on land. Or maybe it was simply because the Vikings thought of the sea as their natural element, particularly since so many of their political disputes seem to have occurred in areas of archipelago, whether around the Norwegian and Danish coasts or in the Orkneys and Hebrides.

Before a sea battle could take place at all, there had to be two opposed fleets within view of each other in a relatively calm and sheltered stretch of water – which was itself perhaps quite a difficult set of conditions to achieve. The two opposing fleets would usually find it easier to stay away from each other and terrorise poorly defended enemy territory elsewhere, rather than risking the hazardous proposition of finding and fixing the enemy battle fleet in the right sort of waters. Nevertheless there always remained the tempting prospect of reaching a rapid decision rather than a protracted attritional one, so naval battles continued to be fought – perhaps even including an artificial element of 'arrangement' – throughout the Viking Age.

In common with battles on land, the initial stages would have consisted of a mutual inspection and psychic probing between the two sides, perhaps with an exchange of diplomatic feelers and surely with pep talks for one's own men as well as demonstrative signals or gestures directed towards the enemy. There would have been a general 'clearing for action' within each boat. In this phase the commanders would have taken care to count the number and size of the enemy's vessels, as well as to gauge the probable strength of their crews. It seems that mariners can tell a very great deal about the intimate state of a crew's morale and competence simply by looking at the state of their hull, sails and rigging. In the freemasonry of the sea it is thus apparently harder to keep secrets than it is between armies on land.

One particularly important question in Viking sea battles seems to have been the sheer size of one's boat. Time after time we read of warships which were considered to be powerful simply because they were big. This was not primarily a factor of the crew numbers that could be carried, but more a matter of the height of the gunwales. A high-sided ship could protect its crew from arrows or thrown spears, and would be difficult for an attacker to escalade. On the other hand it could itself drop either missiles or a boarding party onto the deck of a smaller boat with relative ease. In the conditions of Viking warfare this all offered some massive tactical advantages that no commander could possibly afford to ignore. Thus Earl Hakon was worn down in his battle with Ragnfrid, 977, because his ships were smaller than his opponent's (*The Olaf Sagas*, p.17); just as at Hackelswick (c.980) the Jomsvikings had an advantage with their 'larger and higher-sided ships', even though they eventually lost the fight (*ibid*, p.39). At the night battle of Helganes, 1044, King Magnus' victory was attributed to the fact that he had fewer men but larger and better equipped vessels (*Sagas of the Norse Kings*, p.154); while in the battle at Roberry at around the same time Earl Rognvald defeated sixty small boats with thirty big ones (*Orkneyinga*, p.65). There was also a seaworthiness advantage with larger boats, so that in the *Saga of the Vopnafirthings* (p.34) we read that Brodd Helgi would not attack a single big boat with a fleet of small ones, because the wind might have blown the latter onshore during the battle, while the former had a better chance of holding itself offshore.

The tactics of Viking sea battles seem to have depended on a very formal type of line-up between the two opposed fleets, which would mainly be expected to meet bow to bow (and the fiercest warriors would be stationed in the bows). At least one of the two fleets would be tied together side by side to make a raft of decks across which foot soldiers (*ie* 'marines') could fight almost as if they were on land. Whichever side felt it was on the defensive would hope to adopt this raft formation before the battle started, with its boats' bows facing the enemy, and then wait to be attacked. The advantage of this configuration was that it allowed a maximum of concentration of fighting power within a small space, as well as flexibility for troop movements from one boat to another, allowing a rapid concentration of forces at any threatened point – or an evacuation of any ship that was cleared by the enemy. However, for his part an attacker would not expect to lash his own boats together until they had become fairly engaged with the defender; or he might grapple and lash them only to the enemy's boats and not to each other. Once grappled, it would be difficult for either side to disengage unless by mutual agreement, since whichever side sensed it had an advantage could probably then redouble its grappling and frustrate enemy efforts to cut free.

It was always seen as a good trick for an inferior fleet to manoeuvre its vessels into action against a few individually-selected boats in its opponent's fleet, thereby hoping to exclude the remainder from the fight and grab back the advantage of manoeuvrability and flexibility. Any navy that was agile or desperate enough might therefore hope to outflank the solid raft of enemy boats, dash in quickly, and kill the enemy commander before the remainder of his fleet could be summoned to his aid. Even if in practice this seems to have been achieved but rarely, it was at least a possibility that could keep hope alive when one was outnumbered, and hence maintain morale.

Whatever the exact method used by each side, this whole approach to tactics must have depended essentially upon missile action against the enemy's crew, followed by boarding to clear the decks of his men in a close quarter fight. Once a boat's entire deck had been cleared, its new owners stood a much improved chance of resisting the enemy reinforcements that could be expected to flow across the raft of other enemy boats lashed alongside, trying to concentrate maximum force against threatened points in the line. Apart from anything else, as soon as the attacker had secured the entire deck of an enemy ship, the same bulwarks that had originally been an obstacle to him could then be used as a defence against the enemy counter-attack. Note, however, that this process presumably did not involve lines of shields still remaining attached to the bulwarks. Those were surely usually for show in port, or at best during the missile phase of action while the crew was still pulling on the oars. As soon as close-quarter combat and boarding began, every warrior would have felt naked without a shield in his left hand, especially since he might well have rejected a mail shirt in the interests of easier rowing.

It was only at the point when the enemy's deck had been cleared of personnel that a victorious boarding party could hope to take breath and investigate the riches stowed in the hold of the captured boat. Hence each individual 'deck clearing' was often seen as the essential unit of profit and loss in these battles, and it may well also have represented a distinct psychological pause for drawing breath and looting the booty – including the captured boat itself, if it could be disentangled and sailed off as a prize. Prudent warriors may have seen it as the best moment to make their excuses and halt their offensive. Only heroic and renowned warriors would eschew the booty and keep on driving relentlessly

Figure 31
Naval battle

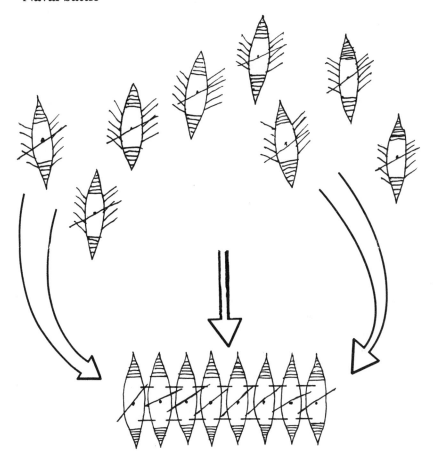

Schematic plan view of an idealised naval battle. The defender has
lashed his boats together to make a 'raft' across which his infantry
may move freely from one point to another. The attacker is trying
to find positions – preferably along the flanks – from which they
may grapple and board. Often they will be able to meet the enemy
only bow to bow, which explains why the most élite troops, both
for missile action and assault, were conventionally posted there.

forward, without a pause, onto the raft's next enemy deck. By so doing they might be multiplying their risks, but they would also be multiplying their potential winnings.

As so far described, all these tactics were exclusively 'anti-personnel', and apparently include no suggestion that the enemy's boats themselves were supposed to be targets for destruction. However, a possible alternative theory of Viking naval tactics has sometimes been put forward as a result of Earl Eric's use at the battle of Svold of a flagship named 'Iron Beard'. This boat had an armoured prow and stern (*The Olaf Sagas*, pp. 90–3), and such boats are also mentioned elsewhere, for example in *Arrow-Odd* (*Seven Viking Romances*, p.46). The question this raises is whether the armour was intended merely to strengthen the stem and stern of an otherwise potentially fragile vessel; whether it was for breaking through the lashings between enemy boats (as it was used in the Arrow-Odd example); whether it was to assist grappling by spearing into the upper woodwork of an enemy bulwark; or whether – as is sometimes claimed – it was intended for actual ramming against enemy vessels. The very habit of lashing the defending fleet together, prow-on to the enemy, may itself have been an anti-ramming precaution, as it sometimes was in other antique navies confronted by the risk of ramming. However, the present author tends to doubt this last thesis, on the basis both that the destruction of shipping seems to have been alien to the Viking mentality, and that the undercut configuration of the prows themselves does not seem to have been designed for ramming below the waterline. Yet we should still entertain the remote possibility somewhere in the back of our minds, since at this distance in time it seems unlikely that the real truth of the matter can ever be properly established.

Whether they were intended for ramming or not, the tone in which these 'barded' boats are reported in the literature clearly indicates that they were seen as in some sense superior to unbarded ones. This may reflect no more than conspicuous consumption and naval-architectural one-upmanship, in that a boat builder who could afford to buy iron sheeting was obviously richer than one who could not: but it may also indicate some extra strength in beaching or docking that the unbarded boat did not enjoy. Against this there may also have been a penalty to pay for barding, in terms of reduced sea-worthiness resulting from the additional weight of iron. Just as warships carrying large crews would have had to pay for their increased tactical hitting-power by decreased operational range, so the barded boat may have been similarly restricted.

In order to analyse naval tactics a little further, we can look at a few examples:

– Of the battle at Hafrsfjord, c.880, we have few details except that Harald Finehair rowed his fleet at the enemy's and then won the ensuing 'hard and long' close quarter combat. Apparently it was the fall of the enemy's champion berserk, Haklang, which set the seal on the king's victory. His defeated opponents then fled in all directions, by sea and land (*Sagas of the Norse Kings*, pp.63–4).

– A 'very tactical' little battle was supposedly fought by Onund Treefoot at 'an island called Bot' in the Hebrides, where he placed his five boats in a line with each flank protected by rocks, so that his attackers – with eight boats – were forced to fight on even terms. Then he lured them forward by pretending to flee, so that they came under a cliff from which rocks were thrown by a pre-positioned ambush party. When the enemy in turn attempted to flee they were caught in a narrow channel and chopped up (*Grettir*, p.7).

– In Earl Hakon's battle with Ragnfrid, 977, the two sides 'fought bow to bow' but were driven landwards by the current. Making a virtue of necessity, Hakon had his men row for the shore and draw their boats up on the beach. He then offered a land battle, but his opponent would not accept it. After an exchange of missiles Ragnfrid sailed away (*The Olaf Sagas*, p.17).

– At Svold, 1000, Olaf Tryggvason arranged his fleet in line and lashed it together. The enemy fleet then rowed forward to meet it and grappled onto it wherever they could. The attackers tried to concentrate large ships against smaller ones, clearing them successively and then detaching them from the central raft. This process continued from the flanks until it came to a final showdown at the centre, on the decks of Olaf's famous flagship, the 'Long Serpent.' (*The Olaf Sagas*, p.91 *ff*).

– At Sotholm, c.1009, St Olaf made up for the small number of his boats partly by the fact that they were larger than the enemy's, and partly by anchoring the raft of his fighting line to some rocks which restricted the enemy's access. When the enemy attacked, Olaf was able to grapple each ship in turn and drag it into a close combat, without being overwhelmed by superior numbers (*The Olaf Sagas*, p.117).

– At Nessie, 1016, St Olaf had originally planned for his fleet to row towards the enemy then lash itself together and wait for combat. He warned his men not to waste their missiles in this phase – 'that we do not cast them into the sea, or shoot them away in the air to no purpose' – but to save them for the main action. In the event, however, it was the enemy who took up a defensive posture and St Olaf himself who rowed forward into the attack. He had fewer men, but on his flagship there were 100 men each in a mail shirt, 'so that he could not be wounded'. This turned out to be the decisive argument in the close-quarter fighting, although it was not sufficient to prevent the enemy from cutting the grapples put out by the attacking boats, and making good his escape (*The Olaf Sagas*, p.151 *ff*).

– At the River Helge, 1025, St Olaf and his allies lured Canute's very superior fleet into an ambush by lining up outside the harbour and thereby enticing him to use the harbour itself overnight, while he collected his boats and rested his men. Then a carefully-prepared dam was broken, sending water and logs rushing downstream into the harbour to drown Canute's men and damage his boats (a rare example of a specifically anti-shipping attack). Canute's flagship was washed alongside Olaf's, although it was so big and well-crewed that it could not be captured. Both sides then parted with honours more or less even (*The Olaf Sagas*, p.308 *ff*).

– At Aarhus, 1043, King Magnus deliberately made a headlong attack against a superior fleet that was waiting for him and had been lashed together as he approached. There was a missile contest and then Magnus electrified his fleet by emerging from his 'shieldburg', amid roars of cheering, to storm his opponent's flagship and clear its decks. He captured a total of seven enemy boats, which was quite a high tally by the standards of the age. It seems that the sheer impetuosity and violence of Magnus' assault was the key factor that carried the day (*Sagas of the Norse Kings*, p.147).

– Around Lessö, 1049, Harald Hard-ruler was initially prepared to fight King Sven of Denmark, who had twice the manpower, at sea but not on land. This would seem to indicate that numerical odds were judged very differently as between the two elements, with raw numbers alone being counted on land, whereas at sea they might be multiplied by advantages in naval architecture. However that may be, Harald then got himself into an epic escape, by sea, in which he was able to slow down his pursuers only by throwing attractive items overboard – from treasure to slaves – which they would want to stop and pick up (*Sagas of the Norse Kings*, p.187).

– At the all-night battle of Nissa, 1052, Harald Hard-ruler accepted battle against the Danes even though he was outnumbered by two to one. Both sides lashed their fleets into fighting lines, with the most important boats in the centre. However, the fleets were so big that many wild cards remained unsecured on the flanks, and these conducted an interesting free-for-all skirmish from which the Norwegian Earl Hakon emerged as the spectacular victor. This turned out to be the decisive factor in the battle as a whole, and Harald's triumph was eventually total (*Sagas of the Norse Kings*, pp.206–9).

– In a surprise night attack, in fog, by his three boats against five manned by 'trolls' in Danish waters, Hrolf Gautreksson (p.71 *ff*), managed to worm his boats inshore of the enemy so that he could concentrate maximum force against one enemy boat at a time, clearing each one's deck before moving on to the next. The last one was nevertheless a very tough nut to crack, being bigger and with taller sides that could not be escaladed. It eventually had to be induced to list (thereby allowing escalade and assault) by placing tree trunks against its off side, although just how this was achieved is not properly explained.

In all the above there is a telling contrast between the scarcity of detail that we have for Viking battles on land – at least at levels anywhere above personal and very 'minor' tactics indeed – compared to the relatively large volume of good circumstantial evidence that we seem to have for Viking naval combat.

Counting the Cost

How did a Viking battle end? We might imagine that a horrific bloodbath was always produced by all that hewing and chopping, especially after one side or the other had realised it was beaten and began to flee. Whether by sea or land, as soon as the fugitives stopped trying to use their shields against the enemy's blows they would be exposing themselves to unrestrained slashes and cuts, and it is almost a cliché that in medieval warfare 'by far the majority of casualties occurred in the pursuit phase'. If they jumped overboard to escape a deck clearance in a sea fight, they might perhaps be picked up later by a friendly ship; but they might just as easily disappear, like Olaf Tryggvason, to a watery grave. If the fugitives could be cornered – against a boat's gunwales, in the ditch of a fortification on land, or perhaps while attempting a river crossing – they might all be cut down, to the last man. This clearly happened on many occasions, whether before or after the fugitives had surrendered, and in small scale 'saga warfare' as much as in bigger battles. If the battle had been fought over a town or a monastery, the whole place stood a significant chance of being put to the torch after the fighting had ended. Atrocity certainly cannot be dismissed as an unlikely or mythical outcome of a battle.

Nevertheless, it seems probable that Viking battles ended inconclusively or 'humanely' more often than our cherished image of Viking atrocity might have us believe. There were a number of reasons for this, which even include a Viking sense of family propriety and respect for the law. When a centralising Norwegian king (eg a Harald Finehair or a St Olaf) defeated rebellious sub-kings in battle, he was quite likely to allow them and their men a 'golden bridge' to safety, once the fact of their defeat had been properly demonstrated to all concerned. Plenty of them found their way to a foreign court – normally in Sweden or Denmark, but quite often as far away as Kiev or Dublin. If the defeated sub-kings were captured in the battle, even then they were more likely to be banished than butchered – although they did admittedly run a certain danger of judicial mutilation as they went. But mutilation was seen as more lenient than death, and it conveyed the coded message that 'I really do like you, cousin, and I fully appreciate all our family ties – but I'm afraid I can't possibly have you contesting my throne ever again'.

Equally in hall-burnings in Icelandic 'saga warfare' (where thirty people might easily be killed within an hour) there were standard legal procedures to be followed by the victims' kin, in order to get atonement money from, or the outlawry of, the burners. The penalties were less if the latter had publicly declared their act than if they had left it as an unsolved night murder (see *Egil*, p.155), and the fines might be further reduced if they could be offset against earlier offences shown to have been committed by the victims. The whole process was perhaps cumbersome and often arbitrary, being followed as much in the breach as in the observance; but at least it was a generally accepted framework for inter-family negotiations. Without it there would have been nothing but pure anarchy.

Norwegian or Icelandic 'civil wars' could thus, in a certain sense, be conducted in a relatively gentlemanly way. The fact is that very many civil wars throughout history have actually been less atrocious than international wars, and far too few historians have stopped to contrast the true scale of horror in, for example, the American Civil War with that of the First World War, or in the Irish 'Troubles' with that of the Armenian massacres. The normal belief is that civil wars are always the worst wars of all: but this is often a serious misreading of the real situation. It is a myth created by the fact that whereas one expects foreigners to be very atrocious indeed, and is unsurprised when they seem to live up to that stereotype, one expects nothing but peace and harmony from one's own kith and kin. In a family quarrel, therefore, one may immediately be far more appalled than the true scale of the violence actually merits – although admittedly the rancour may still tend to last longer and be harder to settle by diplomacy.

The further from home a Viking travelled, and the larger the scale of his operations, the more he would be perceived as an alien, and the further he would tend to stray from 'laws of war' that could be equally well understood by both sides. His victims might only too easily be appalled that he did not observe such conventions as, for example, that one should stop a battle as soon as the enemy king had been killed, or that one should never try to burn down monasteries. For any foreign race which fell victim to the Vikings, it was doubtless difficult to communicate with them sympathetically or understand the rules by which they were playing. Yet in the shock of their assault it was also doubtless difficult to remember that one's own kith and kin had also probably committed just as many atrocities and breaches of etiquette as these new and alien aggressors. For example the king of Mercia had mutilated the king of Kent after capturing him in battle in 798 (ASC), while there had been a strong tradition of church-burning in Ireland during the century before the Vikings appeared; yet it is the Vikings who tend to get all the blame for such things in the chronicles (see the article by Halsall).

Even though they appeared deeply alien to most of their foes, the Vikings did nevertheless somehow manage to strike deals and make alliances with many of them. They often grew to understand local politics intimately, and therefore learnt to play by very similar rules to those of their 'hosts', even if the laws of war were never fully observed by anyone – and Vikings somehow always tended to retain a sticky reputation for cheating. In terms of the ethical and psychic factors which determined how a battle might end, however, there seem to be no particular grounds for thinking that the Vikings were any more ferocious or atrocious than anyone else.

Quite apart from such considerations as these, Viking battles may have faded

Table X

A few selected Viking battles

(*ie* large scale battles rather than 'saga' combats or raids. Note that this is by no means anything like a complete list, but it may be of some help in chronological orientation. The battles are located in their modern countries, which may not be the same as those of Viking times – *eg* both Nissa and the River Helge were owned by Denmark when the battles were fought there, but are in Sweden today.)

Year	*Place of battle*	*Comments*
841:	Fontenoy, France	Between the successors of Charlemagne, not Vikings: but it led to the Treaty of Verdun to partition the Frankish empire.
844:	Quintos-Maafir, Spain	Bad defeat for Vikings at hands of the Arabs.
866:	Brissarthe, France	Hæsten and the Bretons kill Robert Capet the strong of Neustria.
871:	Ashdown, England	Victory (short-lived) of the Wessex English over Vikings.
878:	Ethandun, England	Guthrum defeated by Alfred, makes peace at Wedmore.
c.880:	Hafrsfjord, Norway	Important victory by Harald Finehair over rival minor kings.
881:	Saucourt, France	Vikings defeated by Louis III.
885–6:	Paris, France	Siege of the city lasting one year; Vikings bought off.
891:	The Dyle, Belgium	Viking defeat by Arnulf (with Saxons, East Franks, Bavarians).
910:	Tettenhall, England	Vikings defeated in their Danelaw.
937:	Brunanburh, England?	Athelstan defeats Olaf Guthfrithson and Constantine's Scots.
954:	Stainmore, England	Eric Bloodaxe, now Earl of Northumbria, defeated and killed.
c.960:	Frædeberg, Norway	Hakon the Good defeats the sons of Eric Bloodaxe.
c.966:	Fitjar, Norway	Hakon the Good wins the battle but dies of wounds.
c.976:	Lymfjord, Denmark	Harald Greycloak killed by Gold Harald, who was then hung.

Table X continued

991: Maldon, England	Earl Byrhtnoth defeated and killed by Sven Forkbeard.
1000: Svold island, N. Germany?	Olaf Tryggvason defeated and killed by a large coalition of warriors from all three Scandinavian countries.
1014: Clontarf, Ireland	Brian Boru's Irish defeat a Viking-Leinster army, but he is killed.
1016: Ashingdon, England	King Edmund defeated by Canute.
1016: Nessie, Norway	St Olaf defeats Earl Sven of Trondheim.
1025: River Helge, Sweden	St Olaf and Canute fight a drawn naval battle.
1030: Stickelstad, Norway	St Olaf defeated & killed by Thore Hund's bonders.
1043: Aarhus, Denmark	King Magnus of Norway defeats Sven Ulvson of Denmark.
1052: Nissa, Sweden	Harald Hard-ruler defeats King Sven of the Danes.
1066: Stamford Bridge, England	Harold Hard-ruler killed by Harold Godwinsson.

out relatively quietly for more practical reasons, such as the mutual exhaustion of the two sides before either of them had achieved its aim. In common with so many battles of the nineteenth and twentieth centuries, Viking combats are often reported as ending with neither army destroying its opponent, but both giving up a costly and futile effort and saving themselves to fight another day – especially if night was falling or the weather was deteriorating. Alternatively one side or the other might have realised it was losing and succeeded in making good its escape – perhaps exploiting a trick of wind or current in a naval battle, or an orderly withdrawal covered by favourable terrain on land. If the enemy had been smitten sufficiently heavily, he would not be keen to launch an energetic pursuit. Throughout history, an 'energetic pursuit' has usually been the last thing an army has wanted to launch when it has just finished fighting an energetic battle, particularly if it lacks large bodies of formed cavalry. In victory there is not quite the same incentive for rapid movement as there is in defeat, and we can see that an army which has 'possession of the place of slaughter' (a favourite phrase in the *ASC*) at the end of a stiff combat will be somewhat disinclined to venture further afield, at least until the morrow.

'Possession of the place of slaughter' was certainly beneficial in itself, in view of the plentiful booty and prisoners that could be found there. The dead and near-dead of *both* sides could be plundered at will by the victor, while the healthy vanquished could be punished, ransomed or enslaved at will. There was also the symbolic value of resting on the battlefield and showing that it was still your territory – even if you knew in your heart that the fighting had lost you a higher strategic advantage (as Robert E. Lee was to fully understand after Antietam). There was normally very little to be gained by quitting the materially and symbolically key ground, especially since it would also be the place where many of your best friends might be lying freshly dead or wounded – or wandering crazed by *herfjöttr* ('war fetter' or 'foot terror', which we might today translate as 'shell shock': *Sturlunga Saga*, vol.1 p.475n.).

Surely not even the supposedly 'bloodthirsty' Vikings would have let their greed, *Real Politik* or battle lust take over completely from their duties towards the casualties on their own side. In the case of the wounded there would always be plenty of constructive care and attention that could be administered, even in those primitive times. At least the basic principle of amputation seems to have been quite well understood – including cauterisation – even if, according to the sagas, gangrene was always a big killer. Many leading Vikings seem to have survived some horrific mutilations, and there are even a few stories of combat medicine in the sagas. Quite apart from magical transplants of feet or hands in the 'lying sagas', there were apparently some dynasties of physicians, at least one of which was founded at the battle of Lyrskog Heath when Magnus the Good personally selected twelve men with soft hands to tend the wounded (*Sagas of the Norse Kings*, p.147). The local people and their houses would be used to help give care and shelter, as would any 'civilian echelon' the Vikings themselves might have brought with them. In common with the myth of the 'unerring Viking navigator', however, we should certainly beware of establishing a new myth of the 'unerring Viking MASH surgeon'. We can be very confident that the fatal mistakes and failures were far more frequent than in the present century – although we have no particular reason to suppose that their incidence among the Vikings was any different from that among the non-Viking races of the same era.

As for the battle-dead, the sagas at least are often very specific that they must be given a decent burial in a mound or chamber-grave – or maybe under a cairn on a prominent headland or hillock. Adam of Bremen said that the Swedes held ceremonies to give the battle-dead to Odin (Wilson, *The Northern World*, p.38), although some of the Vendel Age practices of throwing weapons into rivers after a victory had largely died out by the Viking Age. Even after the advent of Christianity there was a feeling that even the much less elaborate funerary proceedings preferred by that particular cult should still pay considerable and appropriate respect to the significant fallen. The exact sites of their graves are often recorded in the sagas, at least in Iceland, and they can often still be identified to this day – as indeed can some of the landscapes in which heroic combats took place (see *eg* the modern plans and sketches at the end of *Gisli's Saga*, and photographs in Magnusson's *Iceland Saga*).

As for the number of casualties in Viking battles, this is as much a matter of mystery as the number of warriors who joined battle in the first place. We have plentiful details of the victims in small-scale 'saga warfare', and in the case of the 'family sagas' there is no particular reason to doubt their general accuracy. Normally they were close to 100% of the inhabitants of a hall that was burnt, but tended to vary from 5% to 80% in ambushes or other fights in the open, depending on the chances of escape. For bigger battles, however, we have few precise references that we can trust. The *ASC*, for example, often talks of 'great slaughter' when opposing armies meet, but is seldom specific about numbers. It may mention the deaths of particular named sub-kings or earls, but it is on only a few occasions that it tells us more. It claims there were 'many thousands of slain' at Ashdown, 871, and again at a battle in Mercia in 910, although surely on neither occasion was the entire Viking army more than a few thousand strong. It says 'many hundreds' were slain at Maldon in 920, which looks more reasonable, and we can believe that a leading Dane was killed in Devon, 878, with forty of his retinue and 800 more 'ordinary' warriors. In 881 Alfred killed or wounded the companies of four boats, and slew those of sixteen more in 884, although as usual this begs the question of how many men were in each boat. In 896 120 Danes were killed at Poole out of six boats' crews, for the loss of sixty-two Englishmen and Frisians. Three boatloads of wounded Danes escaped from the battle, but two ran aground later and their crews were hanged. In 1001 at 'Aethelingadene' the Danes killed eighty-one men of Hampshire and held the place of slaughter, but suffered heavier losses themselves – may we speculate about a hundred? That sort of figure would seem to be the most likely scale of casualties in many of these battles, especially when the defeated side was able to withdraw.

After the battle the final act would be the arrival of the wingéd Valkyries to carry their chosen ones, the fallen warriors, to Odin's hall in Valhalla, whence they will eventually sally forth, one day quite soon, to fight a last and final battle that will end the Viking Age forever and usher in an age of bliss.

The Vikings' Place in the Evolution of 'The Art of War'

'I'd like to thank those who've listened and enjoyed the story, and since those who don't like it won't ever be satisfied, let them enjoy their own misery – Amen.'
The Saga of Göngu-Hrolf, p.125.

If we can talk of an evolving 'art of war' at all, it surely tends to evolve in fits and starts, sometimes taking several steps forward, all in a rush; and sometimes taking several steps backwards. In the case of the Vikings we can probably agree that they did not take many (or even any) retrogressive steps apart from those that had already been taken by other and larger post-Roman empires. However, they equally probably brought few really new elements to their strategies, operational arts or tactical skills. All they did was to bring together such elements as they did possess with exceptional energy and enthusiasm, and gave a powerful new meaning to the already perennial and familiar concept of the 'seaborne barbarian'. In particular, they mightily emphasised the point that one does not have to fight battles, let alone win them, in order to get geld.

The Vikings were not, in fact, particularly good at winning battles, and they must have been defeated every bit as often as they were victorious. They doubtless saw their many unexpected raids against undefended soft targets as the best sort of victory; but whenever it became a matter of lining up and matching shield-walls against a well-armed opponent, they must surely have been treading on very much less firm ground. Often they would try to cheat their way out of trouble or – assuming it did not amount to the same thing – rest content with diplomatic negotiations which may or may not have ended in a payment of geld. Otherwise they might have made little more than a menacing demonstration, perhaps by a distant and relatively harmless exchange of missiles. But if it did finally have to come to close-quarter combat, the Vikings seem to have been quite as likely to lose as to win, since in general terms their armament and methods were scarcely distinguishable from those of their opponents.

Admittedly the Vikings might hope to use strategic mobility to concentrate an experienced and battle-hardened force against a hastily-raised local levy of untried green troops, and one of their most widely-acknowledged assets was a deep mastery of deception, surprise and the unexpected. The success of their 'pop up factor' was notorious throughout Europe, and it was made trebly frustrating to its victims because the Vikings were normally fighting far from their home base. This made it almost impossible to launch effective counter-raids, in the form of surprise attacks on Trondheim, Roskilde or Birka. The Wends and North German Franks did nevertheless land some very telling blows of this type, probably little different in style from those of the Vikings themselves; but the English, Irish, French and Byzantines found themselves almost completely disarmed against such targets – apart from the somewhat less satisfying possibility of raiding the local 'Danelaws' in Normandy, Dublin, along the East coast of England or on the lower Dnieper.

For all the apparent one-sidedness of Viking strategic mobility, a well-organised and confident defender could and did in many cases use his own strategic mobility to make a counter-concentration of high quality troops, who could very easily be more than sufficient to meet the threat. The devastating 971 Byzantine counter-attack against Vladimir's cheeky invasion of Bulgaria is a model of this type of operation; but many other equivalents can be cited from France, Ireland and England. The assets of a defender could also, if granted sufficient time, be greatly strengthened by a network of fortresses designed to negate Viking domination of any given area. The Vikings were not best noted for their siegecraft, at least in the offensive, even though they seem to have been resourceful in such areas of engineering as the improvement of fortifications or the overland portaging of boats. Their techniques for capturing an enemy fortress probably extended little further than diplomacy, *coup de main* and starvation, none of which could absolutely guarantee success within the time-scale required to maintain the momentum and unexpectedness of a mobile campaign. In these circumstances the Vikings almost always bounced off well-organised opponents, and could make headway only in inconclusive raiding campaigns, or in campaigns of occupation only when the enemy was unused to war or divided by internal political dissensions. It is noticeable that for all their much-vaunted military muscle the Vikings managed to erase only one race permanently from the map of Europe – the Picts – and even then it was surely not out of any deliberate policy of genocide.

Nor should we think of Viking seamanship as in any way revolutionary. Doubtless they did make some small improvements to the existing state of naval architecture; but their navigational skills were not especially innovative. Their epic voyages across the North Atlantic were highly uncertain and risked by only a brave few, while the vast majority of voyages were probably restricted to short hops on fine days, with beaching at night as well as throughout the whole of every winter. Losses must have been high to shipwreck and – perhaps ironically – to piracy, although the naval battles would almost always be conceived as anti-personnel rather than anti-shipping operations. The main infringer of this last rule was the Imperial Byzantine navy, which tried to burn its opponents' boats with Greek fire; but in northern waters there was no such weapon, and ramming does not seem to have been practised.

At sea as on land it was only the strategy of raiding that could be made to work on a regular basis, since neither the interception of enemy fleets on the high seas, nor their blockade in harbour, was normally technically possible. An enemy fleet might be disarmed by a direct assault while it was either beached or deliberately awaiting battle in calm shallows; but otherwise it would tend to be elusive. It could normally escape a naval sweep and go raiding elsewhere almost at will, with the result that most wars would tend to see both sides studiously avoiding each other, but energetically ravaging the poorly-armed civilians or monks who were unfortunate enough to be close at hand.

Overall, the Viking achievement at sea seems to have been a matter more of quantity than of quality, and it earned its place in the annals of warfare – as opposed to those of exploration – mainly through its sheer scale and persistence. The Vikings created a bigger and more experienced 'critical mass' of boats, sailors, navigators and 'marines' than had ever before been seen in northern waters, with which they overcame a set of climatic (and tidal!) challenges that the still bigger but more pampered navies of the Mediterranean had never had to face. In that sense the Vikings pushed back the frontiers of the art and adapted existing technology to different circumstances; but they were not necessarily attempting anything that was conceptually new. Nor did it take very long for their neighbours to catch up and match Viking maritime practice. Alfred was already building bigger boats than theirs by about 890, while the ports of the Netherlands and North Germany continued to flourish and grow, albeit intermittently, throughout the period. The Viking eruption certainly provided a stimulus and a standard to be bettered; but it was relatively transient.

One might argue that the independence of Norway, Sweden and Denmark was never seriously infringed, while the 'overseas empire' – in the Shetlands, Orkneys, Hebrides and Man, as well as in Iceland and even in Greenland – was left to pursue its natural course as specifically 'Viking' territory throughout the middle ages. Yet the lion's share of the 'Empire' was surely located in the Danelaws of England, Ireland, Russia and France, in all four of which the Vikings became assimilated into the local population with almost indecent haste. Unlike the Portuguese in Africa, who lasted over four hundred years, or the Spanish in South America who lasted for three hundred, the Vikings maintained a distinct identity in these places for less than two hundred years: approximately the same as the British in India (albeit considerably longer than the Germans in Africa). Perhaps that was enough to leave an indelible cultural stamp upon the territories concerned, although it would be difficult to detect the influence if one visited Dublin, Rouen or Kiev today. In York, however, there is an excellent Viking museum. Harald Finehair did not live entirely in vain.

Sources

An important problem with all aspects of the Vikings, civil and military and at home as well as abroad, is that we still know very little about them, and certainly very much less than we do about such civilisations as those of classical Greece or Rome, or even of Viking Age Byzantium. The Vikings were sometimes described by their Christian or Arab neighbours with more or less detail and accuracy (although rarely with sympathy or comprehension), for example in the *Anglo Saxon Chronicle* or in some of the Frankish annals. However, they themselves left very few written records apart from several hundred runic inscriptions on sticks or stones. These sometimes carried (tantalisingly short) direct and personal messages, although they would become really numerous only from a period after the Viking Age had already been well launched. More lengthy written works (in Latin) would also start to appear after the conversion to Christianity, for example the relatively late and often fanciful *History of the Danes* written by Saxo Grammaticus. In common with the non-Viking sources, such works were written by ideologically Christian authors and so, since conversion to Christianity was the moment at which some authorities believe the Vikings lost their distinctive character *as* Vikings, there remains an important sense in which we can say that we have very little contemporary writing 'from the inside' of truly Viking society.

The best we can do to win an 'insider' perspective is to pursue archaeological, and not literary, research. Boat burials, for example, have been a particularly rich source of material – and by definition they were a pre-Christian form of burial. The excavation of forts, trading centres and other settlements has also produced a wealth of information during the past century. This includes indications, from treasure-hoarding and the destruction or abandonment of buildings, of just when and where there is likely to have been major insecurity and war. Such techniques as place name evidence, dendrochronology (*ie* the dating of each year's weather from the rings on tree trunks) and linguistic reconstitution can all add extra pieces to the jigsaw. However, none of this can possibly add up to a complete or reliable picture, least of all for such transient events as battles or tactics. It therefore cannot be stressed too much or too often that very very few of the statements contained in any modern book about the Vikings (especially including the present one) can be substantiated in much more than a very tentative form. We have plenty of ambiguous artefacts which cannot be interpreted with any sort of certainty, just as we have numerous hypothetical theories which are largely unproven and often pretty amorphous. At the end of the day the central lesson really *must* be that we simply do not know the truth.

Most of the sophisticated historical literature that was written about the Vikings from within their own world was produced in Iceland from about 1170 onwards, and mainly in the 1200s, although it was often based on earlier oral traditions and poetry. It was deliberately written to be attractive, entertaining and alluring, in all of which it still succeeds very well indeed. But it must be stressed that it is also notoriously full of historical innaccuracies, guesswork or just plain fantasy. This is because it was written more than a century later than the battle of Stamford Bridge, and many hundreds of miles away from the main seat of the most important action – regardless of whether that is defined as the power struggles within Scandinavia or as the establishment of 'Danelaws' throughout Russia, the British Isles, and Normandy. In England, for example, the two main sets of Viking assaults came in about 835–96 and 980–1018, both of which periods fell considerably earlier than Stamford Bridge in 1066. Despite strong Icelandic recognition that these interludes were generally important for the Viking story as a whole, therefore, they ultimately seem to have won little better coverage from the saga writers than did such subjects as the magical barrow-wights of Courland or the man-lifting giant vultures of Slabland.

The period in which the action of most sagas is set is called either the 'Age of Settlements' or (somewhat confusingly) the 'Saga Age' (mainly c.874–1030, *ie* from the initial settlement of Iceland up to its first generation after conversion to Christianity). Yet many of the sagas were actually written only in what is sometimes referred to as the 'Age of the Sturlungs'. This lasted for the particularly violent and confused eighty years of Icelandic history which culminated in the final acceptance of Norwegian kingship in 1262–4. From the perspective of that troubled time the Saga Age often looked like an ideal period of law-abiding local democracy and national independence – although many of the sagas still contain tales of horrific violence modelled on the immediate concerns of their authors from the later period. The point should therefore be repeated that the sagas may often tell us more about the internal conditions of Iceland in the 1200s than about those of the Viking world and the Viking Age.

The sagas are conventionally divided into the following general categories:

a) High historical works or 'kings' sagas', especially the *Heimskringla* series, but also such works as *Orkneyinga*. We might even include the Greenland and Vinland histories (even though they include no actual kings) as well as the basic archival source material for Iceland itself, notably the early *Islendingabók* and *Landnámabók* together with the *Sturlunga Saga* for the later period. Most of these works turn out to be far less reliable than they purport to be, although they can occasionally give us a tantalising peep into the world of Viking strategy and tactics 'as it might have been or as it ought to have been'.

b) The more intimate but also supposedly truthful 'family sagas'. These can be compared with modern historical novels, insofar as they weave an imagined personal psychological or moralistic story into an historically factual background of genealogy, normally within the known topography of Iceland – but quite often they stray into (far less factual or carefully recorded) overseas areas as well. *Egil*, *Njal*, *Eyrbyggja* and *Laxdœla*, for example, fall directly into this group.

c) The mainly-fictional 'romances' and the entirely fanciful 'lying sagas'. *Arrow-Odd* is an excellent example but there are many others, such as *Göngu-Hrolf* and *Hord and the Holm-Dwellers*. Sagas such as *Grettir the Strong* are possibly based on rather more historical truth than most of the above, but still ultimately come down on the 'romantic' or 'lying' side of the wall.

Interesting general discussions of all this may be found in Foote and Wilson's *Viking Achievement*, in Sawyer's *Viking Age* and *Kings and Vikings*, and in the prefaces to most of the modern English editions of the sagas themselves. At the end of the day, however, we must still always be very wary of believing too much of what we read in the sagas. They offer us an infinitely amusing and instructive peep into what might have been – but absolutely no historical certainty at all.

When we turn to twentieth century writings about the Vikings, we find that an apparent plethora of 'general overviews' appeared around 1960–80, all covering much the same general themes and laying bare the fruits of modern archaeological research. Some of the more obvious examples are Foote and Wilson's wonderful *Viking Achievement*; Michael Gibson's *The Vikings*; David Wilson's *The Northern World* and *The Vikings and Their Origins*; Gwyn Jones' *A History of the Vikings*; Loyn's *The Vikings in Britain*; and Sawyer's *Age of the Vikings* and *Kings and Vikings*.

More recently there has been an ever-intensifying academic interest in this whole subject area, although the present author, alas, has been unable to peep in at much of it. Apart from anything else, the (astonishingly unusual) millenial anniversary of the battle of Maldon has provoked welcome books from both Donald Scragg and Janet Cooper, while from Neustria we have seen some very lucid and informative work from Jean Renaud. Of particular interest to the present book is John Haywood's *Dark Age Naval Power*, which reassures us that excellent writing is still being produced, even in our own new 'Dark Age', just as it always was throughout the days of Aethelred the Unready.

The whole body of relatively recent 'Viking' literature, from around 1960 onwards, must be considered as almost the 'state of the art' as far as the non-academic historian is concerned. Yet within the academic world itself it is all already pretty *passé* and even obsolete. We therefore wait with interest to read the new burst of Viking books that will soon doubtless be showered upon us by the rising new generation of academic experts. One predicts that there will be a veritable flurry of controversial new re-interpretations in all areas of this subject during the next decade.

Medieval Sources

Little more than half of the Icelandic sagas were available to the present author at the time of writing, and a far lesser proportion of the West European chronicles. Nevertheless, it is hoped that the sample, when taken alongside the modern secondary sources consulted, will be sufficiently representative to fulfil at least most of the present purpose.

Anon, G.N. Garmonsway, ed, *The Anglo Saxon Chronicle* (London, Dent, 1953, 1972): The essential source for English history at this period, despite deep suspicions of its poetic and propagandist distortions and its 'magic numbers' designed to enhance the reputation of King Alfred.

Anon, translated by G.W. Dasent, *The Story of Burnt Njal* (London, Dent, 1861, 1903): Epic psychological drama of blood feuds and narrow escapes, ambushes, duels, murders and convoluted pleading through the law courts. Written in Iceland about 1280 and set around 1000 (including an account of Clontarf, 1014).

Anon, translated by Hermann Pàlsson, *The Confederates, and Hen-Thorir* (Edinburgh, Southside New Saga Library, 1975): written around 1270 with considerable borrowing from the Nieblung cycle. The Confederates are powerful men who attempt to outlaw the richest man in Iceland, but are frustrated by a mixture of bribery and clever legal footwork. Hen-Thorir is a miser who comes to a sticky end.

Anon, translated by Alan Boucher, *Tales from the Eastfirths* (Reykjavik, Iceland Review, 1981), including *Thorstein the White*, *The Vopnafirthings*, *Thorstein Rod-Stroke* and *Gunnar Thidrandi's Bane*: These stories were probably written between 1200 and 1240 and describe events in the Vapnafjord area of north-east Iceland, notably the feud between Geitir and the oppressive Brodd-Helgi, who had killed his first man at the age of twelve.

Anon, translated by Jeffrey Gantz, *Early Irish Myths and Sagas* (London, Penguin, 1981): Folk tales mainly from before the Viking era, but committed to writing only towards its close.

Anon, translated by Hermann Pálsson and Paul Edwards, *Eyrbyggja Saga* (Edinburgh, Southside New Saga Library, 1973): One of the most famous epic 'family sagas', written c.1255, which apparently inspired Sir Walter Scott. It includes plenty of blood-feud but little military detail.

Anon, translated by Eleanor Haworth and Jean Young, *The Fljotsdale Saga and the Droplaugarsons* (London, Dent, 1990): Written about 1500, it is 'the last of the sagas', giving an episodic account of the lives of the Droplaugarson brothers in north-east Iceland.

Anon, translated by George Johnston, *The Saga of Gisli* (London, Dent, 1963): Written in the early 1200s, it is a classic tale of an honest man who lapses into crime and outlawry, finally being tracked down and killed.

Anon, translated by Hermann Pálsson and Paul Edwards, *Göngu-Hrolf's Saga, A Viking Romance* (Edinburgh, Canongate New Saga Library, 1980): Written in the 1300s it purports to be set in Russia and England, showing how Hrolf (not the same Göngu-Hrolf who founded Normandy) overcomes all magical dangers (not excluding a double foot transplant) and fights his way – via the battle of Ashington – to the crown of Russia.

Anon, translated by G.A. Hight, edited by Peter Foote, *The Saga of Grettir the Strong* (London, Dent, 1972): A muscle-bound but cantankerous Viking who kills his first man when aged fourteen and goes on to perform a series of spectacular and widely-celebrated feats – often on the wrong side of the law – until finally betrayed by witchcraft c.1025. Written c.1325.

Anon, translated by Alan Boucher, *The Saga of Gunnlaug Snake-Tongue, together with The Tale of Scald-Helgi* (Reykjavik, Iceland Review, 1983): Written c.1290, it recounts an Icelandic blood-feud just after the year 1000 which is pursued all around the Viking world.

Anon, translated by Alan Boucher, *The Saga of Hallfred the Troublesome Scald* (Reykjavik, Iceland Review, 1981), including *The Tale of Thorvald Tassle*: Written around 1210, Hallfred's story was very influential upon later saga writers and tells of a poet-adventurer who lived by his wits and his sword at the courts of several Viking kings.

Anon, translated by Alan Boucher, *The Saga of Hord and the Holm-Dwellers* (Reykjavik, Iceland Review, 1983): Written about 1275, possibly by Styrmir the priest, it is a tale of adventure and magic ranging around Norway and Finland and ending with a mobilisation of the population to root out Hord and his outlaws in their final lair in Iceland.

Anon, translated by Hermann Pálsson, *Hrafnkel's Saga and Other Stories* (London, Penguin, 1971), including *Thorstein the Staff-Struck, Ale-Hood, Hreidar the Fool, Halldor Snorrason, Audun's Story* and *Ivar's Story*: *Hrafnkel* itself is one of the most famous and realistic of the sagas, set in Fljotsdale and describing how a murdering bully is punished but then reforms – but not so far that he does not eventually take revenge upon the wronged man who had originally brought him to justice. It was perhaps written around 1262 by Abbot Brand Jónson of Thykkvaby monastery, one of the most active Icelandic writers.

Anon, translated by Hermann Pálsson and Paul Edwards, *Hrolf Gautreksson, A Viking Romance* (Edinburgh, Southside New Saga Library, 1972): A late saga (c.1330?) and the sequel to *King Gautrek*, possibly by the same author, it relates Hrolf's adventures and battles through the Baltic and Ireland to win a fair lady and establish a North Sea empire.

Anon, translated by Magnus Magnusson and Hermann Pálsson, *Laxdœla Saga* (London, Penguin, 1969): One of the longest and most famous epics, this is the story of two families as they evolved over 150 years from the initial settlement of Iceland, culminating in a fatal love-triangle around the time of the conversion to Christianity. Written about 1245, it draws widely upon many sources including *Landnámabók*, other sagas such as *Sturlunga*, as well as Homer, Nieblung and the later European tales of chivalry.

Anon, translated by Hermann Pálsson and Paul Edwards, *Orkneyinga Saga, The History of the Earls of Orkney* (London, Penguin, 1981): Probably written at Oddi in South Iceland about 1200. A unique history, used as a source for *Heimskringla* (just as was the *Fœringa Saga*, for the Faroes).

Anon, translated by Hermann Pálsson and Paul Edwards, *Seven Viking Romances* (London, Penguin, 1985), including *Arrow-Odd, King Gautrek, Halfdan Eysteinsson, Bosi and Herraud, Egil and Asmund, Thorstein Mansion-Might* and *Helgi Thorisson*: Written at different dates between 1250 and about 1320. Despite some 'historical' content, these are essentially fantastic tales, influenced by both Homer and the European chivalric romances, set in all parts of the Viking world and extending into deepest Giantland (*ie* Permia, which lies to the East beyond the White Sea).

Gwyn Jones, *The Norse Atlantic Saga* (Oxford, Oxford University Press, 1964, 1986): Collected texts with interpretations, on the settlement of Iceland, Greenland and America. Very interesting – and wide-ranging in more than the geographical sense.

Saxo Grammaticus (a Sjaelander who lived c.1140s–early 1200s), translated by Peter Fisher, edited by Hilda Ellis Davidson, *The History of the Danes* (London, Boydell and Brewer, 1979), Book Nine (pp.275–97): Quite a full but fanciful and rather garbled account of the legendary hero Ragnar Lothbrok (early 800s) and his immediate successors as kings of Denmark up to Gorm the Old (died c.950). The subsequent seven books seem to have been more historically based than the first nine.

Snorri Sturluson (?), translated by Hermann Pálsson and Paul Edwards, *Egil's Saga* (London, Penguin, 1976): Vibrant and epic account (written c.1230) of a formidable Viking, who killed his first victim at the age of six, went on to raid around the Baltic and in England (including participation in the battle of Brunanburh, 937), and yet was also a famous poet!

Snorri Sturluson (1178–1241), translated by Samuel Laing, *Heimskringla* ['The Circle of the World']; Part One *The Olaf Sagas* [*ie Olaf Tryggvason's Saga* and *St Olaf's Saga* together with *The Tale of the Greenlanders*], 2 vols (London, Dent, 1914, 1964); Part Two *Sagas of the Norse Kings* (London, Dent, 1930, 1961). Note that other editions split it up in different ways, *eg* Penguin extract *Harald Hard-ruler's Saga* (London, 1966) as a completely separate book. *Heimskringla* was written at Oddi around 1230, and is essential reading not only for its historical narratives but for the supposed underlying *mores* of Viking politics and warfare. It also includes several important battle-pieces. Although one knows that significant parts of it are fanciful, anachronistic or downright inaccurate, it still leaves an indelible impression of how things might have been, or ought to have been. Since, furthermore, its author was himself an actor in the violent politics of a technologically little-changed Icelandic world, the 'way of doing things' that he portrays is doubly alluring.

Sturla Thordarson (1214–84), translated by Julia McGrew and R. George Thoma, *Sturlunga Saga* 2 vols, (New York, Twayne, 1970): A collection of thirteen historical sagas (not all by Sturla himself) written at various times throughout the 1200s, and dealing mainly with the 'Age of the Sturlungs' rather than with the earlier 'Saga Age'. *The Saga of the Icelanders* is by far the longest and an especially important historical source; but it should not to be confused with *Islendingabók* (written by Ari Thorgilsson 'The Learned', 1067–1148, who is also thought to have had a hand in *Landnámabók*).

Modern Works

Arbman, Holger, *The Vikings* (translated and edited by Alan Binns, London, Thames and Hudson, 1961): Wide ranging and entertaining account from 'the generation before last'. It suffers, however, from a lack of references.

Bennett, Matthew, 'The Myth of Viking Ferocity' in *Slingshot* (Journal of the Society of Ancients) No.116, November 1984: Useful short summary of why the Vikings were not as 'atrocious' as they are often made to look, citing Frank (*qv*) and Klaus von See's article (in German) in *Zeitschrift fur Deutsche Vortforschung*, No. 17, 1961, pp.129–35.

Blöndal, Sigfús, revised by B.S. Benedikz, *The Varangians of Byzantium* (Cambridge, Cambridge University Press, 1978): An excellently deep analysis of the Varangian phenomenon as seen from Constantinople, although lacking much concept of the strategic issues on the fringes of the empire – or of anything at all on the Caspian Sea.

Brooks, N.P., 'England in the Ninth Century: the Crucible of Defeat', in *Transactions of the Royal Historical Society*, 5th Series, No.29, 1979, pp.1–20. The classic refutation of Sawyer's 'small army' theory, which nevertheless manages to reduce the vast original 'Stenton army' by quite a wide margin.

Caldwell, Colonel C.E., *Small Wars, a Tactical Textbook for Imperial Soldiers* (First published 1896; and London, Greenhill, 1990): A fascinating analytical guide to the role of force in the 'fit of absence of mind' that was the high British Empire, not excluding some very 'Viking-like' recommendations for the conduct of atrocities such as the gratuitous destruction of native villages.

Clausewitz, Carl von, *On War* (P. Paret and M. Howard, eds, Princeton, 1976):

The all-time classic analysis of strategy, written partly by the widow of a Prussian general who had betrayed Napoleon in 1812 . . . and partly by that general himself.

Corbett, Julian, *Some Principles of Maritime Strategy* (London, 1912): A wonderfully elegant British 'commanding the seas' riposte to the bluntly unimaginative 'decisive battle' school of seapower as advocated by Alfred T. Mahan. One sometimes has to pinch oneself to remember that this was written before the Great War, and not after the Anglo-American squabbles about 'Mediterranean Strategy' during the Second World War.

Coupland, Simon, 'Carolingian Arms and Armour in the Ninth Century' in *Viator*, 1989 pp.29–50: A good summary showing that contemporary drawings portray arms in use more accurately than is often assumed.

Foote, P.G. and D.M. Wilson, *The Viking Achievement* (London, Sidgwick & Jackson, 1980): A long, monumental and wonderful summary of modern scholarship in the field, concentrating mainly on the political, social and technological development of Scandinavia itself, but with a very useful section on its poetry and mythology.

Frank, Roberta, 'Viking Atrocity and Skaldic Verse – The Rite of the Blood-Eagle' in *English Historical Review*, April 1984, pp.332–43: A densely scholarly proof that King Aella's body was figuratively left as carrion for eagles rather than literally subjected to a formal 'blood eagle' operation – hence there is no proper contemporary evidence that such a rite as the 'blood eagle' ever existed. It seems to have been nothing but an invention of sensationalist late-medieval clerics.

Gibson, Michael, *The Vikings* (London, Wayland, 1972): A lively and attractive short overview.

Halsall, Guy, 'Playing by Whose Rules? A further look at Viking Atrocity in the Ninth Century' in *Medieval History*, Vol. 2, No. 2, 1992, pp.2–12. Useful short summary of the argument that the Vikings were simply more 'alien' than their contemporaries, rather than actually more 'atrocious'.

Hardy, Robert, *Longbow, a Social and Military History* (Yeovil, Patrick Stephens, 1976, 1992): A noted contribution to the literature, although fullest for centuries subsequent to the Viking Age.

Harrison, Mark, *Viking Hersir 793–1066* (London, Osprey, 1993): Very useful modern 'popular' illustrated coverage of the Viking warriors, with good stress on archaeological evidence and weaponry, as befits a curator of the Royal Armouries.

Hayes McCoy, G.A., *The Irish at War* (Dublin, Mercier, 1964): Eight radio lectures including a pithy piece on Clontarf by Rev Prof John Ryan.

Haywood, John, *Dark Age Naval Power, a Re-assessment of Frankish and Anglo-Saxon Seafaring Activity* (London, Routledge, 1991): Fascinating analysis of North Sea piracy and counter-piracy from Roman times to Charlemagne and

Louis the Pious. This puts claims for Viking 'novelty' in maritime affairs very firmly in their place.

Heath, Ian, *The Vikings* (London, Osprey, 1985): An excellent short and 'popular' illustrated introduction to Viking warfare.

Hopkirk, Peter, *Foreign Devils on the Silk Road* (London, John Murray, 1980): Mainly about modern times, but contains some useful background on the origins of trade routes in Central Asia.

Hunter Blair, Peter, *An Introduction to Anglo-Saxon England* (Cambridge, Cambridge University Press, 1962): A clear and concise account, somewhat more modern than Stenton, although not necessarily better.

Jones, Gwyn, *A History of the Vikings* (Oxford, Oxford University Press, 1968): A very interesting and discursive account, leading to many diverse speculations. Highly recommended.

Leyser, Karl, 'Early Medieval Warfare' in Janet Cooper, ed, *The Battle of Maldon, Fiction and Fact* (London, Hambledon, 1993), pp.87–108. Posthumously published analysis of the extent to which Carolingian kingship depended on constant warfare and plundering.

Loyn, H.R., *The Vikings in Britain* (London, Batsford, 1977): A wide-ranging scholarly account.

Lund, Niels, 'Danish Military Organisation' in Janet Cooper, ed., *The Battle of Maldon, Fiction and Fact* (London, Hambledon, 1993), pp.109–126: Nice detailed discussion of the Danish levy system.

McEvedy, Colin, *The Penguin Atlas of Medieval History* (London, Penguin, 1961): Invaluable short and readily-comprehensible guide to the bewildering ebb and flow of tribes, races and civilisations across Europe, 362–1478.

Magnusson, Magnus, *Iceland Saga* (London, Bodley Head, 1987): Useful brief introduction to Icelandic history, including summaries of some of the main sagas.

Major, Albany, *Early Wars of Wessex* (Poole, Blandford, 1913, 1987): A rather dated 'classic' which nevertheless still has some insights into the military landscape of south-west England in the time of Alfred and his successors.

Muckelroy, Keith, ed, *Archaeology Under Water* (New York, McGraw-Hill, 1980): Interesting partwork with some revealing articles on the Vikings.

Obolensky, Dmitri, *The Byzantine Commonwealth* (London, Weidenfeld & Nicolson, 1971): An elegant overview with fascinating perspectives on both the Rus and the Varangians, as well as the Bulgarians, the Arabs and all the other opponents of Constantinople.

Renaud, Jean, *Les Vikings et la Normandie* (Rennes, Editions Ouest-France, 1989): Excellent modern analysis of the Viking activities in 'Valland', with particular reference to the establishment of the Norman state. The author is an expert philologist but also abreast of archaeological discoveries.

Renaud, Jean, *Les Vikings et les Celtes* (Rennes, Editions Ouest-France, 1992): An equally good summary of Viking operations around the Celtic fringe, including Orkney, the Hebrides, Ireland, Man, Wales and Blrittany (– but where is Scotland?).

Reuter, Timothy, 'The End of Carolingian Military Expansion' in P. Godman and R. Collins, eds, *Charlemagne's Heir: New Perspectives on the Reign of Louis the Pious* (Oxford, Oxford University Press, 1990): The important thesis that Charlemagne 'turned defensive' around 800.

Sawyer, P.H., *The Age of the Vikings* (first published 1962; and London, Arnold, 1971): Famously iconoclastic overview based heavily upon numismatics, but also making excellent use of the boats and other archaeological evidence. Interesting, among other things, for his stress on the peaceful nature of the Vikings and the smallness of their armies.

Sawyer, P.H., *Kings and Vikings, Scandinavia and Europe AD 700–1100* (London, Methuen, 1982): A wide-ranging if diffuse scholarly consideration of the nature of kingship, and of society in general, across the Viking world.

Scragg, Donald, ed, *The Battle of Maldon, AD 991* (Oxford, Basil Blackwell, 1991): A wonderful collection of modern scholarly essays not only about the battle itself but also about the whole 'second era' of Viking assaults on Britain.

Smurthwaite, David, *The Ordnance Survey Complete Guide to the Battlefields of Britain* (London, Webb & Bower, 1984): Essential general guide to British battlefields today although neccessarily limited for the Vikings, for whom only around ten per cent of the battles are covered.

Stenton, F.M., *Anglo-Saxon England* (Oxford, Oxford University Press, 1943, 1962): The standard modern single-volume treatment of the subject, which ages only slowly and gracefully.

Wallace-Hadrill, J.M., *The Barbarian West, 400–1000* (London, Hutchinson, 1957): An interesting background on the Frankish Empire.

Whitelock, Dorothy, *The Beginnings of English Society* (London, Pelican, 1965): Key texts and interpretations.

Wilson, David M., ed, *The Northern World* (London, Thames and Hudson, 1980): Very good illustrated partwork including the Wends, Slavs and Saxons as well as more familiar 'Western' subjects.

Wilson, David M., *The Vikings and Their Origins* (London, Thames and Hudson, 1980): A useful introduction, particularly for pre-Viking Scandinavia.

Wise, Terence, *Saxon, Viking and Norman* (London, Osprey, 1979): A 'popular' illustrated overview.

Index

This necessarily selective and short index tries to concentrate on the more significant people, places, artefacts and events mentioned in the text, and omits the more fleeting references. Note that entries for a particular place include references to its inhabitants (*eg* an entry under 'Ireland' may refer to 'the Irish'). Some subjects occur constantly throughout the book and their appearances are not itemised separately here, *eg* modern North America; the Anglo Saxon Chronicle (*ASC*); Anglo Saxons in England (but see especially pp.65–6); Denmark; France/the Franks; Iceland; the Icelandic sagas (but see especially pp.212–5); Norway; Rome; Scandinavia; Sweden; 'Vikings' (defined on pp.13–20), and 'Vinland the Good'.

The most important references to any entry are shown in italics, but titles ('Emperor', 'King', 'Earl' etc) are not normally given.